Abigail Leonard is an international reporter and news producer, previously based in Tokyo, where she was a frequent contributor to NPR, *Time* magazine, and *New York Times* video. Before moving to Japan, she wrote and produced news documentaries as a staff producer for PBS, ABC and Al Jazeera America. Her work has earned a National Headliner Award, an Award for Excellence in Health Care Journalism, an Overseas Press Club Award and a James Beard Media Award Nomination. She was a 2011 East-West Center Japan Fellow and 2010 UN Foundation Journalism Fellow. She now lives in Washington D.C. with her husband and three children.

Four Mothers

FOUR

A Year in Motherhood Around the World

MOTHERS

ABIGAIL LEONARD

Sceptre

First published in Great Britain in 2025 by Sceptre
An imprint of Hodder & Stoughton Limited
An Hachette UK company

First published in the United States by Algonquin Books, an imprint of
Little, Brown and Company, New York

The authorised representative in the EEA is Hachette Ireland, 8 Castlecourt Centre,
Dublin 15, D15 XTP3, Ireland (email: info@hbgi.ie)

1

A CIP catalogue record for this title is available from the British Library

Hardback ISBN 9781399734387
Trade Paperback ISBN 9781399734394
ebook ISBN 9781399734417

Typeset in Sabon LT Std

Printed and bound in Great Britain by Clays Ltd, Elcograf S.p.A.

Hodder & Stoughton policy is to use papers that are natural, renewable
and recyclable products and made from wood grown in sustainable forests.
The logging and manufacturing processes are expected to conform
to the environmental regulations of the country of origin.

Hodder & Stoughton Limited
Carmelite House
50 Victoria Embankment
London EC4Y 0DZ

www.sceptrebooks.co.uk

For my parents, and their parents

INTRODUCTION

"LET'S GO AROUND AND everyone tell us what you did before you became a mommy," the principal said, smiling at our group, which was perched awkwardly in front of her on small yellow classroom chairs. We were all mothers—no fathers had come to this introductory session at our children's school, a colorful space in a dense commercial district of Tokyo. I shifted uncomfortably in my seat, pregnant with my third child, and tried to conjure a vision of my pre-"mommy" life.

Five years before, when I was pregnant with my first, I had moved to Tokyo from San Francisco. But sitting in that classroom, with its rows of hiragana characters on the wall and small school shoes lined up by the door, it was hard to remember the version of myself that had made the decision to do that: the one without children, who was steeped in the myth that work-life balance was relatively simple to achieve, and who was still easily drawn to adventure. Back then, I had told myself it was the sensible choice. My husband was spending one week a month in Tokyo to open the Japan office of a renewable energy company, and it was more practical for him to be there full-time. I traveled frequently too, as a journalist, but I wasn't sure how feasible that would be with a new baby at home, and so I rationalized that an international move would at least make my maternity leave more interesting, and when the baby was a few months old, I would take advantage of the country's quality public daycare and do freelance reporting. What could go wrong?

I signed up with an experienced Japanese obstetrician who, importantly, spoke English. The interior of his clinic was pale pink, and he greeted patients there with grandfatherly kindness. But as I would find out, at night he sped across Tokyo behind the wheel of a ruby red convertible to deliver babies at the three different hospitals where he had admitting privileges, like some sort of fighter pilot in scrubs.

A few days after he delivered mine, I shuffled past other women in loose-fitting clothes pushing their own plexiglass bassinets around the maternity ward with their similarly crinkly newborns in tiny, terry cloth yukatas. In the corner of the room a vending machine hummed, offering hot tea and adult diapers. The whole scene was comic and strange and so disconnected from the world waking up outside that I felt like I'd tumbled into a new reality, my own kind of rebirth. I navigated out to the hospital balcony, and as I looked across the endless cityscape that still felt so unfamiliar, it occurred to me that I might have made a terrible mistake. Thousands of miles from the comfort of my family and now with a new baby, I was filled with a deep longing for home.

Mothering is thrilling and also confounding—even more so in a foreign country, where so many of the conventions are different. And in the months after my son was born, I felt completely overwhelmed by the endless micro-questions of new parenthood, whose answers vary by culture. Like whether to co-sleep, when to introduce solids, and even whether babies should wear socks.

Still, despite the daily uncertainties, there were advantages to being in Japan. We had arrived at a time when support for young families was becoming a national priority. The country's birthrate had been declining at such a precipitous rate that, in 2012, the government made raising it a centerpiece of its long-term economic plan, and enacted programs aimed at encouraging families to have more children. When we moved there in 2015, we became beneficiaries of many of them: The cost of childbirth was covered by a government-funded lump sum payment, as was the five-day stay in the hospital afterward. Then in the months that followed, a caring public health nurse made home visits to check on my son and me. Our follow-up medical care was covered by national health insurance, and we received a "blue book" in which doctors kept careful track of his growth, development, and inoculations—a highly effective national recordkeeping system.

In addition to public interventions, there were longstanding cultural traditions that made the country remarkably family-friendly. At spotless community centers around the city, retirees read and sang to young children. Other grandparent-aged volunteers swept local parks with straw brooms, and smiled sweetly at children rushing past—the whole blissful scene an affirmation of the Japanese philosophy that one should "respect the aged and be gentle with children."

About six months after I had my son, I went back to work, covering Japanese news for American outlets. It was exciting to return to the professional world, where in many ways I still felt most comfortable. And as I reported on many of the social policies the government enacted, while simultaneously living out what they meant for families on the ground, I came to understand the contours of Japanese motherhood: a status upon which the country bestows a bevy of social services but demands significant personal sacrifice in return, particularly with respect to mothers' professional ambition. It occurred to me that being "pronatal"—designing policy to increase the birthrate—is not the same as being pro-woman. Until just a few decades ago, the typical Japanese family survived on a single income—the father's. Today, most families are dual income, but in many ways, the professional and domestic spheres have not caught up to that reality: Women still do almost all the household labor, and workplaces can be inhospitable to female employees, which helps explain why the country has one of the lowest rates of female managers in the world.

I was conscious that because I wasn't raised in Japan—and neither were my parents or my partner—and I did not work for a Japanese company, my experience of motherhood there was not typical. The country's policies and culture did not shape my life as much as they would have if I were Japanese. But I came to appreciate that being an outsider allowed me to question some of those conventions. Had I become a mother in the United States, I probably would have just accepted parenthood as it came to me, passed down from my own parents and steeped in my own cultural context, without any point of comparison.

As it was, when I attended that introductory meeting at our children's school and the principal asked us to tell everyone, "what you did before you became a mommy," something about the question bothered me. I was, admittedly, sensitive to perceived sexism because by that point I was pregnant again, and concerned with how being a parent would continue to affect my career and creative output. But the premise of her question seemed to confirm that even as women were pushing for professional equality, there was still a perception that careers were something they dabbled in before getting married and procreating.

What I did before was the same thing I was still doing: working as a journalist. Except that now, I was also juggling the demands of domestic life. And, as was true for all the women in that room, that meant filling out daily school forms that chronicled what our children had eaten, when they'd used the potty, and a description of the results. There were exact specifications for the lunchboxes we should send, along with detailed instructions on how the food inside should be prepared. I was immensely happy to have children, and grateful to live in a place that cared so much about their welfare that adults kept track of every fleeting aspect of their development. But I resented the assumption that all of us assembled mothers had made the same choice to devote our days to the pleasure and mundanity of childrearing. It seemed to deprive us of any agency about how to inhabit the role of parent.

Perhaps the principal could have framed the question differently to ask: *Who* were you before you became a mother? Because I would have been the first to admit I was not the same person who had moved to Japan heavily pregnant, hoping for the best. That was made all the more clear when we later moved back to the US, after nearly seven years away. I had left the country without children and returned with three, and so much of American culture was now both familiar and strange. I approached motherhood back in the States with the same curiosity that I had in Japan. It was inspiring to be around so many professionally empowered women, but it also struck me that the sense of choice many American mothers had felt false. They were encouraged to succeed at work and at home with no commensurate support system; they had professional opportunity but lacked the public framework to make it reasonably attainable without significant wealth or full-time family support.

It was the inverse of the problem Japanese mothers had. Here, mothers were expected to be professionals, but there was no universal daycare, no immaculate community centers where volunteer grandparents sang to small children—no real infrastructure for young families. After so many years abroad, I could see the negative space where those programs should have been and the suffering their absence caused. Many of my friends battled to stay relevant at work and cobble together childcare; some were pushed out of the workforce because daycare was too expensive, others were stuck at awful jobs because their families needed the health insurance. What real choice did these women have about how to be mothers, professionals, partners? They were just surviving.

As I had come to understand, the way societies support families is critical to how women experience motherhood. Because while parents might feel like they have the freedom and responsibility to raise their children as they want, the truth is that many of the big decisions, like how much time to spend with their children and how to divide the emotional and physical labor with their partner, are heavily determined by the social structures of the place they give birth. And often women are asked to sacrifice freedom for support, when what they should have is *both*.

I became curious about whether there were other countries that were closer to getting it right, and what living there would be like. Could a system that was more responsive to parents' needs improve their relationships, their children's lives, even their sense of self? I began to report on that question and this book is the result: It follows four women—from the US, Japan, Kenya, and Finland, who all had babies around New Year 2022—through their first year of motherhood, to draw an intimate portrait of their lives and compare the support they received.

I chose those four countries because they speak to broader trends. First the US, the country I know best, with its remarkable history of female professional achievement but an unusually weak social safety net. I wanted to understand whether they were connected or if it might be possible to have both gender equality and a strong benefits system at the same time. Of course, asking that question always leads one to Nordic countries. And so I went to Finland, where I was particularly interested in whether strong social programs could make up for difficult personal circumstances. And even if generous programs were effective in a small country like Finland, could they also work on a much larger scale? That took me back to Japan. It is one of the world's largest economies, and Tokyo, with thirty-nine million people, is the biggest city on the planet. Yet the country still maintains one of the most generous social welfare systems anywhere. As I began to understand during my own time there though, its strict gender roles can undercut those benefits for both men and women. With lessons from these systems, I wondered if it would be possible to build an entirely new one. To answer that question, I went to Kenya to see how its recently implemented maternal support programs work with long-standing traditional community care.

In each place, I found a mother whose story seemed to speak to those larger issues. My hope is that these character studies do more than a simple side-by-side policy comparison could to show how social programs shape parents' relationships, career options, and deep anxieties. As the poet Muriel Rukeyser wrote, "What would happen if one woman told the truth about her life? The world would split open." I was grateful these four remarkable women were willing to tell the truth about their lives. The first year of parenthood is a wild journey of transformation, and they let me ride along with them for all of it. They and their partners patiently answered all my questions and let me shadow them in their local communities. When I couldn't be there in person, we spent countless hours on the phone and Zoom, and I worked with talented local reporters who were there for important events and helped chronicle their daily lives.

At the start of the year, the women were all middle class and urban, to make comparisons easier, and also because that represents a growing majority of the world's parents. But as the year unfolded, their circumstances changed and their lives took unpredictable turns, as all of ours do.

Some patterns did emerge. Each woman seemed to exist at the center of three concentric spheres of support: first her close family and friends, then her wider local community, and finally her country, or in other words the social, cultural, and state safety net. The less support she had in those spheres overall, the less agency she felt in how to be a parent.

I won't pretend that these stories provide solutions to all the thorny challenges that make mothers' lives harder than they should be. But hopefully they do show how much parenthood is shaped by the broad systems our societies have built over time. And in a moment of rapid technological and economic change, they might help us consider how to create new systems that preserve and build upon long-established ideas about community support and interdependence.

As the women described to me their own experiences, I was surprised by how much it helped me make sense of my own. I saw many of my struggles reflected in theirs: the loneliness of new motherhood, the realignment of relationships with one's family and one's self.

It also helped me realize I had missed something fundamental during my time in Japan: that motherhood there is venerated in a way that is so different from what I was used to seeing in the US, I had overlooked it. There was real value attached to raising the next generation, so being a mother was seen as its own kind of calling. Watching the extraordinary efforts of these four women reinforced the idea that motherhood deserves respect, even awe. And it helped me acknowledge all the work I had also done to care for my children.

I hope parents and non-parents alike find something meaningful in these women's stories, and that it leads them to question the norms and implicit demands we all take for granted in our own families and countries. Like how much we give to our children, and how much we expect from our partners, our extended families, our social services, and our medical systems. Broadly speaking, we cannot choose our society any more than we can choose our parents, or our children for that matter. But we can seek to improve it. One place to start is with the understanding that mothers are full humans with needs and desires and differences among them, who through pandemic and war, sleep deprivation and pelvic pain, do the hard work of raising the next generation. Their labor—and the hard work of fathers and other caregivers—is worthy of policy that acknowledges that reality, and of respect.

PART ONE

TSUKASA
JAPAN

TSUKASA IS SCARED. IT isn't the emotion she'd expected to feel at this appointment, but when the doctor tells her the baby in her stomach is a girl, all she can feel is fear. The world can be dangerous for little girls—and onerous for women—and she worries she might not be up to the task of protecting a daughter. She stares at the flickering ultrasound screen until she feels her anxiety sharpen into resolve. She vows to teach her daughter to be "wise as a serpent," to know when the world is asking something of her it should not, and to feel comfortable in her body—amazed by it even, by the power it holds.

It's a revolutionary thought, and one that would have never crossed her mind when Tsukasa herself was growing up in Matsumoto, a traditional alpine town in Nagano Prefecture, ringed by the snowy foothills of the Japanese Alps. Tsukasa, a slight woman of thirty-three with soft curls and dark glasses, has family in this region going back five generations—manufacturing on her father's side, porcelain vendors on her mother's. She left when she was admitted to a prestigious university in Tokyo, known for educating the Imperial family, and there she threw herself into studying Western culture and French language. She had hoped to find a job that made use of those skills but graduated just after the subprime mortgage crisis had hobbled the world economy. "It was the ice age of employment," she says.

She eventually found a position doing administrative work for a company that built and operated parking lots. It was the kind of place where women are required to wear heels and show respect for their male colleagues by pouring their tea and pushing the elevator buttons for them. She left after six years when she found a position at a major video-streaming service.

In her new role, for the first time, she found real pleasure and meaning in her profession. "I finally felt self-actualized," she says. And her husband, Kaz, filled her evenings with music. He's a successful songwriter and composer and looks the part: head shaved on one side, with long blue hair on the other. Then there was her love affair with Tokyo itself. The city's scale was surreal: The entire population of Matsumoto could fit into just one of Tokyo's twenty-three central wards. Quiet Shinto shrines sat tucked behind teeming intersections; and giant towers soared above jewel box restaurants that could seat only a handful of diners. The narrow streets of their Kagurazaka neighborhood were lined with hundreds of those tiny eateries, including their favorite, an okonomiyaki restaurant where they spent many blissful evenings. "I simply love good food. My husband always says to me, when you eat, you look so happy," Tsukasa laughs.

Then the nausea started, the fatigue, the sensitivity in her body. The feeling was familiar, and it filled her with joy but also foreboding. She had celebrated the onset of these sensations twice before, only to have them stop, replaced by a sudden lack of queasiness that served to remind her of what she'd lost. The first miscarriage happened at about eight weeks. She was able to get pregnant a second time, thanks to a daily regimen of medicinal herbs, she says.

But then at Tsukasa's two-month appointment, the doctor told her the baby had stopped growing. Tsukasa could see there was no heartbeat but still didn't quite believe it. Not until she started bleeding did it really hit her.

After that, she remembers the white walls of the operating room and the sound of her own frantic breathing. Somewhere down the hall, babies cried. The vigor of their screams provoked an ache that mingled with the pain of the procedure. A riot of panic overtook her as the doctor removed the lifeless mass from her body. She listened to the other infants wail, knowing hers had never taken a breath.

But that is all in the past now. In her third pregnancy, after four years of trying, she knows things are different. She is past the tenuous early stage, and the prolonged sluggishness and sickness portend good things. Her doctor does not prescribe medication for her debilitating nausea—she's long known the medical system's reluctance to treat women's discomfort or even pain with drugs— and so she soldiers on, seeking out anything sour to cut the bilious feeling in her gut. Mostly, though, she just stops eating. She loses over eleven pounds in the first half of pregnancy. As her energy wanes, her doctor tells her he does not want to take any chances, especially after her previous miscarriages, and prescribes bed rest. "The response to everything is more rest," she laughs. So at the midway point of pregnancy, she goes on leave from her job.

Thankfully, her manager is understanding. She's a woman not much older than Tsukasa, a promising sign of the changing landscape of Japanese professional life. Tsukasa is entitled to maternity leave starting six weeks before the birth. She will receive two-thirds salary for the first six months then fifty percent after that. She'll take one full year, as most mothers do, but her job is protected for two if she does decide to extend her leave. The country has had maternity leave since 1947 and on top of that, the government enacted a package of new supports in 2012 to try to stem Japan's steep population decline.

Tsukasa now has a choice: She can stay here in Tokyo with Kaz or return to her hometown of Matsumoto to deliver the baby. Going home seems like the right thing to do, the well-worn path many expectant Japanese women take. But it would mean being separated from Kaz for long stretches until the baby is born because he needs to be in the city for work. He's a source of stability for her and she worries about how she'll cope without him, particularly because on top of this move, there will be yet another one: Kaz has been offered an assistant professor position at Osaka's College of Music, which means they will need to relocate there from Tokyo after the baby is born. It's hard to untangle her anxiety about moving so many times, from her broader unease about impending motherhood. "I can't wait to have the baby but there's also so much uncertainty, one move and then another, so it's a mix of excitement and worry."

It seems all she can do is press ahead, and she soon finds herself on a bullet train speeding toward Matsumoto. The vertical density of Tokyo gives way to wide stretches of countryside; calm rice paddies between clusters of tile-roofed farmhouses. An occasional kei mini truck kicks up dust.

She exits the train into a mountain breeze that is a relief after Tokyo's oppressive summer heat. Her mother is there to take her to her childhood home, a narrow, modern house not far from historic Matsumoto Castle. The "crow castle," as it is called for its ebony façade and parapets that unfurl like wings, was built more than four centuries ago by a powerful samurai clan. Some ancient architectural savant designed it to look as if it has five tiers—their tile roofs carving crescents into the sky—but in fact, the castle has another, hidden level. That one was filled with rows of finely tuned armaments, including naginata, long poles affixed with pointed blades. They were the weapon of choice for onna-bugeisha, the rare female warriors who fought alongside men. One of the most revered was Jingū, a formidable fighter who went on to become empress. According to legend, she rode into battle wearing men's clothing that concealed her own secret: the baby inside her. She was celebrated for succeeding as a man while never forsaking her duty as a woman.

For Tsukasa, growing a baby is a battle unto itself, and the exhaustion is incapacitating. The first few months at home pass in a haze, and she sleeps through half the day while outside, the sun bakes the alpine valley. When she is awake, she spends time with her mother, who is separated from her father. They are not legally divorced but have lived apart since Tsukasa was young. Their split was hard for her and left her feeling forgotten at times. "I do sometimes wonder, 'If you can't love your family, how can you love others?'" She wants her child to grow up in a home filled with affection and parents who care deeply for each other.

For the time being though, separated from Kaz, it seems that all she can do is prepare the house for the baby. "This is how I spend my time now," she says, laughing as she folds a soft baby onesie. The tatami floor is covered with piles of tiny clothes she laundered in the washing machine then hung on a line outside to dry. Her parents' house, like most homes in Japan, does not have a dryer. Sunlight is a natural disinfectant, and the machines are generally considered an unnecessary use of space and energy. Even dishwashers are a relatively new addition to domestic life and are still seen by some as an extravagance. For the most part, women are simply expected to do housework as their mothers did before them.

Tsukasa was thrust into this homemaker role when she arrived at her mother's house, a strange kind of maternity leave with no baby. She can feel her professional identity slipping away but also finds she has a willingness to sacrifice for the new life inside her, a kind of awakening of maternal purpose.

Then one day, around her sixth month of pregnancy, as the heat subsides and flamboyant hydrangeas emerge around the city, she feels a sudden, robust hunger for life—and food—that draws her out of the house and into the warm embrace of a local bakery she'd frequented as a girl. It smells the same as it did then, an intoxicating blend of sweet and savory. The scent would have turned her stomach a week ago, but now it fills her with immense joy.

When she enters, a woman in a green apron and baker's headscarf greets her from behind a display case filled with glistening sweets and cakes. On the lowest shelf are neat rows of the profiteroles the bakery is known for. Tsukasa orders one and the woman hands it to her in a small paper bag, affixed with a pink sticker. Outside the shop, she unwraps it, mindful of the powdered sugar. With each bite, cool cream spills from the center. The taste is transportive. It reminds her of walking this neighborhood's spotless cobblestone streets as a girl, past well-tended gardens and neat rows of potted bonsai; shoes precisely aligned in every genkan entryway—a tidiness that only underscored the disorder she often felt in her own life.

This sunlit bakery had been a bright spot in a childhood marred by darkness, the worst of it during elementary school. Around fourth grade, a male worker at Tsukasa's school followed her into the bathroom, where he told her he could help her practice swim strokes and began to touch her, in sensitive areas she knew he should not be touching. She says it hurt. And then he began to expose himself to her as well. The sexual abuse continued. He found ways to perpetrate it subtly so no one would know. It was horrific and destabilizing. The man was about forty and an authority figure. "I was so pure then, there was no way I would have disobeyed someone in his position, I thought it was strange and I was uncomfortable, but I couldn't fight back."

When she did finally manage to escape the abuse, she was in a state of shock, and in the years that followed, she felt a deep sense of shame. She acted out, rebelling against all authority figures, including her parents. Now she is back in the prefecture where, she says, the man still lives. "For many years, I tried to forget about it, but now that I'm back, it does sometimes enter my mind that he's still here." She has never told her mother what happened.

In a culture that prizes group harmony, speaking out can be seen as unnecessarily disruptive. Perhaps for that reason, in Japan, only an estimated five to ten percent of sex crime victims go to the police—so for each offense reported an estimated ten to twenty are not—and among children, the rate of reporting is likely even lower. That leads to the misperception that such crimes are rare, so even when survivors do come forward, they are frequently not believed. In 2017, Reuters intern Shiori Ito accused Noriyuki Yamaguchi, one of Japan's best-known television journalists, of raping her when they met to discuss a possible job. When she reported the alleged assault to police, investigators had her reenact the incident using a life-size doll. Yamaguchi denied the allegations and was never charged with any offense.

Yamaguchi had ties to the late Prime Minister Shinzo Abe, and when Ito took him to court herself in a civil claim, it set off a political firestorm that subjected her to so much hostility she had to leave the country. After appeals, a high court finally ruled in 2022 that Yamaguchi should pay her about thirty thousand dollars in damages—but it also ordered her to pay *him* about four thousand for the hit his reputation had taken when she accused him of using a "date rape drug," something the police never tested for. Ito told reporters at the time that she was inspired by the American

#MeToo movement, but no similar wave of accusations and stories followed hers in Japan.

When Tsukasa was eighteen, about a decade after her own assault, she found refuge in the church when a Christian congregation welcomed her. "I wanted to be loved for who I was and to have something to believe in," she recalls. Her trauma was so severe, she was sure she didn't want marriage or children, but that changed as the priest and his wife modeled a healthy relationship. "Seeing them I realized that having a good partner would help me heal. It gave me hope that family could be good." She finally felt comfortable enough to talk about what had happened with friends she made at the church, and they comforted her as she cried. "I dealt with my pain and that process led to liberation," she says.

A few years later, she met Kaz, her now-husband, at a church event. He was kind and creative and shared her vision for a happy family life. By the time they married, Tsukasa says, she'd overcome her fear of men, but it had taken fifteen years. She wants her pregnancy to mark another turning point, when she will exorcise any shadows that still haunt her. "A mother's thoughts affect the fetus, so I know I have to resolve this issue; I've tried to heal myself, for her."

IN LATE FALL, AS the mountain ravines around Matsumoto flush scarlet and gold with autumn foliage, Tsukasa goes to the public hospital and checks in at one of the little pink kiosks for her eight-month appointment. After the exam confirms everything is fine with the baby, her doctor gives her some disappointing news: Kaz will not be allowed at the birth because of the current hospital policy; no one from Tokyo can visit since Covid rates are higher there. She's been willing to live apart from him for months but had still expected him to be with her for the delivery.

Tsukasa presses the doctor: *So can you take a video? Live, you know, so he can watch as it's happening?*

But he is adamant.

I'm sorry, we don't have enough staff to do that, the doctor responds. Then he adds calmly: *Even after the delivery, your husband should not come see the baby until she's a month old. You can't risk infecting a vulnerable newborn.*

There is no arguing, the system does not make exceptions. It was only recently that fathers began to take part in their children's births at all. They weren't allowed in Japanese delivery rooms until the late 1970s because hospitals saw their presence as an unnecessary distraction and most workplaces didn't give them the time off. Then in the 1980s, one of the biggest newspapers in the country published a series called "Childbirth Revolution" that introduced the Lamaze method and it took off throughout Japan. Suddenly fathers had a supporting role to play. Still, as recently as 2006, only a third of Japanese fathers witnessed the birth of their child. Since then, it has risen to about two thirds. That's compared to ninety percent of fathers in the US and ninety-five percent across much of Europe and Scandinavia.

Tsukasa is dismayed that Kaz won't be there—not only because she wants him to see his daughter's birth but also because she needs him there to help her deal with the pain. Her hospital, like most in Japan, does not offer pain medication. In 2023, just sixteen percent of birthing women in Japan received an epidural, and that's double what it was in 2020. In her final weeks of pregnancy, Tsukasa grows increasingly anxious about enduring labor alone. "I wanted anesthesia so I don't suffer too much but the hospital told me they don't provide it." She remembers the panic and pain she felt during her miscarriage procedure and worries labor and delivery could be similar. She has frequent nightmares—flashes of her own childhood trauma and visions of violent armies locked in bloody battle—that shake her awake. She calls Kaz so he can soothe her back to sleep. During the day, she speaks with members of her church group who tell her they will pray for an easy birth.

Christians make up just over one percent of the Japanese population and Tsukasa found refuge in that small community, outside the mainstream culture that failed her when she was sexually abused. But somewhere between half and two thirds of the population is Buddhist, and in Japanese Buddhism, the pain of childbirth is believed to bond the mother and child and prepare women for the trials of motherhood. Suffering itself is considered virtuous, and in this case, foundational to parenthood.

On top of that, there is widespread skepticism about opioids throughout Asia that dates to the nineteenth century Opium Wars: the Chinese fought to stop British and other foreign traders from exporting opium from India to China, because it was causing an addiction crisis with significant social and economic costs, and to this day, opioids are strictly controlled by the Japanese government and difficult to prescribe.

Dr. Mihyon Song, the director of the Marunouchi no Mori Ladies Clinic in Tokyo, thinks antiquated ideas around pain management are a problem. She says there is no reason a woman should have to feel pain during delivery. "I think pain medication at birth should be more widespread, but there isn't adequate availability of anesthesia departments." That means it's still only an option for women in certain regions of the country, and to those who can afford it. The few hospitals that do offer epidurals often only do so during "business hours," though many babies are born overnight. Instead of medication, doctors sometimes encourage pregnant women to diet in order to keep their babies small so delivery will be easier, asking them to resist natural cravings, a different kind of agony, that can even be hazardous when it results in underweight babies.

It seems that on top of skepticism about opioids and Buddhist beliefs about suffering, there is simply an indifference to women's pain, from the almost entirely male medical establishment. Dr.

Song is the rare female obstetrician. That is in part because, as was discovered in 2018, ten top medical schools routinely altered female applicants' test scores in order to accept male applicants with lower scores due to a "silent understanding" among admissions boards that women would leave the medical profession once they had children. Dr. Song was one of a minority of women—about ten percent of her class—at a top medical school. Her father, a surgeon, encouraged her to become a doctor so she worked hard to get high scores in math and physics. When she heard about the test fixing, she says she resented that the admissions boards had led everyone to believe the process was fair. And then in the fallout after the news broke, was shocked again to learn their bias against women had become an open secret among students taking the exams, who had come to accept it as normal.

Since then, medical schools pledged to stop altering the tests and female applicants now routinely out-perform their male counterparts. Dr. Song says things are changing in other ways as well. In just the past few years, more women have started asking for pain medication. A recent survey found half of Japanese mothers said they would choose to use it for their next birth if they could. Still, the idea that pain bonds a mother and child endures. As one survey respondent explained, "I believe mothers will love their babies more if they give birth with pain and I am not interested in pain medication."

KAZ ENCOURAGES TSUKASA TO be strong during birth when they meet one last time before her due date, at a nearby hotel. Her doctor probably wouldn't approve but their separation has been so hard on both of them they decide it's worth the risk. Over a long kaiseki dinner, they decide on a name for their baby: Rota. It's a reference to a type of musical composition, and also easily pronounceable, good in case they move abroad as they hope to do someday. Their time together feels so short, and the next morning when it's time to leave, they are both in tears.

When she gets back to Matsumoto, Tsukasa distracts herself by helping her family prepare for the traditional New Year's feast. Her mother hangs a shimekazari rice straw garland on the front door and lays boughs of ripe red berries called senryo, which literally translates to *thousand coins*, to invite prosperity. Tsukasa does the best she can, given her unwieldy shape, to help her parents set out the big, premade osechi-ryōri platters overflowing with giant crab legs and whole yellowtail.

Tsukasa is delighted to see her close childhood friend Kyoko, when she visits for the New Year's holiday, but as they sit next to each other at the dining table, she can feel a simmering tension between them. Kyoko is trying to get pregnant. She is entitled to a generous new government policy that reduces the cost of IVF by seventy percent to about twelve-hundred dollars per cycle. Still, Kyoko has not yet conceived and Tsukasa thinks that has made it hard for her to confront Tsukasa's pregnancy. Tsukasa understands; can still viscerally remember her own four years of trying, and wishes her friend would see her as a source of comfort rather than a reminder of her own disappointment. "I really miss her, it makes me sad, but I just watch over her quietly," Tsukasa says.

She doesn't even mention to Kyoko the other happy news she is celebrating: Kaz video-called that morning to tell her he's won a Japan Record Award, the equivalent of a Grammy, for a song called "Citrus" that he co-wrote for the boyband Da-iCE. He didn't think he would win—there were so many other strong contenders in his category—but, as he tells her, it's starting to feel real as artists across the country reach out to congratulate him and ask when they can schedule time to work together. He tells Tsukasa he thinks the coming year is going to be very different from the last. Tsukasa gestures to her stomach and laughs: *You think?*

Two weeks later, the notional becomes real for her as well. It begins as a slight cramping but then grows more intense. By four p.m., the contractions come at somewhat regular intervals; by five p.m., they are so intense, she has to grab something to steady herself; and by six, they are less than five minutes apart, so she calls the hospital. The nurse tells her to try to have dinner first. She and her parents eat katayakisoba, a Chinese fried noodle dish with savory ankake sauce. Tsukasa struggles to eat through the pain.

When they finish, her father says, *Okay then?* and loads her suitcase into his Volvo sedan.

It is only a five-minute drive to the hospital, but time seems to stretch like putty, every second lengthening to allow her to feel the full force of it.

By the time Tsukasa arrives at the hospital's circular drive, she is in agony. A guard motions for her to use an after-hours entrance, and her father helps her inside. He carries her luggage until they reach the entrance to the ward, then gently hands her over to a pair of nurses, who escort her to a labor room and help her into a gown. Her pain is now intense—worse than the miscarriage surgery and much worse than she'd feared. A wave of nausea brings her dinner back up. A nurse cleans her, and when Tsukasa has more or less recovered, instructs her on how to breathe: a focused exhalation, as if she is blowing out candles. The nurse stays a few minutes to help Tsukasa practice, then tells her that she has to leave but will be back to check in shortly. Tsukasa feels anxiety tighten its grip. Alone in the dark room, she urges herself not to panic.

She tries to fix her mind on an image of her church group praying for her. But she can feel herself losing her way. She's sweating, though she's not sure if she's hot or cold. Waves of contractions seize her like a vise around the midsection and she struggles to remember what the nurse had said about how to stay calm. There is the emptiness where her husband should be—where he would have knelt to comfort her. She feels a deep loneliness with each searing spasm. For the next three and a half hours, a nurse checks on her every thirty minutes, but it isn't enough. She tries not to contemplate how much worse things will get because it only makes the pain worse in the moment. *I just want someone to hold my hand*, she thinks.

The Japanese feminist poet Yosano Akiko brought the experience of childbirth into public consciousness when she wrote about it for a Tokyo newspaper in 1909. At the time, she had borne eight children and would go on to have five more. She wrote that each time labor pains began, she was filled with hatred toward men: "There are those who view women as physically weak and what I want to ask them is whether a man's body could bear childbirth . . . Could a man suffer over and over in that way?" Women risk their lives bearing children, she goes on, and that's comparable to sacrifices men make for the country, like going to war. But there are no comrades in the birth experience, and it can be profoundly lonely, she writes: "Gnawing my lips, holding my body rigid, waiting on inexorable fate . . . the indifferent world goes strangely calm, I am alone."

The next time the nurse comes, Tsukasa explains that in her birth plan, she requested that someone be with her. Could she stay? Please?

I'm sorry, the nurse tells her. *We don't have enough staff— there are many other women giving birth, and I have to get to all of them.*

Tsukasa watches the nurse go. Half an hour later, she returns with aromatherapy oils to put on Tsukasa's pillow.

The pain surges keep coming, each peak higher than the last, until about 10:30 p.m. when Tsukasa is gripped by a new and terrifying sensation. "Suddenly, I just can't breathe. I'm not even aware of my breath, it's gone." The feeling is beyond panic. She is filled with the urgent need to scream for help but can't, and she is alone in the room.

Then her water breaks, warm and wet. A nurse arrives and sees that Tsukasa is struggling to breathe. The baby's heart rate is dropping, too. The midwife quickly slips an oxygen mask over Tsukasa's face and moves her to the delivery room.

The world goes fuzzy as she waits for the baby to move down her birth canal.

You can breathe, yes you can, she hears a midwife gently assure her.

Tsukasa tries to take a breath, but her body won't do it. She is desperate. Her hand reaches for something—anything—to grip and finds a thin metal rail on the side of the bed. She clutches it and wills her body to relax. She inhales tentatively.

It helps that she is no longer alone. In the delivery room, four midwives attend to her—bringing drinks when she is thirsty and helping move her hips to encourage labor to progress. She is so grateful to be ensconced in this circle of proficient and caring women, it is almost mystical. With each breath, the baby moves a little farther down, and about an hour later, finally begins to emerge.

Would you like to touch the head? a midwife asks.

Tsukasa puts her hand down to feel the top of her daughter's head. Even in the midst of her pain and disorientation, it is astonishing to touch her baby for the first time.

Then at the last moment, a male obstetrician is there with them. He instructs her to move her feet higher on the table and the midwives tell her to breathe as hard as she can. She exhales audibly and it feels as if everything stuck inside her releases all at once. There is a searing pain and a midwife cries: the baby's out! Then there she is, in the midwife's arms, ready for Tsukasa to hold. As soon as the cord is cut, the baby wails.

At the sound of her daughter's cry, Tsukasa's own eyes fill with tears. She feels a wave of relief, then awe: Her body made this tiny person; it defies comprehension. Her skin tingles with joy.

Thank you for being born, you did a great job, too, she thinks as she looks at her baby.

She takes in the shape of her face, the sweet swirl of dark hair and thinks how cute she is. It makes her feel incredibly special to have created her. And she has a strong sense that she now belongs to a lineage of powerful women. "I'm convinced women are stronger because they've experienced this," she says.

Nurses help her to a private room with a wide view of the snowcapped mountain range that hovers above the city. She'll stay there for the next five days and enjoy beautifully prepared meals, both Japanese and international cuisines. Italian pasta trimmed with bright herb garnishes; fresh fish and vegetables; and, on the last night, a celebratory French meal. She won't pay anything for the delivery and postnatal care, will instead use the government-issued vouchers that cover the cost of birth and their seven-day hospital stay.

But on this first night—January 17, 2022—as the baby sleeps in a bassinette beside her, clothed in a soft, white yukata, she calls Kaz to share the news. He doesn't pick up. It's late and he went to sleep without even knowing his wife was in labor—unaware his life has come to a critical inflection point. He awakens the next morning to find a text message from her: He is a father.

CHELSEA
KENYA

IT IS NOVEMBER, RAINY season in Kenya, and even on this humid evening, bathed in the fluorescent light of her studio apartment in
Nairobi, Chelsea is radiant, with long braids down her back and
a perfectly round bulb of a stomach. But at thirty-eight weeks
pregnant, she is uncomfortable sitting for long periods—though
it is still better than standing—so she lengthens her spine, lays her
hand on her belly and sighs. "I'm a bit tired; I just want to give
birth soon because I feel like I've been pregnant for a while and
I'm ready for something new," she says with a soft smile.

Her friend Vee, who lounges next to her on the chocolate-brown
couch, laughs knowingly, her eyes still fixed on the bright television screen. Vee is here to help Chelsea prepare for the baby and
has seen how difficult it's been for her, at just twenty-three, to balance a new job at a local bank and the demands of pregnancy. Vee,
a young woman with shorter braids and a kind smile, can sense
Chelsea's apprehension building as the due date approaches—like
lightning on the horizon, getting more vivid as the storm draws
near. Other friends have described the pain of birth and what
follows: the interrupted nights, the busy days. Vee and Chelsea

sometimes lay awake at night talking about what it will be like, a continuation of the conversation that has flowed between them since they met through childhood friends here in Uthiru, a residential neighborhood of low buildings and wooden shopping stalls. It is middle class, to the extent that there is such a thing in Nairobi, and the area has its own microclimate that makes it rainier than the rest of Nairobi. During the storms, tree branches often fall on electrical lines so there are frequent power outages, and Kenya Power trucks rumble along its ruddy dirt roads.

She rented this apartment before she got pregnant, and it isn't the place she would have chosen to raise a child: It's small and, along with the recurrent problems with electricity, there is the more concerning issue of maji, water supply. The property manager determines when residents have running water, and most days, it's only for a few hours in the evening. So she runs the bathroom tap then to collect water in a yellow jerrican and uses that the rest of the time.

The idea of caring for a newborn here makes her stomach tighten. But, she says, brightening, she won't be in this apartment much longer. "We might, probably, move in with my boyfriend, so yeah, there's plans to move to a different house."

Chelsea grew up in another boxy apartment building not far from here with her mother. Her father was out of her life too early for her have any clear memories of him, only a general recollection of her mother's dissatisfaction. Relatives later filled in the rest, describing how he drank heavily and would frequently beat her mother. By the time Chelsea was two, her mother, Ada, had had enough and left him. At the time, Ada was a waitress at the InterContinental Hotel, a luxury property next to the Kenyan Parliament that caters to international business travelers. It was a glamorous, though relatively low-paying, position, but Ada still made sure her daughter never lacked for anything. Chelsea attended good schools and always went on class trips, no matter the cost. She even got a bicycle before many of her peers, and it was so exquisite she can still remember how they coveted it, and assumed she must have come from great wealth.

It was a modern, urban childhood, filled with school uniforms and bustling city streets. But her mother would also take her on the eight-hour bus ride to visit her family upcountry, in their ancestral homeland, a city near Lake Victoria set among green hills and fertile pastures. Life felt different there, more tight-knit and traditional. But Chelsea learned it came with its own risks: fewer speeding motorbikes but more malaria-carrying mosquitoes. When she was eight and staying with her grandparents there, she developed spots that looked like ringworm. No one could determine what they were or how to treat them, even local doctors. As they grew big and swollen along the crown of her head, her grandfather suggested perhaps she'd been bewitched, that someone had used witchcraft against her. He gave her an herbal remedy to apply morning and night, and it was the only thing that worked, she says. To this day, she still relies on traditional medicine to treat certain ailments like ulcers: a practitioner puts oil on her stomach and then applies a glass with a small flame inside it to draw out the "evil eye of witches." Like Tsukasa, who used herbs when she was trying to get pregnant, Chelsea still makes room in her modern life for ancient practices.

Mostly though, Chelsea uses local clinics that practice Western medicine. Her stepfather, who entered her life when she was a teenager, used to be a doctor at one of them. He was kind and nurturing and present for her in a way that her biological father never was. After Ada gave birth to their son, Chelsea's half-brother Daniel, the four of them lived happily together in Nairobi. Then Chelsea left for a top university in Eldoret, a smaller city several hours by bus from Nairobi, surrounded by farmland and bisected by the Sosiani River. She loved its natural beauty and excelled in her classes on tourism and computer science.

During her last year there, Ada called to tell her that her stepfather had fallen off his motorbike and bruised his leg, a common occurrence in Nairobi, where at one point an entire ward of Kenyatta National Hospital was devoted to motorbike injuries. He was confident it was minor, a contusion that would heal in time. But it didn't—his leg became increasingly discolored, then whole patches turned black. Still, he casually—perhaps stubbornly—dismissed his symptoms, until finally, he could no longer walk, and Ada prevailed on him to seek medical treatment. By then he was so immobile that several men had to carry him from the house and help him to the clinic, where staff determined his case was beyond their capabilities and referred him to the national hospital.

There doctors diagnosed him with deep vein thrombosis, a blood clot in his leg. And they discovered that an errant piece of the clot had broken loose and lodged in his lung, causing a pulmonary embolism. It was too late to save him; he arrived at the hospital at two in the afternoon and died there at seven that evening.

When Ada called to break the news, Chelsea was distraught: *I'll come home, Mama, to be there with you, we'll get through it together*, she said.

But Ada told her to stay where she was and not interrupt her education.

Chelsea only found out months later how depressed her mother had become and that it had driven her to drink—to the point that her organs began to fail. Chelsea watched the same horrific timeline unspool: By the time Ada got to the hospital, nothing could be done to revive her liver and kidneys, and she died, just five months after her husband. So at twenty-one years old, on the cusp of full adulthood, Chelsea became an orphan. After she graduated from university, she moved back to Nairobi and set out alone in the sprawling capital city, the vast financial and cultural nerve center of East Africa.

"One thing I've learned is that when someone is grieving, they're not supposed to be alone because that's when the intrusive thoughts come," she says. She tried to soothe her own depression with drinking, but it only fueled an incipient alcoholism, the very illness that had taken her mother.

"I would drink morning to evening, then go out for more drinks in the evening and stay out until morning again," she remembers. She neglected to eat and lost so much weight that rumors circulated she had contracted HIV. Rather than rally around her, her family and close community in Nairobi effectively disowned her. Relatives upcountry heard she was drinking and chastised her. One uncle was particularly cutting when he snapped: *You're not the first one to lose a mother.*

Somewhere in the haze and throb of nightclub dawns that bled into dim, somnolent dusks, she found someone who did understand her pain and offered comfort: a man named Joseph. He was broad-shouldered, bearded and handsome, with a warmth she found intoxicating. They weren't an obvious romantic match, though. Joseph was nearly two decades older than Chelsea and from a different ethnic community.

Chelsea is Luo, an ethnic group from the Lake Victoria region that has produced members of the country's political and academic elite, including Barack Obama Sr., a senior government economist in the seventies, and Raila Odinga, the former prime minister. Joseph is Kalenjin, a group from the Rift Valley known for leading an early anticolonial resistance movement which has, since independence in 1963, played a dominant role in Kenyan politics: Two of the country's five presidents have been Kalenjin. Though both groups are politically powerful and from the same corner of the country, they are still culturally far enough apart that even in modern-day Kenya, theirs was an unlikely romantic union.

And there was one more thing: Joseph was married. But as he explained to Chelsea, he was estranged from his wife, who lived abroad. That left Joseph lonely, just as she was. They continued to talk, and as they grew closer, the murky fog of Chelsea's grief began to lift.

"For some weird reason, he helped me come out of that because he was just there for me, he was really supportive and when we got close, I had someone to talk to. I could see he was more understanding and wasn't judging me," she says. In a world where she felt she had no one, it seemed she had finally found *the* one. And a few months later, she was pregnant.

It came as a surprise, the result of a faulty morning-after pill, she says. "I don't know if I took it too late, I don't know what happened, but somehow it didn't work." The emergency contraception, called Postinor-2 (or P2), is popular among young women in Kenya, says Dr. Rosa Chemwey Ndiema, an obstetrician who used to own a pharmacy near what she describes as "an elite, Christian-based university that doesn't promote premarital sex." One of the bestselling drugs at her pharmacy was P2. Ndiema had to make sure to have enough of it in stock on Fridays because most other pharmacies were closed over the weekend. "I can assure you, you can run a whole pharmacy just selling P2," she laughs.

The problem is the pill can be unreliable, as Chelsea discovered. Both doses have to be taken within a narrow timeframe for it to work. There are many better options: The government subsidizes contraception, so condoms and Depo-Provera, a contraceptive injection, are free in most public clinics, and IUDs are heavily discounted. Still, there's so much stigma around women being sexually active, Ndiema says, that they don't use preventative methods and instead rely on P2 as an emergency solution.

Ideas around contraception go back to the colonial era. In the 1920s and 30s, British officials wanted to increase Kenyan birth-rates to "expand the availability of cheap labor." But when the 1948 East African census revealed previous statistics had undercounted Black Kenyans, some colonial officials began to worry about an "unmanageable population" and encouraged contraception. Still, aggressive birth control programs proved hard to implement and on top of that, the Christianity that missionaries brought to the region stigmatized birth control, as well as abortion.

The British colonial penal code said anyone who performed an abortion could be imprisoned for fourteen years and a woman who did it herself could be imprisoned for seven. At independence in 1963, Kenya's new government kept those harsh guidelines in place. Then in 2010, the country's new constitution made abortion legal in "emergency cases"—when a pregnancy results from rape or compromises the mother's health. Still, an assertive antiabortion movement, comprised mainly of Christian organizations backed by American antiabortion groups, has pushed back against any further relaxations to the law. The American government itself has also curbed abortion access here: Since 1973, the Helms amendment has effectively prohibited US foreign assistance funding from supporting abortion services around the world. And conservative administrations since Reagan's have put in place a so-called Global Gag Rule that makes foreign health organizations ineligible for American grant funding for health services if they provide any kind of abortion support, even referrals and even with their own, separate funding. That policy has historically been rescinded by Democratic administrations and reinstated by Republican ones. In 2017, President Donald Trump restricted twelve billion dollars in health funding to aid recipients globally. President Joe Biden reversed the policy, but then in 2025, President Trump reinstated it, just four days into his second term.

Despite that, abortions are still common in Kenya; there are an estimated thirty per hundred births (in the US, it is about twenty per hundred births). That number is hard to verify, though, because most medical facilities will only perform them "undercover," Ndiema explains, and charge exploitative rates. Women who can't afford to pay use knitting needles, drink bleach, or go to cheaper "backstreet places." Conditions there can be unsanitary and women frequently contract sepsis or have other complications. For that reason, incomplete abortions account for more than half of all gynecological admissions at the country's main national hospital. Many women require long hospital stays and nearly two hundred die annually.

Chelsea says she didn't consider terminating the pregnancy. "I decided that I was going to be a mom, I knew there would be challenges but that was the decision I made." A year after her parents died, she was bringing new life into the world. She immediately stopped drinking and felt an enlivening sense of purpose. "I could feel that this baby came to save me."

CHELSEA GAZES OUT HER apartment window across a variegated sea of corrugated metal roofs, to a water tower in the distance. It fades in and out of focus. Her eyes are tired—at nearly thirty-nine weeks pregnant, her whole body is. She's been nauseous for several days and woke up this morning to throbbing pain in her lower back as well.

Maybe it's worth getting a checkup to make sure the baby is all right, she thinks.

She calls an Uber, and on the forty-minute car ride, watches everyday life slip past. It's both reassuring and isolating to see the frenetic world carrying on, even as her own body feels so thick and unfamiliar. A group of boys chases after a beat-up brown soccer ball; a woman wearing gumboots carries a large, plastic sack on her head; a cow grazes at the side of the highway; and a Maasai boy herds goats on the median. Chelsea closes her eyes.

Yes, the baby is fine, the doctor tells her calmly, after he completes the examination. But you, my dear, are already two centimeters dilated. He tells her she can go home and return when she feels real contractions, but she worries about making the long trip again, so he admits her that evening. She messages Joseph, but he still lives in Eldoret and can't make it in time.

The next morning, her friend Vee arrives, and Chelsea breathes a sigh of relief to have a companion. Then a nurse examines her and says the dilation is progressing slower than expected. So a little before noon, the doctor suggests they induce labor. She agrees—she just wants to get it done—but only realizes afterward that the drip they put in her arm to strengthen contractions will make her labor much more intense.

Four hours later, the pain is so excruciating she's scared she won't be able to endure it. She asks for medication—gas or local anesthesia maybe—but the nurse tells her they could cause complications, and she wouldn't advise it. But the pain continues to get worse and she can feel anxiety rising hot in her chest. Please, she asks an hour later, could she get an epidural? The nurse calmly explains it will cost about three hundred US dollars. Chelsea can't afford that, so she surrenders to the experience and grips Vee's hand.

In private hospitals like the one where Chelsea delivered, "you get what you pay for," says Dr. Ombaba Osano, a lecturer and pediatric specialist at the University of Nairobi. "If you want to pay for more expensive, more effective pain medication, you'll get it, whereas at public hospitals you are limited to what the government has provided." Epidurals are expensive and also require skilled personnel to administer, so just two percent of birthing women in Kenya receive one.

How do you feel? Vee asks Chelsea gently.

It hurts, can't believe how much it hurts. And I'm so tired, I don't think I can do it, Chelsea murmurs. It is after nine at night and she hasn't eaten all day; she was so nauseous and over-whelmed, she only had a soda. Vee tells her to breathe. A nurse examines her again and tells her it is time to push. Chelsea finds the nurse's steady presence calming, but can't summon the energy to follow her directive.

Chelsea, listen to me, you need to push, the nurse repeats urgently; *You're choking this baby.*

Chelsea does—as best she can—and then finally, miraculously, the baby is out. But in the disorienting aftermath, Chelsea knows something is wrong. The newborn doesn't make a sound as a clutch of medical staff surround her to administer some kind of intervention. Chelsea's catches a first glimpse of her child and can see her skin is bluish; she looks wildly at the nurses for reassurance.

She's swallowed some fluid during delivery, one of them explains.

Chelsea watches as they apply suction to her baby's mouth to clear her airway, then rub her feet to stimulate resuscitation. At last, the tiny infant takes her first breath. The room relaxes and Chelsea, too, inhales deeply for the first time as a mother.

Women in Chelsea's Luo community traditionally delivered at home, and the placenta, which was believed to hold extraordinary power, was buried in the ground to connect babies with their ancestors. The ritual continued into the twentieth century, when the British pushed to Westernize birth practices. "By the 1930s, few areas of colonial medicine were more central to the 'civilizing mission' than maternity work," writes Lynn M. Thomas in *Politics of the Womb.*

Missionary hospitals trained traditional birth attendants in Western science so they could use it in home births, which accounted for the vast majority of deliveries. As an indication of how few hospital births there were, in 1945, the country's three main hospitals handled only about three hundred births between them—a tiny fraction of the overall number in a country of five million people—and few, if any, were to Black Kenyan mothers.

Mama Asande Bonyo began having children just a few years later, in her round, thatch-roofed hut on a floor covered with animal skins and reed mats. She still lives on the same plot of land she did then, near the shores of Lake Victoria in the town of Kendu Bay, the birthplace of Barack Obama Sr. and the center of Chelsea's ancestral homeland. Bonyo's government-issued identification says she is eighty-seven, but she says she is not sure exactly when she was born. She knows it was the year the locusts came—Bonyo means locust—which would make her ninety-one. She is frail and wheelchair-bound, but she recalls with clarity what it was like to give birth when Kenya was still a British colony.

"Back then, people gave birth to a lot of children. We did not plan children, we just gave birth until we could not give birth anymore." She herself had eight, under the guidance of a nyamrerwa, or traditional birth attendant. "Your family would just call her and she would come to the house. Sometimes she would come late and find that you have given birth, and in that case, she would cut the umbilical cord." Nyamrerwa used centuries-old local practices and were skilled at turning the baby if it wasn't facing the right way for birth. "They were mostly older women," says Bonyo, "and they helped so many mothers, especially those whose babies were not in the right position."

The infant mortality rate around that time was high though— almost 180 per 1,000 infants, six times what it is today—and no one even kept statistics on maternal mortality, an indication of priorities at the time. In the following decades, the government pushed to ensure that all birthing mothers had access to medical care and infant mortality began to decline. Then with the AIDS pandemic in the late 1990s, fewer women used nyamrerwa birth attendants because they did not have the equipment hospitals did to prevent disease transmission during birth.

But it wasn't until 2013 that things really changed. That year, the country made all prenatal visits and childbirth free of charge. At the time, still less than half of all Kenyan mothers delivered in hospitals, but after care became free, it increased to close to ninety percent. Still, the quality of birth care remains uneven: in part because the healthcare system, which was originally modeled on the British National Health Service, has since incorporated elements of the American system, with private employer-based insurance and that helped produce the current two-tiered system.

At expensive private hospitals, birthing mothers have a "high-end delivery environment" similar to that in wealthy nations, says Dr. Osano, who has worked in both private and public hospitals. There are well-appointed rooms, tubs for water births, and patients can bring their own doulas, a modern iteration of nyamrerwa birth attendants.

Public hospitals, by contrast, which are largely free at point of service and can't turn patients away, get massively overcrowded, though Osano adds that the healthcare workers there are usually better qualified. Dr. Ndiema, the obstetrician who used to own the pharmacy that sold emergency contraception, now runs the maternity ward at Kenyatta National Hospital. The ward was designed for about sixty-five patients, but she has had to accommodate as many as three hundred at a time (many are there because lower-level regional hospitals can't care for them, due to lack of running water, gloves, or a trained obstetrician). That means three or four women in active labor might share single a bed. "It's really bad,"

Ndiema says. "Sometimes we run out of bed space and women have to labor in the corridors or on benches." She examines each woman and sometimes performs invasive procedures like membrane sweeps, then changes the linens to protect the other women in the bed from infection. She says the solution isn't more funding, which the hospital gets through donor organizations, but better organization. "What we could do is decentralize, equip and empower the lower-level clinics so that they only refer high-risk patients," to national hospitals like hers.

Chelsea's delivery at a small private hospital, though painful, is comparatively smooth. Still, she runs into trouble when it is time to leave two days later. The National Health Insurance Fund will cover the cost of her bed during admission—about four thousand Kenyan shillings or thirty dollars—but the private insurance she gets through work only agrees to pay seventy-five-thousand shillings ($500) of the hundred thousand shilling ($750 USD) medical bill, though her limit is high enough that it should have covered everything. The difference she owes is about two-thirds of her monthly take-home pay, more than she can afford with her minimal savings. "At the end I was just bombarded with an extra bill," she says. Thankfully, clinic staff negotiate on her behalf and allow her to leave without paying.

So, the day after giving birth, Chelsea walks out the sliding glass door of the maternity hospital, proud of the baby in her arms and impressively well put-together in a ribbed, maroon dress. Vee is waiting there to help her get home, and she admires the infant, eyes shut tight beneath a plush white blanket and pink hat. "Her name is Ada," Chelsea tells Vee as she looks down at her new baby with wonder. "I named her after my mother."

ANNA
FINLAND

IT'S STILL EARLY EVENING, but Anna is tired. The work of manufacturing a flesh-and-blood human turns each day into an endurance event, and it doesn't help that outside her bright, blond-wood flat in Turku, Finland, the sky is already a deep wintry black. Late November and so far north, there are just six and a half hours of daylight. The streetlights that flickered on around 3:30 in the afternoon cast concentric circles in the snow and tall cranes draw triangles in the sky. This part of the city, a salty-aired district near the harbor, was industrial until only a few years ago, when residential construction began to draw young families.

Anna, thirty-six, cuts an elegant figure at eight months pregnant, in a long, formfitting black dress, her dark blond hair slicked into a tight ponytail. Still, she feels leaden on her feet as she clears the remains of dinner from the table with her partner, Masa, who wears a charcoal haori jacket and tabi split-toe socks, black hair wound high in a top knot. Anna bends to scrape extra food into the waste bin, but her belly proves too much of an impediment, so she pauses in an effortful hunch, holds her breath, and empties the plates.

Alright then, she exhales and smiles wearily at Masa, forty-five, who's come into the kitchen behind her.

You okay? he asks, as she leans against the counter.

She can feel a tightening in her stomach but nods anyway. These irregular contractions come and go so she greets them with a degree of nonchalance; this is her second child and she knows the grip of true labor. Liv, nine, her daughter from a previous relationship, is in her bedroom watching Disney shows on an iPad, pink headphones atop a torrent of long blond locks. Anna separated from Liv's father less than a year after she was born, and since then, they have shared custody and successfully coparented. That's fairly common: More than half of Finnish babies are born to unwed parents. That rate is similar to other Nordic and Western European countries but slightly higher than the US and Kenya, where it's closer to four in ten, and significantly higher than Japan, where just two percent of children are born to unmarried mothers. Still, it represents a seismic shift from Finland in the 1960s when almost all babies were born to married parents. The stigma has faded since then, and there are few tax incentives to encourage marriage.

Anna and Masa have no plans to wed, only to prepare for this new baby, a son, who could come any time. And they feel ready. Anna has already washed and folded the durable little clothes she received in the "baby box" that Finland gives all expectant mothers who attend appointments through the public system. It's one reason that 99.5 percent of expectant mothers get prenatal care at public clinics. In addition to clothes, the box includes toys, diapers, thermometers, picture books, bedding, and a mattress that turns the box itself into a crib. Since the 1970s, it has also included condoms. The program started in 1937, in response to high child mortality and poverty, and all Finnish babies receive the same box as a way to give them a chance at an equal start in life.

Anna has unpacked and organized the baby supplies but never got around to deep-cleaning the apartment. "The baby isn't going to look at the corners of the room like, 'Oh, it's so messy.' So I think these things are secondary," she laughs. That's the way she responds to many of life's small stressors, with an equanimity she ascribes in part to being raised with the Finnish ethos of "sisu," stoic perseverance.

It could also be because many of the big stressors of child birth and parenting are mitigated by strong social programs. According to the World Happiness Report, Finland is the happiest country in the world. Dr. Alexandra Schmidt, an American physician who is in Helsinki doing research at the Finnish Institute for Health and Welfare, says it's more nuanced than the ranking would suggest. "I think *happy* is the wrong word; it's more like *content*. And I think it's easier to feel that way when you know there's a system in place to help if things go wrong. Pregnant women are confident in the system and trust it will work for them."

Finnish maternity leave begins a month before birth, so Anna's just started hers. She'll receive nearly ninety percent of her salary from her job—she's a concept designer for large events—from now until her baby is two weeks old, and then about seventy percent for the following nine months. That's based on her income; higher earners get a lower percentage, though big firms sometimes top them up to full pay. Mothers with low or no income get a minimum allowance. Anna's only plan from now until the baby arrives is to relax and attend to her own needs; his will soon take precedence.

She reties her cloth belt, which now falls mid–rib cage, exhales audibly, and asks Masa, *Are you going to the boat tonight?*

No, no, I'm helping at that festival this week. He looks at her expectantly, waiting for her to remember.

The silence stretches. She is tired. Finally it comes to her and she nods with relief.

They are new to this life of shared meals and integrated schedules. Masa only moved to Finland a few months ago from Amsterdam, where he was a performance artist and, for additional income, a massage therapist. But now, with his work permit still in process, he works as a cleaner on a cruise ship, eleven-Euro-an-hour labor mostly done by recent immigrants from North Africa and Eastern Europe. It isn't the life he'd envisioned for himself when he visited Finland a year and a half ago to work on a theater project and met Anna on Tinder.

It was summertime, long languid days and wildflowers in bloom, the season for something airy, she explains. "I was just swiping, not taking it too seriously, and then I saw this peculiar-looking guy who seemed like he had just survived some sort of an explosion," she recalls with a deep, warm laugh. His profile said he worked in the arts so she thought they might have something in common and, because he was just visiting, it would be fairly casual. When they met, though, she sensed something special about him, "something very good." She thought he saw her as perhaps "too posh," but still they were drawn to each other, and met again and again. "It wasn't the sex," she says. "That's something very different. No, I found something magical about this person. He's not a he; he's not a she; he is a creature and his magical qualities are unexplainable."

They were happy together, and as Anna told Masa, at thirty-six, she felt like the window for her to have another child was closing. So six months after they met, they were thrilled to learn their ineffable fascination had resulted in pregnancy. Anna knew it in her body even before the test confirmed it and was overjoyed. "Things clicked and it felt like, this is gonna work," she says.

Then came the hard part: reorganizing their lives to accommodate a new one. Anna needed to stay in Finland with Liv, whose father lives nearby. But Masa is a Dutch citizen and had deep roots in Amsterdam, so he was reluctant to leave. It was especially hard to disentangle from the communal residence where he lived with an assemblage of people from different creative fields. They were inspiring and collaborative, but many were also financially strapped, and as he dithered about what to do, they got frustrated: *Are you staying or not? And what do we do with your space if you leave, will you be back?*

Their questions inflamed his already tense phone conversations with Anna, which frequently devolved into fights. She wanted him in Finland well ahead of the baby's arrival, but it all felt uncomfortably rushed to Masa. "Originally I thought I would have more time, but I moved very rapidly, almost forcefully," he says.

He finally made it to Turku, and as they began to explore the city together, they also explored the idea of shared parenthood. One morning, on one of the city's bright yellow, electric buses, Masa watched a woman effortlessly collapse her stroller to the size of a backpack as she boarded. Anna hardly noticed but Masa was transfixed. Whereas before, he'd ignored strollers almost entirely—the ambient noise of other people's parenthood—now he noticed every detail: How the tires attached to the frame, the quality of the suspension system. He'd found a tangible aspect of childrearing that could be his contribution. He certainly couldn't approximate what Anna was doing, creating blood and bone, but he could find a conveyance for it, with a tight turning radius. But those little mechanical marvels carried exorbitant price tags and awakened a deep worry that even if he did resurrect his art career, he still might not be able to provide the kind of stroller his family should have, the kind of life.

"I'd like to be equally supportive," he explains, "but I'm grateful Anna supports my vision even though I'm very much struggling."

Anna is sympathetic but doesn't share his anxiety about parental responsibility. She's already a mother and long past what she calls her "rebel days," a raucous stretch of young adulthood that followed a relatively traditional upbringing on the outskirts of Turku. As a child, she spent hours in its pine forests—tall, straight trees atop a tufted green carpet—where she and her friends created potions from berries and mushrooms, nibbled on roots, and romped alongside tawny foxes and swooping birds. Now, she laughs, her own daughter plays "real estate agent" in their small city apartment.

Anna, too, leads a somewhat different life from her own mother, who owned a shoe boutique downtown when Anna was young, across the street from the bank where Anna's father worked. Anna was in daycare part-time and otherwise with her grandparents. When the economy soured in the late eighties, her mother closed the shop and spent several years raising Anna and her two brothers. Anna went to art school and built a career in the design industry, which she continued fairly easily after giving birth to Liv.

Her path is reasonably well-worn for Finnish women of her generation. The prime minister, Sanna Marin, is roughly the same age as Anna, and heads a governing coalition of five political parties all led by women, most of them also in their thirties. Anna says this government's election was a watershed moment for Finnish families: "It became clear that being a mother and taking care of the state weren't mutually exclusive; motherhood happens and it's okay to be a mother."

She doesn't feel the need to keep her family and professional lives separate or to engage in the maternal code-switching that women in other places might—commiserating with friends in

graphic detail about the crude realities of childrearing while acting at work as if their children don't exist. In fact, Anna says the
debate over working mothers seems so resolved that the conversation has largely moved on to fathers and non-birthing partners,
"that they should have the same rights as mothers and also be
entitled to spend time with their kids."

For Masa, though, it's not so simple. He needs to rebuild
his career before he can even consider how to integrate it with
fatherhood. And what is a father's role, after all? He wrestles
with the question in part because he lost his own dad at a young
age and was raised in Matsuyama, Japan, by a single mother, a
kind woman who educated deaf students. Masa's older brother
sometimes played the paternal figure, but Masa remembers him as
being domineering, even harsh, and isn't an example he wants to
emulate. So now, Masa will need to find his own way.

A MONTH LATER, THEY join Anna's parents at their house for Christmas. Her mother has filled the space with traditional Nordic
decorations—geometric mobiles and a ram figurine made of
straw. When Anna was young, almost all Christmases were
snowy, but that's become less common. This year, though, heavy
flakes began to fall overnight. "It's very classic, beautiful like
old times, so it's nice Masa gets to experience it this way," she
says. She dashes with him through the icy afternoon air into the
warm sauna, where she sprays water on the hot rocks to produce
a satisfying hiss of steam—the vapor, known as löyly, rising to
fill the wood-paneled chamber. A Finnish proverb describes saunas as "the poor man's apothecary," and they're treated with
almost religious reverence. Until the twentieth century, women
even gave birth there, because it was understood to be the clean-
est location in the home.

I like the idea of a home birth, Masa muses when Anna describes that tradition. At a workshop he recently led in Romania, a man had told him about the "magnificent, natural experience" of his partner's home birth. Anna is unmoved. *I've given birth before and I don't see our bathroom doing the job very well,* she says, smiling at him. Home births are rare here, just 0.2 percent of births. Anna will deliver at a public hospital, like almost every Finnish mother.

Of course, the mother has to be comfortable, Masa replies gently.

Finland's maternity clinic system is a point of national pride. The year Anna will deliver, 2022, marks a century since the first birth center opened in a renovated log cabin at a children's hospital in Helsinki. The centers are staffed by midwives, who have long played an integral role in birth and oversee maternity care, only consulting obstetricians when medically necessary. Midwifery was one of the first professions available to women, and since the eighteenth century, has required at least four years of specialized training in Finland. The University of Turku, just down the road from Anna, made that training free in 1816, and half a century later, the country had more licensed midwives than doctors. The national emphasis on birth care was by design: Finland was frequently at war and lower infant and maternal mortality ensured a steady supply of manpower. It's an ideology that explains much of early family policy, here and around the world.

Still, the system has had remarkable success. Finland's infant and maternal mortality rates are among the lowest in the world. A *Women's Health Reports* paper argues that aspects of the Finnish model could help the US decrease its maternal mortality. Specifically, the authors point to Finland's "decentralized network of primary health centers that serve local communities and support both the physical and psychosocial well-being of expectant mothers." The clinics are publicly funded, and birth is essentially free.

As Anna's due date draws closer though, she begins to worry Masa is not being as careful as he should be. Around the New Year, less than two weeks before the baby is due, Masa's friends from Amsterdam are coming to town—a couple that was part of the performance community he left behind—and Masa is eager to see them. But there has been an uptick in Covid cases, and Anna doesn't want Masa to meet them indoors. He thinks it's worth the risk; he hasn't seen any close friends since he moved to Finland and hates having to choose between them and the new family he's building.

He tells her earnestly, *I have difficulty prioritizing one thing and the rest is secondary, I'd rather stay on a more horizontal plane.*

Listen, Anna responds, *I'm going into labor sometime in the next two weeks. If you're home with Covid, where will I go when I leave the hospital with a newborn?*

Masa is silent. In that moment—in a home, in a country, where he's only just moved—he suddenly feels the additional dislocation of new parenthood. The baby is not even born, and he's already being asked to sacrifice the creative and personal freedom he'd cultivated for most of his life.

When his friends arrive later that week, he meets them for a long walk then says goodbye outside the restaurant where they're going to dinner.

This is bloody ridiculous, he says as they part, his eyes burning with disappointment.

Anna is appreciative, though. And a few days later, she goes into labor. Masa is there to massage her feet and keep her relaxed in the large delivery room, an armchair in one corner and a birthing ball in another. The midwives work in shifts—three over the course of Anna's labor—but pass information seamlessly. Anna tells the first one she doesn't want an incision or stitches if it can be avoided, and the third makes sure of it. Studies show midwife-based systems have better health outcomes and lower costs, perhaps because doctors are more likely to use instrumental or surgical interventions.

The only time Anna sees a doctor is when she receives spinal anesthesia. "I took every kind of pain relief available," she recounts with a smile. That's common: ninety-two percent of Finnish women receive some form of pain relief during labor, one of the highest rates in the world.

The birth itself is quicker than Masa had anticipated. First he sees the top of his son's head and soon his whole face is visible. Masa takes out his phone to record and a minute later, the baby is in the world. He had expected the kind of shouting and medical commotion he'd seen on television, but there is none of that. "It's amazing that new life is born but at the same time, you expect something really big and then it's actually not that big," he reflects afterward. "I know it wasn't easy, but it was way less dramatic than the image I had before."

The midwife cleans the baby and when she hands him to Masa, he has a soft smile on his face that Anna has never seen before.

"No niin," Masa says in Finnish to his son: *There you go, it's done.*

After the delivery, the staff move Anna to a recovery room. Typically she would share it with another mother and baby, but she has it to herself. "It's luxurious, yes, indeed," she smiles.

Her daughter, Liv, comes to meet the baby and is quiet when she first sees him, taking in the moment. But when Anna's parents arrive to pick her up a short time later, Liv is effusive and reports how "super cute" he is, clearly proud to be his big sister.

The rest of the day, Anna and Masa take turns cradling the baby, remarking on the beauty of his jet-black hair, which peeks out from beneath the little white hospital bonnet. Masa has the same gentle smile as the first time he held him. Still, even in their postnatal bliss, they know there is a major issue to resolve: what to name him. They still haven't been able to agree. First they choose Eemeli, but hospital staff keep mistaking him for a girl, and they have second thoughts. So they put off the decision and just call him by the nickname Paavo, a traditional Finnish name.

That's still his name two days later when Anna is cleared to go home. As it was with Tsukasa, whose baby was born just a week after Anna's, birth and delivery are covered by the public health system. So she pays nothing and leaves—that's it.

From the hospital, Anna goes directly to her parents' house to introduce them to their new grandson. "They are in love," Anna says, gazing down at her tiny newborn, "especially my father here, he has lost his heart to this charming boy." They toast with sparkling wine and have blinis, Russian-style pancakes with sour cream and fish eggs, which Anna is thrilled to be able to eat again. Pregnancy is over. The next phase has begun.

But Masa isn't sure what that will look like for him. As he watches Anna settle deeply into a chair to nurse their baby, he is in awe. "There's a bond or natural connection," that he says he hadn't previously understood. He'd seen Anna parent Liv of course, but this feels different, primal. If she can grow and sustain this new being, what's left for him to do? Anna senses his apprehension but is confident he'll find his way. She's seen how he's become a warm presence for Liv, comforting her when she needs it, but careful not to overstep.

"He'll take care of us. The way I've seen him take care of Liv, I have no worries," Anna says.

Masa, though, is much less sure.

SARAH

US

SARAH HAS COME A long way. Not strictly in geographic terms—she grew up just forty minutes away in Utah Valley, known locally as "Happy Valley." The majority there was Mormon, and as Sarah describes it, "you had to put on the persona of a happy, golden family that followed all the church teachings and lived a perfect, righteous life." But as an adult she's built something different, more authentic, here in West Jordan, a fast-growing Salt Lake City suburb surrounded by Oquirrh Mountain peaks so breathtaking, it's clear why early pioneers found something holy about this place.

Her house sits in a cul-de-sac of nearly identical gray clapboard homes. Their gabled roofs echo the alpine range in the distance, now crowned with snow. It is early December, and for the past three weeks, she and her husband, Brian, have methodically scrubbed every room. "Nesting," she explains, and not the sort of work husbands back in Happy Valley would typically undertake. But at thirty-four weeks pregnant, it is getting harder for her to do it alone. "I've always been overweight so I'm used to having to accommodate for a big belly," she says as she rescues a pastel baby headband from the floor and returns it to a rack with a dozen

others, "but now I try to bend over and think, 'Oh, that hurts.'"
She laughs in Brian's direction and reveals her wide, flawless smile.

Sarah, thirty-three, works as an educational technology specialist at a public school that serves low-income students. Brian
delivers Amazon packages for a third-party delivery service,
from one of many unmarked commercial spaces across from a
sprawling Amazon fulfillment center. He is auburn-haired with
dark-rimmed glasses and an athletic build—thanks in part to that
delivery job, which allows him to run all day. It suits him better
than his previous position at a call center that was so sedentary and
stressful he developed anxiety attacks, acid reflux, and gout. Sarah
encouraged him to find something different, and as soon as he
started working the delivery route, his health issues resolved. Still,
it doesn't pay particularly well, and the only insurance options are
high-premium, high-deductible plans, so they rely on Sarah's job
for insurance.

Their dual-income household would have made their family an
oddity back in Happy Valley. When she was growing up there, her
father was an IT manager for Brigham Young University's College
of Nursing and her mother worked in the home to raise their seven
children, including Sarah's disabled brother Evan. That's what
women have always done in her family, which traces its lineage to
the original "Utah pioneer company" that traveled from the eastern
US to establish the Church of Jesus Christ of Latter-day Saints here
in Utah. Like those earlier Mormon women, her mother subscribes
to the belief that, as Sarah puts it, "your role as a female is to be a
good wife and mother, that is your end-all, be-all." (The church's
official position is that "fathers are to preside over their families in
love and righteousness and are responsible to provide the necessi-
ties of life… Mothers are primarily responsible for the nurture of
their children.") Sarah's mother never asked for help, even offered

to care for neighbors' children on top of her own seven—an outward projection of total maternal competence and ease.

She raised Sarah and her siblings in a ranch house on a street with others like it, around the corner from the elementary school and not far from the leafy campuses of Utah Valley University and Brigham Young University. Many of the families in the neighborhood were just as large, and after school, children spilled outside as mothers kept watch. They were all members of the local "ward," an LDS geographic designation that means they attend the same church—its low steeple visible from her family's front yard.

Sarah, a high achiever by nature, threw herself into the dutiful, devout daughter role and became a "goody-two-shoes" with an air of righteous superiority. But that posture hid the prickly truth that she was never truly comfortable. She didn't feel divine revelation so much as obligation. By the end of high school, she was old enough to know that if she stayed close to home, it would be the beginning and end of her story. So she applied to one of the few colleges she knew outside Utah—an LDS university in Idaho. But when she got there, she realized she'd only dug herself in deeper.

"If you can get more for Happy Valley than Happy Valley, it was where I went to school," Sarah says. Religion was at the center of university life. The campus temple—white marble spires topped with a gilded angel—loomed above the athletic fields. The school's honor code prohibited tank tops, shorts, premarital sex, alcohol, and coffee. The rules didn't bother Sarah as much as the creeping feeling that the internal righteousness she'd so painstakingly cultivated as a child was no longer enough. To her dismay, her adult body defied the culture's ideal female form—slim and blond. And that would make it harder to do what so many of her female classmates told her they'd come there to accomplish: find a man to marry.

That was never Sarah's goal, but she still nodded agreeably as girls in her classes strategized about the best way to land a husband and explained that they'd chosen majors like early child education to prepare themselves to care for their own children. Then she watched as one by one they got engaged to their boyfriends.

The LDS religion has always emphasized procreation as a way to accommodate celestial spirits waiting to take human form. The culture encourages its members to marry young and have large families just as their pioneer forebearers did. Life in the mountain west was hard and the "weaker sex" had to be strong. They raised children and took on tough farmwork; many were also trained in obstetrics as well as traditional healing methods like blessing and anointing. That culture is still evident in the current social media trend of women who publicly embrace traditional gender roles. Many are Mormon, including Hannah Neeleman, a lithe blond woman with eight children and ten million Instagram followers. They watch as she scores loaves of sourdough, and milks cows straight into her homemade, noncaffeinated turmeric latte. She gave birth to her children by candlelight without pain relief and competed in the Mrs. World pageant twelve days postpartum. "I feel like we're doing what God wants," she told the British newspaper, *The Times*.

That idea of a traditional marriage in which the mother doesn't work outside the home is largely a fantasy, though, perpetuated by church leaders who won't admit how much class plays a role, says Margaret Toscano, an associate professor at the University of Utah and noted LDS feminist. Toscano is a demonstrative speaker, with wavy dark hair that falls loose at her shoulders. She says there have always been Mormon women who needed to do paid work to provide for their families. (Neeleman's husband, Daniel, is notably the son of the billionaire founder of JetBlue.)

Sarah knows well how punishing traditional gender roles can

be. Her older sister Julie married a man she met through church shortly after college, but grew depressed by what she described as his constant recriminations that the house wasn't neat enough, the children too disorderly. Julie tried to escape what she felt as domestic entrapment through books, but that seemed to enrage her husband. Still, it took Julie years to divorce him, in part because, though she had a chemistry degree, she had not had a job for two decades and worried she wouldn't be able to support herself and her children without him.

The church has a more complicated history with gender, however, than those strict roles might suggest. The original Mormon pioneers were radicals who criticized many traditional institutions, including traditional marriage, Toscano explains. And they believed in a Heavenly Mother, alongside the Heavenly Father, that Mormon feminists have long argued is a true goddess and not simply a "heavenly housewife." Still, by the early twentieth century, Mormons were embarrassed by their history of plural marriage, Toscano says, and wanted to be accepted into mainstream culture, so they embraced the conservative family ideal. When strains of feminism have periodically emerged, church leaders stamp them out. Toscano herself was excommunicated in 2000 for publicly advocating that women should be ordained as priests. It came at a particularly painful time because she had been raising four young daughters in the church. Still, she says, though the church periodically excommunicates LDS feminist leaders, it has never been able to fully expunge the movement. "That silences the group for a while, but feminism always rises back up."

In college, Sarah began to view herself as a feminist but couldn't find a like-minded community in the church; the leaders had so effectively suppressed it. So by the end of college, she was pretty much done with Mormonism, and she joined a wave of young women leaving organized religion. Americans have been getting less religious for decades, but now is the first time women have led the exodus, because more women in these communities now identify as feminist and they don't want to be associated with institutions that uphold traditional gender roles.

Sarah says people in her generation are more likely to read about feminism and different approaches to gender online, and less likely to believe that ideas outside the LDS community are part of "Satan's plan" to lure them from the church, as she had been taught. "When you start actually breaking it down, the more you're like, this doesn't add up, this is just church leaders trying to protect themselves."

Women leaving the church could have dire consequences for organized religion, since mothers typically pass down the faith to children. The Mormon church had intended to fit into American society by embracing traditional family structures, but as the culture has moved on, it hasn't kept up.

When Sarah graduated, she found a teaching job in Salt Lake City rather than back in Happy Valley. The state capital, with its relative diversity and open-mindedness, was like a warm soak after a chilly day; she could finally relax. Perhaps this was where she might find herself and others like her, and maybe even the kind of equitable relationship she desired. Neither the bar scene nor the church scene was appealing, so she joined a Facebook singles group. One of the first posts she read was a welcome message to new members, from Brian. Sarah responded with a friendly hello and the two started exchanging personal messages, then he asked for her number.

They got along on the phone, with the same crackling senses of humor, but Sarah was skeptical it would go anywhere because he was LDS and so committed to its doctrine that he'd gone on a two-year proselytizing mission. She knew a red flag when she saw one, so before they even went on a date, she told him what she was all about.

I am no Holly Housewife, she declared on the phone. *My job is not to keep a nice, clean house and to cook and clean for you. I won't do that, I refuse, so if that's what you're after, you are barking up the wrong tree.*

Brian was surprisingly receptive and told her that he was on his own journey away from the church. After he returned from his mission in Fresno, he married his first wife, with whom he has a son, Mason, now ten, but the relationship soon began to unravel. When they divorced, he felt like a failure. "The church teaches about eternal marriage and eternal happiness," he says. "So when my first marriage came crashing down around me, I was like, why did this happen when I worked so hard to achieve something?" Divorce is possible in the church but highly stigmatized—"Satan's work," according to the LDS manual. Though Brian had committed his entire twenty-eight years to the faith, when he divorced, it no longer welcomed him.

Then he found Sarah. She was different: similarly disillusioned with religion but also intent on creating the happy family life Brian craved. On their first date, they talked about how they would raise children, and from there, the conversation never stopped. "We've spent every day together since then," Brian says, grinning widely at her from across the kitchen counter, clearly enamored.

They were married a few days before Christmas, so she wouldn't have to take time off work. Brian's only request was that it be an LDS ceremony. Even after everything the institution had put him through, he still wasn't ready to leave it completely. Traditionally, Mormon weddings are held in temples, but because Sarah was no longer an active member and Brian's divorce hadn't officially been sanctified, they didn't meet the "worthiness requirements" for a temple ceremony. So they married in a Mormon church, a local chapel open to the public, unlike temples, which only admit members in good standing. A bishop Sarah knew from childhood officiated, and to her, it was perfect.

THREE YEARS LATER, THEY celebrated their anniversary at La Frontera, a restaurant on West Jordan's main road. The host led them to a booth next to a blue-tiled wall and a server followed with water in oversize red Coca-Cola cups and a squeeze bottle of salsa. The menu was a profusion of Southwestern comfort food: chile relleno, ribs, both Mexican- and American-style steak. They ordered margaritas, a favorite of Sarah's since she left the church for good, and settled into easy conversation.

Sarah asked Brian if he'd seen the news that after BYU lifted its ban on "homosexual behavior," it issued a statement clarifying that the school *still* prohibited same-sex dating.

It's so ridiculous, she vented, another example of the church's tenacious resistance to modernity.

She looked for him to agree, but sensed something had changed. For the first time, a lengthy silence stretched between them. Brian shifted in his seat, as Mexican music floated from the open kitchen and hung in the air. To the extent that he had had a plan, this wasn't it. But he also knew he had to say something, and so he let the words tumble from the deep place they'd been lodged: *You know, I'm bisexual.*

Wait, what? Sarah exclaimed, her voice tremulous with shock, but also some amusement at the abrupt turn their conversation had taken.

Brian explained that he'd known he was attracted to men since he was fourteen but had suppressed his feelings because of the strict interdiction of homosexuality in the LDS church, which teaches that, "the attraction itself is not a sin, but acting on it is." God had intended for him to procreate and that meant he was only allowed to have sexual experiences with his wife, so he'd done his best to push down his feelings and ignore them.

He had planned to tell Sarah, but not on their anniversary. "I didn't want to ruin the mood and be like, 'Surprise! Your husband likes guys,' and have Sarah potentially be like, 'Oh, no, this is definitely not going to work out anymore,'" he recalls later. Still, he knew how open-minded she was, and so when the topic came up on their anniversary, a celebration of their love, he decided he didn't want to leave anything unsaid between them. "I came out to her *because* I wanted all my secrets out in the open, at least to her. Like there was nothing hidden anymore."

Up to that point, Sarah had committed herself to building a relationship that rejected strict gender roles and valued acceptance. Now, she faced her first real test of those ideals. That night and through the following days, Sarah replayed their conversation and tried to parse her genuine feelings.

She is a logical thinker, comfortable in the binary language of technology, and as the shock subsided, her analytical instincts reemerged, and she found herself returning again and again to the same question: What had changed? "The hardest part for me was that I felt like this should have changed things—it should be earth shattering—but also, why should it?" she says. She and Brian were still in love, and he'd been honest with her even though it put him at risk of another painful breakup. They were both employed and lived in a state consistently ranked among the most family-friendly in the country and, if things continued on the current path, they were still going to have a fulfilling life together. She knew it logically and intuitively. She was at peace.

As it turned out, she had more pressing worries. Getting pregnant proved significantly harder than getting married or coming to terms with Brian's sexuality. So her doctor recommended a medicine called letrozole, a breast cancer drug that's also used to help women conceive, but she was reluctant to take it because her insurance didn't cover fertility. The medical staff were undeterred and offered to code it instead as treatment for an irregular cycle, an odd twist of American healthcare that makes payment dependent on the goodwill and savvy of providers.

Even after she started the medication, though, pregnancy remained elusive. Months slipped by; each negative test brought a fresh feeling of failure, as she came ever closer to the ominous half-year mark, at which point her doctor would refer her to a fertility specialist. That, Sarah thought, would likely be the end of it. A single round of in vitro fertilization costs upward of ten thousand dollars—almost ten times what Tsukasa's friend Kyoko paid in Japan, with its subsidized program—and patients frequently require multiple rounds. Sarah had friends who'd done it, but she couldn't imagine spending that much money, more than her entire life savings. She and Brian talked about how far they were willing to go: What was a baby worth? What would that choice cost them in future financial security?

We have to do it, Brian said. He wanted another child, and felt he had finally found his ideal partner.

But Sarah shook her head. *I really just don't think I can*, she replied. It was simply too expensive.

"The hard part is in a state that's so pro-family, where the goal is to have more kids, to procreate, the major insurance company doesn't cover fertility," she reflects.

Most states don't require health insurance companies to cover IVF, in part because insurers argue it would force them to raise costs for everyone. But in several Northeastern states—Massachusetts, Connecticut, and Rhode Island—that have required insurers to cover infertility for three decades, premiums are estimated to have increased less than one percent as a result. Still, with so many women shut out, private companies saw an opportunity. Led by Apple and Facebook in 2014, they began to offer coverage for egg freezing as a way to recruit and retain female talent. Now, more than forty percent of all large companies cover infertility, according to a Mercer survey—though with deductibles, copays, and the cost of medication, it can still be extremely expensive—and that still doesn't reach the majority of American women. It can also make those who *are* covered hostage to their employers. When Twitter CEO Elon Musk—who used IVF to conceive at least eight of his children—laid off half his workforce in late 2022, among the employees let go were women in the middle of treatment. As *Wired* magazine reported at the time, several said they couldn't afford to continue on their own, so along with their jobs, they lost the choice of when—and perhaps whether—to become mothers.

For Sarah, even after her family offered to help pay, she still couldn't justify it, couldn't come to terms with the hardship it might impose on them. And so she pressed on, telling herself each month that she would be fine whether or not she had a baby, until she approached the fateful five-month mark. Then, a yearning revealed itself, and she realized she did care, very deeply.

"My feelings about it were tied to my fear of not being able to conceive: If I don't want one, I won't be heartbroken when I can't," she says. When she arrived at that critical point with nothing to show for it, she could no longer deny her heartbreak and mourned the loss of a motherhood she never had. She typed a plaintive message to a friend: *I just want a baby.*

That day, she couldn't keep her mind off it at work and decided she needed a break from the clockwork of conception. She came home and told Brian: *Pack a bag, let's go.* They put their dogs in the car, and as Brian drove south, Sarah called hotels and finally found one with a room in Moab. The next day, they hiked through the otherworldly red-rock outcroppings at the foot of Corona Arch, a hundred-foot-high span of ruddy sandstone. The dogs scrambled to get up the slickrock face, but finally, they all managed to make it to the top of the trail and looked out across the red and purple layers of the valley, carved by the serpentine Colorado River. It was transportive.

"And it happened to be the weekend I was ovulating," Sarah recounts impishly. Like Anna, even before she had symptoms, she knew she was pregnant, felt it viscerally, even cosmically. Then a pregnancy test confirmed it. Religion was no longer part of her life, but this felt fated; she had finally accepted that she did want a child, and then learned she was going to have one. So she thought, *Yep, we're there, this will be good.*

A FEW MONTHS LATER, Brian initiated another tricky conversation, this one about polyamory. It started elliptically, a broad discussion circling the idea of introducing other partners into their relationship.

Finally, Sarah asked him directly: *Are you wanting to explore that, then?*

Maybe, he paused, then added definitively, *but I'm not gonna do anything that could harm us, or you know, hurt our relationship.*

He suggested they join an online polyamory group, and when they did, it was a revelation, Sarah says. "I never would have known this existed or was as prevalent as it is had I not joined that group." There were about four hundred people from their local area, including someone she knew from her master's degree program.

As many as ten percent of Americans have been polyamorous—in a consensual non-monogamous relationship with multiple partners—according to research by Amy C. Moors, Research Fellow at the Kinsey Institute at Indiana University and co-chair of the American Psychological Association's Committee on Consensual Non-Monogamy. Moors, who has a wide smile and dark glasses, explains that just as people have a sexual orientation, they could also have a relationship orientation. "I think these things might be fluid, where people could be monogamous or non-monogamous, and some people really feel in their heart they were born polyamorous."

Through the local group, Brian learned about the parameters of polyamory, and he and Sarah began to understand that what they wanted was ethical non-monogamy: a consensual, openly-conducted relationship guided by honesty and communication. That's different, Sarah explains, from the polygamy of the early Mormons, because polyamory is egalitarian. There are just as many women with multiple relationships, and they can enjoy them apart from family relationships. Her support was put to the test, though, when she went with Brian to a polyamory event where they met Nick, a slender young guy with shaggy blonde hair. Sarah liked him immediately—he was so laid back, nothing seemed to faze him—and he and Brian hit it off. They started to see each other, and Sarah would sometimes join them for dinner.

Let me know if it's a you-and-him thing, and I'll be scarce, she tells Brian one evening as they're getting ready. *I don't want you to feel like you always have a third wheel and can't do anything alone. But also, you know, I'm here, so it's probably hard for you just to be like "Okay, we're off, bye!"* she laughs warmly.

Brian encourages her to come. They are effectively in a "poly-mono relationship," in which just one member of the couple dates outside the marriage. Tristan Taormino writes in *Opening Up: A Guide to Creating and Sustaining Open Relationships* that while some people might view such a relationship as inherently unfair, the goal is to construct it in a way that meets everyone's needs, and to strive for balance rather than symmetry. "That means no one is compromising too much or feeling too limited by the agreement." Moors estimates that only a modest number, just five percent according to a small study she did, of polyamorous relationships work that way and it can be because one partner or is bisexual or,

Moors says, because of a "life event," like the birth of a baby, for example.

That event is now drawing ever closer. The houses on their cul-de-sac are strung with twinkling lights. Inflatable Santas wobble jovially in front yards. Sarah counts down the days until Christmas break and her due date soon after. Christmas finally comes and with it a gentle snowfall that blankets the mountain valley, but two weeks later, just before the baby is due, there are still no signs of labor. Her doctor determines she is slightly dilated and does a membrane sweep, manually loosening the amniotic sac from the uterus, to help things progress. Sarah feels a slight cramping but nothing else. Frustrated, she calls her older sister Jess, a nurse practitioner and lactation consultant who lives in Fairbanks, Alaska. Jess assures Sarah it will happen and tells her to try to be patient.

Maternity work runs in the family. Their great-grandmother was Patty Bartlett Sessions, midwife for the Utah pioneer party, who delivered nearly four-thousand babies. She sometimes rushed from birth to birth, first in tents, as the covered wagon caravan of believers crossed the country, then in log-adobe houses, once they settled in Utah Territory. And as midwives often did then, Sessions attended both births and deaths—which were sometimes concurrent. As with Mary Miranda Rogers, a patient whose baby's arm became lodged in her birth canal, the rest of his body still in her womb. Late on the second night of labor, Sessions sent for an Apostle to bless the woman as she died. Afterward, an examiner reported the infant had "torn the womb to bits with his feet." Birth was dangerous: In the middle of the nineteenth century, about one in every hundred women died in childbirth.

In the 1930s, when antibiotics and medications to treat heavy bleeding were invented and hygienic practices improved, American maternal mortality dropped sharply. But then in then in the 1990s, it began to creep back up. Between 2003 and 2013, the US was one of only eight countries where maternal mortality rose. The American maternal death rate is now roughly three to five times that of other high-income countries, including Finland and Japan. Outcomes vary widely within the country, though: Black women are more than three times as likely to die from pregnancy-related complications as white women.

American birth has always been racialized. James Marion Sims, known as the "Father of American Gynecology," opened the first women's hospital on a small farm in Alabama—located there because nearby slave owners were interested in improving enslaved women's fertility. Just as in colonial Kenya, women's fertility was seen in crass economic terms in the Antebellum South. Sims's nurses were enslaved women, as were his patients, who were also test subjects for his procedures. He operated on at least ten enslaved women without anesthesia. One of them, Anarcha, was subjected to at least thirty painful surgeries. Sims went on to open a larger women's hospital in New York City, where many of his subjects were poor Irish immigrants. With their help— nonconsensual as it was—Sims developed innovative surgical methods to make birth safer, and also invented tools including the speculum, familiar to any woman today who's had a gynecological exam. Still, wealthy white women were the first to benefit from those advances because they were more likely to be able to afford expensive medical procedures.

Such disparities persist to this day. Sarah, like nearly three-quarters of white non-Hispanic women, has private insurance to cover her birth care, compared to only about half of Black women. The CDC says lack of access to care, which insurance provides, is a key contributor to pregnancy-related deaths—and that four in five maternal deaths in the US are preventable.

Under the 2010 Affordable Care Act, known as Obamacare,

states could receive federal funds to expand Medicaid, health coverage for low-income Americans. States that accepted the funding after the law went into effect in 2010 saw a significant rise in coverage for women of reproductive age and also reduced maternal mortality, especially among Black and Latina Americans. But ten states chose not to expand Medicaid—most of them Southern states where the majority of uninsured Black and Latina women live, and which have the highest maternal mortality rates. Why would they reject funds that could keep new mothers alive? "One distinct possibility is implicit racism," writes Mark Hall, director of the Health Law and Policy Program at Wake Forest Law School. "This degree of pitched opposition by states to a major federal domestic initiative has not been seen since the civil rights era of the 1960s." The program was associated with the first Black president and seen as likely to disproportionately help poor people of color.

Sarah acknowledges she has it better than many American women—she isn't much worried about her own safety and can even choose the type of delivery she wants: unmedicated, perhaps in the hospital's birthing tub. But first, she needs her labor to start. Four days after her due date, the doctor tells her he doesn't want to wait much longer because she has risk factors that would make her more likely to need an emergency C-section. That evening, he gives her misoprostol—a drug several states are trying to restrict because it is also used in medication abortion— to start contractions. She soon begins to cramp. As he gives her a second, and then a third dose, the contractions grow more intense, and for the next several hours, the seizing pains come just half a minute apart. A nurse checks her progress and Sarah looks at her expectantly.

Still not fully dilated, she determines. Sarah exhales sharply with frustration.

From there, the pain only gets worse, makes her want to crawl out of her skin, it's so intense. She bends over in agony as Brian crouches on the floor to comfort her. He finds her hand and holds it tight. She begins to cry and seeing that brings tears to Brian's eyes as well; she's usually so unemotional, so in control. He wishes he could do more to soothe her, and tries to help her breathe.

I think I need an epidural, she whispers to him through clenched teeth. She had hoped for a "Wonder Woman" natural birth but, like seventy percent of American birthing mothers, Sarah ultimately accepts pain medication.

"Natural childbirth" was promoted by the British obstetrician Grantly Dick-Read in a 1933 book by that name, as labor and delivery with limited intervention, and for Read it had religious connotations: He argued that natural childbirth was God's intention. In some ways it's a similar martyrdom to Japan's Buddhist view of pain as a virtue.

American feminists have taken varying views on "natural childbirth." First-wave feminists welcomed the advent of pain medication, but in the 1960s, second-wave feminists called for a return to non-medicalized birth, saying it gave women more control. More recently, feminists have criticized the exaltation of "natural childbirth," and argued it creates an unrealistic ideal and suggests women who don't conform are unnatural, or even bad mothers.

Sarah is disappointed, at first, that she's opted for pain medication, but when it kicks in, she soon relaxes, and fifteen minutes later, their daughter Vivian is born. It is surreal. "Oh my gosh, this thing just came out of me, like, wow, that really just happened." A nurse asks Brian if he would like to cut the cord. He declines. "Weird stuff grosses him out," Sarah explains with a laugh. So she does it instead. But as the nurses clean Vivian, the baby doesn't make a sound, and Sarah can see the concern on their faces. One nurse rubs her tiny arm, trying to get her to cry. The infant offers a little squawk then stops.

We've got to do more than that, the nurse says to her firmly; *We need you to cry so we know your lungs are good.*

Finally, Vivian wails. The nurse is satisfied, and she lays the red-faced newborn on Sarah's chest. Sarah realizes that she is now, incomprehensibly, someone's mother. In that moment, she feels stuck between a past that still seems present and an almost unimaginable future.

She has two days to orient herself before the doctor determines she and the baby are ready to go home. Then afterward, she gets the bill. Sarah had read her insurer's explanation of benefits to determine how much birth would cost and specifically tried to save enough in her flexible spending account to cover it. So she is surprised when the bill is two thousand dollars more than she'd anticipated—just as Chelsea was when she found out her private insurance wouldn't cover the full cost as expected.

She takes her concerns to the hospital billing department.

Yep, looks like you're right, you were overcharged—good catch, the administrator tells her brightly. *We'll just need to process that change, it should take about a month.*

Patient advocacy groups estimate that somewhere between fifty and eighty percent of American hospital bills contain errors. After Sarah's is corrected, she pays about three thousand dollars out of pocket for an uncomplicated birth, fully insured, at the state's largest healthcare network, Intermountain Healthcare. When President Barack Obama addressed Congress in 2009 to first make the case for Obamacare, he touted Intermountain as a model of "high-quality care at below-average costs." And he was right: a three-thousand-dollar birth is pretty much the best one can hope for in the US, roughly average for an uncomplicated delivery covered by private insurance. But it's more than women pay for birth in Finland, Japan, Kenya, and almost every other country in the world.

Sarah doesn't dwell on the price—that's just the way it is and will always be, she supposes. But it's very different from Tsukasa's experience in Japan, where she gave birth just two days before Sarah did. As Sarah leaves the hospital, which sits on a ridge overlooking the valley, she sees that it snowed while she was in the delivery room. The tiny office parks and temple spires below look soft and white. As she straps Vivian into her new car seat, Sarah worries the snowfall will make the roads slick. She is settling into new motherhood already.

The day they get home, Sarah's third day as a mother, she is surprised by how comfortable she is in the role. Brian lovingly fetches whatever she needs to breastfeed and tells her how well she's doing. She savors the encouragement. "I was feeling so good and so confident, like we had this figured out," she says, smiling. Then the next day, she says, "it all hit the fan."

PART TWO

TSUKASA
JAPAN

TSUKASA LEAVES THE HOSPITAL through its sliding glass doors, directly into a fierce alpine wind. Her daughter, Rota, at a week old, takes her first breath of fresh air and Tsukasa is now a mother in the outside world. Her father guides them both to his Volvo and she sits gingerly in the backseat with her baby.

She can't wait to finally see Kaz, who boarded a bus from Tokyo earlier that morning. They drive to meet him at a stop along the main road that, Tsukasa realizes as they pull up, does not match the magnitude of the occasion. There is no time to dwell on that, though, because there he is disembarking, the glow of Tokyo still on him, his hair dyed a different color than the last time they were together.

He anxiously approaches their car and Tsukasa opens the door to give him his first look at his daughter. He wills himself to appreciate the significance, here in this parking lot in a wide, flat valley, so different from the dense skyscraper metropolis he just left, as other passengers move casually around him in search of their own rides. Then Tsukasa gently transfers the infant into his arms. She feels so incredibly small.

This girl looks like my husband, Tsukasa thinks when she sees their faces next to each other. Watching him hold her, with joy and also nervousness, is like nothing she's ever experienced. "I can't describe how happy I am," she says.

From there they drive to her mother's house. Kaz spends the night, but has to get back to Tokyo for work and so he leaves the next day. Her father goes too, and Tsukasa is alone in her room with Rota. She covers its familiar tatami floors with new supplies—a wraparound breastfeeding pillow, soft baby kimonos from the hospital, assorted bottles—and feels a deep longing for Kaz.

She is following a centuries-old tradition called satogaeri shussan, in which Japanese women rely on their families, principally their mother and sisters, to care for them in the first postpartum month. As the oral tradition holds: "Exerting yourself after giving birth will haunt you for the rest of your life." So the new mother traditionally rested on a futon for a month, until it was finally time to put the futon away and "raise the floor," a celebratory event to this day.

Tsukasa rests as much as she can and tries to avoid getting cold by staying inside, eating warm foods, and avoiding things that could give her a chill, like washing her hair. Kampo, the Japanese version of traditional Chinese medicine, focuses on treating imbalances in the body with temperature regulation and diet. And it holds that cold can slow recovery. "I don't want to get chilled because I need to look after the baby," Tsukasa explains. Kampo fell out of favor in the nineteenth century when the government adopted a medical system based on Germany's that focused instead on pathogenic interlopers—viruses and bacteria. Then, after World War II, the Allied occupation forces prohibited, in racist terms, kampo's "barbaric and unhygienic practices." Still, kampo never really went away, and in recent years, made a comeback: It is now part of the standard curriculum at Japanese medical schools. And so Tsukasa, following kampo principles, plans to leave her mother's house only once in the next month, for her two-week checkup.

That's pretty typical, says Tomomi Yamamoto, the director of nursing at Seibo Hospital in Tokyo. She wears a starched white uniform and has an air of well-deserved authority. She's been a midwife for nearly four decades and says she always makes sure her patients get the support they need after they leave her ward. "If it's not possible for family members to do the caregiving, we'll make arrangements so the new mother can receive support elsewhere, including from public institutions." There's a good amount of infrastructure for that now, because in 2019, the government announced that all new mothers would have access to postpartum care centers, where midwives provide round-the-clock care and guidance on how to breastfeed and look after babies. Women can come immediately after delivery or later in the year—like when infants start getting fussy around three months—and even stay there for up to a week for free, or at a heavily subsidized rate.

Yamamoto says that sometimes public care is preferable because it's not as emotionally fraught as staying with one's own mother can be. "I think often when new mothers feel frustrated, it's because how they were raised by their own mothers is affecting them."

So it is for Tsukasa, who is now back in the hometown she still associates with the most traumatic episode of her life, and with never quite feeling safe. Perhaps now though, with her new daughter, there's an opportunity for a fresh start. She can care for her daughter as she had wanted to be cared for.

She lies next to Rota, who is asleep with her little pink fists framing her face. Tsukasa still can't believe she's her mother and can't resist taking one more photo to prove it. She sends the picture to Kaz and he immediately video-calls her. Tsukasa beams at the sight of his face, excited to share her every thought with him.

She tells him it's hard to believe she was once such a tiny baby. "It's just amazing that there was a time I couldn't do anything, couldn't even hold my head up. I mean it's natural but that cycle is so amazing."

Even more inconceivable is that she herself was once cared for and loved and told how cute she was. It seems so different from the pervasive loneliness that defined her later childhood. She can still remember crying for her mother to hold her and the disappointment she felt when her mother was too busy to do it. Tsukasa's parents separated when she was quite young and her mother went back to work soon after. With her dad also out of the house, she remembers being a "latchkey kid" for most of childhood. She would come home from school to this same house, and in its cold quiet, feel a deep longing for her mother.

As she begins to lose herself in contemplation, the familiar, earthy smell of her mother's miso soup brings her back to the present. This time is not easy for her mother either. Her own elderly parents live here, as well, and rely on her for shopping, cooking, and other daily tasks.

"It's a precious experience to get to stay here with everyone; my mom and grandparents, and there's also a little dog," laughs Tsukasa. "But it can be a little tense and it's definitely difficult for my mother." And it also seems like it has been difficult for Tsukasa's friend Kyoko. She has not come to see Tsukasa since Rota arrived a week ago, though she lives only a few blocks away. Tsukasa doesn't push it. She understands that Kyoko is stuck on the other side of the parental divide and she doesn't want her to feel left behind. "She's so focused on wanting a child of her own, I worry seeing Rota will make her depressed."

The next few days pass quietly, as Tsukasa cares for the baby, and her mother cares for her. Even with her mother's support, it's a real adjustment from her week in the hospital, where nurses attended to her around the clock. "I never expected caregiving would be this intense, so mentally it's tough but the baby is adorable," she says as she holds Rota to her shoulder and gently pats her back.

The stress of it seeps into the cracks of her relationship with her mother and hardens there, making them both inflexible when problems arise. Like when Tsukasa struggles to produce enough milk. She'd planned to breastfeed exclusively, as about half of all mothers in Japan do, a significant increase since she herself was a baby. But at the hospital she had trouble with her production, so the midwives recommended she breastfeed every three hours and supplement with formula. Since then, she's tried to stick to that schedule even when it's tough.

Her mother sees the baby fussing and thinks it's not worth the trouble. *You grew up drinking formula*, she reminds Tsukasa, *you don't need to be so nervous about it.*

This is what the nurses told me to do, Mom, Tsukasa responds sharply. *Breastfeed every three hours, and even if she's asleep, wake her up.*

Oh, just give her more formula and let her sleep. It's really fine, Tsukasa-chan.

The suggestion infuriates Tsukasa, seems to undermine all the exhausting work she's been doing.

That's what the hospital told me, all right? So don't you tell me anything else! She storms from the room.

A 2017 study found that Japanese postpartum mothers reported significantly lower rates of subjective well-being than Finnish mothers. "Finnish mothers got more support from maternal and child health clinics, and I think that support was good for them, compared to their Japanese counterparts who got support from grandparents," explains Tuovi Hakulinen, one of the study's authors. "The Japanese tradition does provide practical support but it doesn't offer new mothers evidence-based information, and the guidance they get from grandparents can be old or traditional so that causes problems."

Tsukasa replays in her mind the argument with her mother and can't quite believe how angry she'd gotten. It isn't just hormones and sleep deprivation; their fight had unearthed memories of her mother fretting about things that always seemed so inconsequential. It feels hypocritical now for her to be so hard on Tsukasa for worrying, and so certain in her own advice, which seems plainly outdated. "My mother doesn't need to raise Rota, all she needs to do is love her grandchild."

When anthropologist Margaret Mead became a grandmother, she wrote that she had expected to feel freedom without responsibility but felt instead "the obligation to be a resource but not an interference." Tsukasa grows increasingly frustrated that her mother doesn't seem to understand that mandate.

There were some good times growing up, though, she reminds herself. Like that golden afternoon she and her mother made a chocolate cake together for Tsukasa's kindergarten teacher. She can still remember how close she felt to her in that moment. And similarly, to her grandparents, when she helped them pickle plums and kumquats from their garden; delicacies that gave the seasons their distinct flavors. Those are the parts of her own childhood she wants to carry forward. "I want to be able to make something like that and have my children say, 'That's delicious, it tastes like home.'" If she is being truly optimistic, maybe it could even remind Rota of her own warm relationship with her grandparents.

For now, Tsukasa focuses on the immediate future, when she will get to bring Rota home to Kaz and see him as infatuated with this infant as she is—as enamored with her fuzzy little mohawk and cheeks so full that her face is nearly a perfect circle. "Before Rota was born, I could only imagine having a sort of dry, objective perception of her, but now my love for her and how I care for her is so saturated with emotion, it's almost impossible to describe."

Finally Rota reaches the critical one-month mark, and Tsukasa brings her to the hospital to see if they can be cleared to return to Tokyo. The midwives note the change in her weight and the baby's since birth; inversely related as they should be. They examine Rota's muscle and eye development, and make sure Tsukasa's uterus is shrinking. Everything looks good. She is finally free to pursue the family life she wants and leave her childhood ghosts behind.

By the time the train reaches her Kagurazaka neighborhood in Tokyo, it is late afternoon. Her apartment building's cantilevered white balconies catch the last of the sunlight. The Family Mart on the ground floor, with its familiar placards advertising onigiri rice balls, is already in shadow. A woman on a bicycle sails past on the wide sidewalk. Tsukasa is reassured to see that life here is mostly as she left it.

Somehow Kaz feels less familiar, though. When she finally gets to the dark wood door of their apartment, their reunion is more awkward than she'd expected. That's because for Kaz, this is the moment when the reality of fatherhood finally hits. Their baby is here in their apartment, and he's not sure what to do. Tsukasa feels pressure to be a perfect mother after only a month in the role herself. As uncomfortable as she was at times in Matsumoto, she now feels fully responsible for keeping their tiny baby alive in a way that she realizes she didn't, wholly, with her mother there.

A few minutes after she lays the baby in her new crib, her spine still freshly relieved from the discomfort of the baby carrier, they hear Rota mew from her crib. Kaz looks at his wife for guidance.

Maybe she wants me to hold her again, Tsukasa suggests.

She re-straps the carrier onto her tired body then lifts Rota to her chest and stands in front of a full-length mirror, fumbling to get each tiny limb in position and nervously consulting her reflection for guidance. She has only herself to rely on.

AFTER SEVERAL DAYS, THE apartment feels more relaxed, filled again with the kind of Japanese pop-rock Kaz composes. Tsukasa has traded her loose, postnatal sweatsuit for a denim dress and Kaz wears dark jeans with a neon cord running the length of the seam. They're easing back into being the creative Tokyo couple they once were.

"I built up a lot of stress when I was home in Matsumoto and didn't even realize," Tsukasa says. But she feels well enough now that she can help Kaz learn to parent. He watches as she scoops powdered formula into a bottle then adds hot water from the electric tea kettle. "This is kind of my baby care internship," he laughs.

He has a buoyant energy, is clearly excited to finally be involved. He offers Tsukasa some cold green tea from a large plastic bottle, and when she declines, fills a porcelain mug of his own and smiles at her. He's still sorry he missed the baby's first month but is more at peace with it now: He shrugs and says they had to follow doctor's orders, that the important thing is they're together now. Then he gestures to his daughter sleeping snug against Tsukasa's chest: "I'm just happy she's here, that's the real feeling."

As much as they look like they did before Rota was born, their life is not the same. They don't go out to their favorite okonomiyaki restaurant much anymore, instead eat a lot of frozen meals at home. Tsukasa is happy to find a delivery service called Nosh— its name a rare Yiddish reference in East Asia—that will bring prepared meals to their house once a week. Not bad, she thinks, when she tries the first one: ginger pork yakiniku with kinpira. She wishes she had the energy to make an entire meal herself but is grateful Kaz doesn't expect that.

Still, there is plenty of cultural pressure to conform to the perfect Japanese mother archetype, embodied by the many mom-fluencers on Instagram. Tsukasa sometimes scrolls through their posts; there are millions tagged #obento (#お弁当), mostly pictures of beautifully constructed children's lunches. It looks like a lot of work. But there is also a nascent counter-movement: Women's magazines run articles with titles like "It's okay, you don't have to cook traditional five-dish meals" and "Side dishes that husbands can also make." Then in 2020, Japanese-American model Shelly led a sort of culinary liberation movement when she said on a live cooking show that potato croquettes were something that should be bought and not made. The hosts looked taken aback, but she went on: "Ever since I got married all anyone wants to ask about is my cooking, but they'd never ask a male celebrity that." The exchange went viral. "Finally someone said it!" one commenter rejoiced. It was, it seemed, a small first step in vanquishing the tyranny of complicated daily meal prep.

For Tsukasa, elaborate meals are out of the question; it takes everything she has just to get out to the grocery store. And when she does, she has trouble even climbing the gentle slope of Kagurazaka Dori, a street she's walked so many times before. "My energy's really declined and my muscles feel so much weaker," she says. Her bleeding has finally stopped, but she seems to have lost any of the vigor the postpartum hormones had once conferred. She's also dramatically sleep-deprived: she often doesn't get to bed until two in the morning, after she's fed Rota and finished the housework. Then she's up again before five when Rota signals with a persistent "fuh-fuh-fuh" that she's hungry.

Kaz can see how hard it is for her and offers to help but she declines; she knows he needs rest to maintain his career. "Composing music is creative work that requires a lot of concentration, so if he doesn't get sleep, he can't think straight," Tsukasa says. He has his job and she has hers, she thinks. Hers has just changed a lot.

His work now takes him out of the house for most of the day. They have breakfast together but then he leaves and when he returns in the evening, he typically works late into the night in his home recording booth: headphones on, microphone illuminated by the glowing computer screen. His compositions have been in high demand since he won the Japan Record Award, but it is a fast and unforgiving industry: He might get a request to finish a song by the next morning, and even if he stays up all night to get it done, he still doesn't get paid unless the band decides to use it. To help his chances, he usually comes up with multiple song pitches, hoping the group likes at least one. Sometimes he will take a long enough break for Tsukasa to have a bath while he watches Rota, but otherwise she spends all her time looking after the baby so he can make the most of the professional opportunities coming his way. She is at peace with it, for now. "At the moment, our professional lives are at different temperatures: his is heating up while mine is on ice."

The benefits she receives make that easier to accept. She is grateful to have a reliable paycheck during her year of paid parental leave, and on top of that, a fifteen thousand yen, or one hundred dollar, monthly child allowance that she'll receive until Rota graduates from high school. In 2022, the year Rota was born, the national government spent about five billion dollars on parental leave benefits, less than one percent of its annual fiscal budget.

With Tsukasa's focus now squarely on Rota, the outside world slips past without her even registering the change of season, until finally it is impossible to ignore. The city bursts with pale pink blooms, and outside her window, petals drift in feathery sakura-fubuki, cherry blossom snowstorms. The Family Mart downstairs offers pink coffee and pink rice in its chirashizushi. Crowds of people walk the streets on their way to or from champagne han-ami, or blossom viewing, picnics.

She can't quite imagine rejoining that world or, more concern-ingly, the professional one. She loved her job at the streaming service, but the idea of balancing it with all her housework has begun to seem so overwhelming that sometimes she fantasizes about taking a different path entirely. As she moves through her chores—folding Rota's little clothes, cleaning bottles—she's sur-prised by how enjoyable it is to think only about life within the confines of this small apartment. "I'd never thought about being a shufu, a housewife, but now I think I might actually enjoy that."

Shufu literally means "main woman," the respected head of household. In premodern Japan, before the 1800s, the only way to get the title was to marry a first-born son. There was typically only one shufu in an extended family group, and she held significant power because she controlled the distribution of rice, a form of currency in an agrarian economy.

When Japan entered World War II, though, life for women changed: Every adult female was enrolled in the Greater Japan Women's Association and all aspects of daily life were managed for militaristic ends. They were trained to defend themselves with bamboo spears and pushed to bear more children at increas-ingly young ages. As the wartime slogan went, "Be Fruitful and Multiply for the Prosperity of the Nation." The government had already outlawed abortion and, in the late 1930s limited birth con-trol under a pronatalist policy to ensure a continuous supply of jinteki shigen, "human resource," for its war with China. Then a 1941 policy banned birth control entirely, putting reproduction squarely under state control.

As ferocious fighting in the Pacific escalated, the nation asked even more of women: That they send their sons off to bloody bat-tle with absolute stoicism. Under so-called "martial motherhood," mothers were forbidden from shedding a single tear when their children, many just teenagers, left for war. Mothers were expected to encourage them to give the nation whatever it needed—even their lives, in suicide kamikaze missions. Women dutifully played that public role but privately they were filled with dread, writes Hillary Maxson, an assistant professor at Pacific University, in *Rethinking Japanese Feminisms*. "Many mothers spoke to pebbles, as if these objects were their soldier sons, expressing the unspoken fears that the state had forbidden them to utter."

The atomic bombs in Hiroshima and Nagasaki marked a horrific end to the fighting. In all, Japan lost roughly three million people, a third of them civilians. For almost a decade afterward, the Allied Occupation, led by the United States with support from the British Commonwealth, oversaw the country's rebuilding. And it enacted a wide range of reforms, including full political rights for women. Allied forces encouraged women in politics, thinking it would contribute to a more peaceful Japan. The new Japanese constitution, authored in part by the American woman Beate Sirota Gordon, ensured "essential equality of the sexes." Women could now stand for office, and in the first postwar election, in 1946, thirty-nine female candidates won, accounting for nearly ten percent of Lower House seats. The next year, the government passed the Labor Standards Law, which established a fourteen-week maternity leave and even menstruation leave.

Many feminists who'd helmed successful labor movements before the war now joined Shufuren, the Housewives Association. Among its members were women who had lost children in the war and wanted to be free once and for all from the awful encumbrance of martial motherhood. As the Japanese Mothers' Congress wrote in 1955: "Because of the war, the pride and joy of being a mother has been shattered. Mothers were even forbidden from expressing the reasonable feeling that they felt in their hearts: that war was detestable. We were not even allowed to shed tears of farewell while we sent our children off to war; we just gritted our teeth." They wanted to wrest back control of motherhood and argued it should be viewed not as a blessing but as a right, with all the attendant protections: maternal healthcare, child welfare programs, and a national commitment to peace. They made clear mothers would no longer raise their children for the state, but instead, expect the state to help them raise their children.

It was a new kind of feminism with markedly different aims from those of their peers in the US, who largely pursued equality through equal professional opportunities. At the same time, as American occupation forces helped shift Japan's economy from agriculture to manufacturing, firms like Toshiba, Sony, and Toyota grew rapidly. But those companies were staffed almost entirely by men, now known as "salarymen." With few opportunities for women to earn a living wage, their economic survival depended on marriage. By the late 1950s, marriage came to be known as women's "eternal employment," something from which they could never retire.

Less than a decade after the war, nearly three quarters of women married to salarymen were housewives. That was a monumental shift from pre-war Japan: In the 1930s, the majority of workers were in agriculture and fishing, and within that sector, there were more female than male wage earners.

The country, traumatized by war, had slid into a kind of gender essentialism: The idea that women should only be mothers. Still, there were some activists who thought the motherhood-centered women's movement had gone too far. Ayako Ishigaki, who lived for a time in New York's Greenwich Village, wrote a controversial article in 1955 entitled "The Secondary Occupation Called the Housewife." In it, she colorfully argued that Japanese housewives' "brains have all turned to mush" and urged them to be more like

American women, who, she wrote, had taken advantage of modern conveniences to escape the entrapment of housework. "We should not get caught up in the uselessness of daily, repetitive chores at home. Stop relaxing with lots of idle chit-chat rather than seeking knowledge. If women let their spirits degenerate, how will we ever be liberated?" It is an argument that would not be lost on Tsukasa today, as she idly flips through momfluencer posts on Instagram.

Ishigaki's essay, unsurprisingly, set off furious debate as many women argued they were already liberated. Like their agrarian predecessors, they argued, they were powerful shufus who held complete domain over the domestic sphere. But in exchange for that power, women had virtually no public voice and did nearly all the domestic work. To this day, Japanese women do six times more housework than men, the most of any OECD nation.

Tsukasa does the bulk of the domestic work in their household. And as she wrestles with her own feelings about shufu life, she has to deal with a reality that only plunges her even deeper into it. She knew they would have to move to Osaka even before Rota was born, but now that the baby's here, relocating feels like an inordinate amount of change to embrace. Tsukasa has lived in Tokyo for sixteen years, and now, at four months postpartum, has just started to go out into her neighborhood regularly again.

As a distraction from thinking about all the things she needs to do to prepare for the move, she puts Rota in the baby carrier and walks through Kagurazaka's dense, narrow streets. The home goods shop on the corner with the wooden and wrought-iron exterior is having a sake tasting. Not yet, she thinks. She turns a corner, past one of the few homes in this area that dates to before the war. It has a tiled roof and sliding doors, and recalls a time when this neighborhood was a hanamachi, a "flower town" or geisha district. Next to it is an entirely different type of building:

a glass-paneled café called Unplan with a female kitchen staff that serves vegan entrées. Welcome to modern Japan. Tsukasa loves this café and the idiosyncrasies of the neighborhood; it's going to be hard to leave.

There is so much to do to get ready, she thinks. She needs to plan a day trip to Osaka, six hours there and back on the train, to get a paper ticket in order to enroll Rota in the public hospital there. "It would be so much better if we could just do this all online," she sighs. Though Japan is home to some of the world's biggest technology companies, the country remains resolutely paper-based. Official documents require all parties to affix personal hanko stamps, a round woodblock carved with an individual's name that works in place of a signature. Notably, women's hankos are typically smaller than men's. The paper-based system is more than just an inconvenience, it's a drag on the economy. It costs an estimated eight billion dollars annually for workers to push all that paper. Then there are the countless unpaid hours mothers spend on it.

The administrative burden of moving seems to stretch endlessly; just getting rid of things she doesn't want to bring to Osaka requires scheduling a disposal service weeks in advance, because larger items can't go in the trash. Then she has to separate the rest of the garbage into discrete categories, each in their own bag: paper, magazines, plastic bottles, plastic bottle tops, cans, glass, batteries, cartridges, folded cardboard, the list goes on.

It's a slog because she also stops frequently to breastfeed, and to entertain fresh worries. One afternoon as she is sterilizing bottles, it reminds her how fragile Rota still is. *Adults can adapt to new environments, but babies are just figuring it all out and a move could really mess that up*, she thinks. *Plus we just left Matsumoto and now we're gonna move her again? Is that okay?* The questions feel so unwieldy that she allows herself the distraction of reading manga on her phone. But when she resurfaces later, the chores are still undone and the house is a mess. She can feel herself slipping into anxious despair.

Then finally, a reprieve: A public health midwife arrives for a scheduled home visit, a service guaranteed to all families during their children's younger years, as part of the Maternal and Child Health Act. It's an organized national effort to make sure every child gets the basic standard of care.

Youkoso, welcome, please come in, Tsukasa greets the midwife with a broad smile. Tsukasa is dressed for the occasion in a crocheted white top and Rota is strapped to her with a gray wrap. The midwife removes her shoes and adds them to a low rack by the door then follows Tsukasa into the main room. There she extracts from her bag a cloth apparatus that resembles a fish scale. She lays Rota inside, checks the dial on top and reports that based on hospital records, the baby is gaining weight well. Then she moves her to a blanket and does a careful physical exam. Rota regards her with curiosity. The midwife points to a patch of rough skin on the baby's arm, something Tsukasa had on her list of things she might need to worry about but wasn't sure.

There's a cream you can use that should help; I'll write it down for you, the midwife tells her.

Tsukasa nods emphatically, ravenous for guidance. Perhaps her own mother could have provided it but their relationship still feels too fraught. And better to have an objective expert ask her the next question: *How are feeling, Tsukasa, and what help do you need?*

It's as if a spigot has turned on and the questions come pouring out.

Will the moving schedule be too much for the baby? What about two moves in such a short time, could that damage Rota somehow? Should she use formula on the trip and how would that work; where can she get hot water? Will these baby carrier straps be strong enough for the three-hour bullet train trip? And what is the right way to use this baby carrier, anyway? Is this strap supposed to go here? But is that position okay for Rota's hips?

The midwife patiently addresses all her questions. Then she asks Tsukasa if she knows about the community center nearby where nurses offer free consultations, and hands Tsukasa a pamphlet. When she finally leaves, two hours after she'd arrived, Tsukasa's whole body feels lighter.

Even with the midwife's guidance, the move is still one of the hardest things Tsukasa has ever done. She struggles to care for the baby and keep their regular routine as she packs and travels, and in the hectic, cardboard-filled weeks that follow. She's grateful Kaz manages many of the administrative tasks once they get to Osaka, and her friend Mari helps her unpack.

As she organizes all the baby gear in their new apartment, her mom calls on videochat to see how it's going. Tsukasa turns the camera toward Rota—lying on the floor beneath a shoji rice paper window, gumming a strawberry-shaped chew toy—and tells her they're slowly getting settled. That she's been able to get most of what she needs delivered. It's challenging to be a one-person operation, though, she tells her mom, a so-called "wan-ope." She's alone in this new apartment in a new city, frantically ordering items online that she hopes will make life simpler—and still trying to figure out how and whether to use her mother as a resource.

You know, everything is available so it's easy but it's also hard, she says lightly.

She doesn't mention that her monthly bleeding recently made a painful return and that she suspects the fibroids she developed during pregnancy are making her symptoms worse. There's a postpartum care salon near the train station but she hasn't wanted to make the long walk there, and then push Rota's stroller back home up the hills next to the cemetery. She's tired enough as it is. So for now she just takes over-the-counter iron supplements and drinks Saji juice, made from a berry that's supposed to prevent fatigue.

It was a different time when her mother was raising her: In the nineties, the housewife was still seen as integral to Japan's miraculous postwar recovery in which it went from an impoverished nation to a world economic power in the span of a generation. As wives, the thinking went, women had supported their husbands while they built those world-changing companies, and as mothers, they were raising the new labor force. When Tsukasa was young, criticizing the "professional housewife" was still almost taboo.

When a recession hit in the middle of that decade, Japan dealt with it by pushing men to work even longer hours. To this day, workers here put in some of the longest hours in the world. That has produced the grim phenomenon of karoshi, death from overwork. In 2022 there were roughly 3,500 workers' compensation claims filed for karoshi deaths and disability, the highest number ever, according to the Ministry of Health, Labor, and Welfare. There were also nearly three thousand suicides recognized as workplace-related.

That extreme work culture extends beyond the corporate world: People in creative fields, like Kaz, also work brutally long hours, an average of thirty-two overtime hours a week. Only seven percent of all US workers report working that many hours per week. "In music, if you don't produce results it's meaningless, it's incredibly competitive," he explains. Even now that they have moved to Osaka, he is still an infrequent presence around the house because, in addition to teaching at the local university, he often has to return to Tokyo to meet with recording artists there.

It's hard, he admits with a sigh. "To be honest, not being able to see my daughter as much as I would like has been painful." Still, he feels pressure to provide for her. "I feel more responsibility than I did before I had kids, for better or worse." That explains why he, like most Japanese fathers, didn't take parental leave. Fathers are entitled to a full year of paid leave—parental leave and then childcare leave—but many believe it would be career-crushing. In 2022, just seventeen percent took any at all.

Tsukasa understands. "Paternity leave is finally being recognized in Japan, but unless the government advocates for it, it's hard for men to participate in childrearing," she says as she adds hot water to a bottle. "I think there's a notion that childrearing is the mother's responsibility."

Kaz had hoped to be more helpful than his own father, a brain surgeon, who in Kaz's recollection never did a load of laundry. "Looking back, I think my father's life was a bit unbalanced. I don't mean to criticize, but he never did any housework." He was likely exhausted though, Kaz concedes. He worked long hours and would frequently have to get up in the middle of the night for emergency surgery. And there was no room for error: "He'd tell me, if I make the wrong split-second decision, the patient's entire lower body could be paralyzed." Kaz knew early on that kind of life was not for him and took a less traditional path. But he can feel himself slipping into similar patterns at home.

He would like to see cultural change, as do many younger Japanese men. In survey after survey, they say they don't want to follow their fathers' and grandfathers' example of devoting their life to a company, only to retire and find that without friends or hobbies, they have become so-called nure-ochiba, "wet leaves" stuck to their wives' shoes.

Many women, too, are ready for a new paradigm. In 2024, after the government increased funding for paid leave, childcare, and other supports, a record eighty-three percent of young women were working and households with a stay-at-home wife fell to a historic low of thirty percent. The overall female workforce participation rate is now higher in Japan than the US, though many

Japanese women do get pushed into lower-paying clerical roles. That rush of women into the labor force surprised even the policy makers who'd designed the programs to encourage it.

There was no longer any question that Japanese women had a hunger for professional actualization, they just needed the public support to do it. The problem now is that although most households are dual income, women are still expected to be primary caregivers. And that has dissuaded many of them from having children, author Sakai Junko told the *Asahi Shimbun*. Despite generous maternal supports, as long as the shufu-salaryman archetype still exists at home, women still feel a real tension between motherhood and career.

Kaz's father is now long retired from brain surgery and has leaned into his new role as doting grandfather. On Rota's Okuizome, her hundred-day celebration, he sends a glistening sea bream from his local Hyogo prefecture. Traditionally, the most senior family member feeds the baby to wish her a long life, and though he's not here to do it in person, Tsukasa appreciates the gesture. She happily prepares the whole fish, its iridescent crimson scales make the meal feel particularly festive.

She and Kaz decide against taking Rota to a Shinto shrine, as full tradition entails. Instead they stay home and marvel that a hundred days have passed since, like hanabi fireworks, Rota burst into their life. Tsukasa pinches a small piece of fish in her chopsticks and brings it close to Rota's mouth, a ceremonial way to wish she will always have enough food.

"And I also hope you have a big appetite because we're about to start giving you real baby food," she laughs. Soon, she will offer her jubai gayu, a light rice porridge. But on this day, her daughter's hundredth, she gives herself a break from thinking about the future and the exhausting micro-decisions like when to start feeding her solids, and simply delights in this new life in front of her.

She thinks of Kaz's father as she eats the sea bream and of how happy his granddaughter seems to have made him. It's almost as though Rota has given him motivation to keep living. "I feel like having Rota has let me connect to this cycle of life," she says. "It's natural so you could just take it for granted but to me it feels almost mystical, like there is a kind of divinity in the chain that links generations."

FOR ROTA'S FIRST GOLDEN Week, the spring holiday when cities empty as people escape to the countryside, Tsukasa's mother comes to visit. In the days leading up to her arrival, Tsukasa is anxious with anticipation, still feeling the effect of their disagreements in Matusmoto. When she finally arrives, she looks at Rota, resting in a baby bouncer on the floor with her chubby legs in a perfect butterfly, and remarks on how much the baby has grown since they were last together. Tsukasa smiles and invites her mother to sit with her on a gray couch next to Rota.

Yes, Rota-chan, you're big now, Tsukasa sings to her, and the baby smiles broadly.

Rota also has more personality now: There is a rattle she prefers, and she lets Tsukasa know when she wants it and when she's losing her patience. Tsukasa thinks it's a healthy sign she's developing her own sense of self.

I brought these for her, her mother says, pulling out several graphic books. She flips through the pages, filled with bright spirals and stripes. *And do you remember this one?*

It's a book from Tsukasa's own childhood. The multicolored cover opens a portal in time. It reminds her, Tsukasa tells her mother gently, of aspects of her childhood she might have changed. She has been waiting for the opportunity to say this.

I think we have a slightly different approach to parenthood, Tsukasa explains, as they sit side-by-side on the couch. *I think you saw me as your possession, you know, to be controlled, and so I think that's where we differ.*

Her mother is silent, reflecting on what Tsukasa has said.

Looking back on when I was raising you, she finally responds, *I suppose it is true that I thought of you as my property.* She pauses and looks down at her hands crossed in her lap. *Perhaps I should not have done that.*

Tsukasa sits in that ripe moment, filled with an aching joy. She studies her mother's face; older now, though her short hair is still dark, with the same straight bangs she's always had. It seems that at last, she has mellowed.

Thank you for saying that, Tsukasa tells her. *I think it's something I only really understand now, with Rota-chan.*

They look at the baby, banging her rattle lightly on the side of her chair. Responsible, somehow, for this progress between them.

You know, Tsukasa goes on, *I hope someday I'll be able to say I'm sorry to Rota, like you did for me, when she tells me she didn't like things I did as a mom.*

Her mother smiles. Happy, it seems, to finally be an example Tsukasa hopes to emulate.

Their conversation is part of a larger evolution for Tsukasa. She has found the strength to tell her mother how she feels, but she is also more sympathetic to how her mother must have struggled with this phase of her own life, after her father moved out and her mother was largely responsible for child raising. Single motherhood has always been difficult here: Women are largely excluded from higher-paying positions, so it's hard for them to support a family; almost half of all single-parent families live below the poverty line, one of the highest rates among developed nations. Tsukasa has struggled to find a balance between maintaining her career goals and taking care of Rota, and she has the benefit of Kaz's sympathy and devotion, as well as his income. It was probably harder for her mother, at a time when there were even fewer supports for mothers.

That evening as Tsukasa is sterilizing bottles, Rota begins to cry. She'd been happily playing on the floor but is suddenly distraught, so Tsukasa hurries to finish one last bottle as the baby's wails intensify. Tsukasa finally scoops Rota's soft little body in her arms and the room stills. Maybe because of her earlier conversation with her mom, a vivid memory engulfs her, of crying for her own mother and not getting what she needed. But as she comforts Rota, that feeling of abandonment eases. "In that moment, I got inner healing of my unfulfilled desire," Tsukasa says. She could see the tableau from both sides, she explains: as the child crying for affection, but also the mother, pulled in two directions. Her mom had been so overwhelmed by daily life, she simply didn't have time to hold Tsukasa every time she cried. "Something inside me changed, thinking about what it was like for my mom when I was a child," Tsukasa says. And it paved the way for forgiveness and a new kind of love. "My mother is amazing; the way I look at all mothers has changed."

If, as psychotherapist Daphne de Marneffe writes, every woman's feminism is a love letter to her mother, then a society's feminism begins at a primal level. In the most hopeful scenario, the next generation of women will work to repair the parts of the system that mistreated their own mothers and fight for better policies that will give them—and their daughters—the best chance at happiness.

WHEN TSUKASA'S MOTHER RETURNS to Nagano, the apartment feels quiet. She and Rota are alone again. And at nearly six months, their uninterrupted time together is almost half over. It's hard sometimes to remember what came before maternity leave or to envision what will come next. Tsukasa finally feels like she's getting a handle on motherhood: Rota cries less at night and sometimes wakes just once in seven hours. And on those days, Tsukasa feels energetic enough to leave the house for a few hours.

She carries the compact black stroller down three flights of stairs to the first level, an elevated carport, and follows the quiet street, past a school where children with little red hats busily kick soccer balls and dig in a sandbox. At the next corner, she stops at a French boulangerie. *Irasshaimase*, the clerk welcomes her as she enters. There are rows of crusty brown breads and a tall basket filled with baguettes. She buys a loaf and thinks how nice it will be to share it with Kaz at breakfast the following morning, when she'll next get time with him. Then at a park a few blocks later, she sees mothers and children gathered for a "children's garden." Smiling retirees read from oversize picture books as the toddler audience squeals with delight. Rota is still too small for the event but it offers Tsukasa a sense of community. She begins to appreciate the relative slowness of life in Osaka. It's not sleek like Tokyo, but it has its charm. "I like the culture," she says. "It's friendly and I can feel the humanity."

She fantasizes about getting a little garden plot at that same park and raising vegetables with Rota. All she wants is to be close to her. "When Rota cries for me I have a sense that I cannot be replaced and that's a meaningful existence; this girl has become the center of my life."

But her mother's visit has also forced Tsukasa to acknowledge that one day, she and her daughter will inevitably drift apart. That she will experience, as her mother did, the exquisite pain of separation from a child. So as she pushes Rota's stroller home from the bakery on this first truly hot day of the year, the muggy gateway to the next season, she reminds herself that she needs to maintain her own identity. She cannot allow motherhood to swallow her whole.

CHELSEA
KENYA

"THERE YOU GO," CHELSEA murmurs, laying her freshly bathed baby onto blue terry cloth. She negotiates Ada's arms into a pale pink onesie and buttons it at her legs, still bent tight as a frog's. Then she lifts Ada to cradle her soft head in the curve of her neck, delighting in the infant's drowsy embrace.

"The first day I was still in shock, like surprised that I'm finally someone's mother," says Chelsea. "But since then it's been okay, she sleeps mostly during the day." She only wishes the same was true at night. "She's not too fussy though," Chelsea says gently and strokes the infant's wispy head. At just a week old, Ada is already making her mother proud.

For Chelsea, the decision to name her Ada after her own mother was easy. But choosing a last name has proven harder. Kenyan children can have as many as four names—to honor relatives, appease ancestral spirits, and affirm community identity—and still disagreements arise within families as relatives vie to have their line represented. Ada though, has just one name. No one in her family suggests another; they have not even come to meet her. Chelsea's aunt, who took Chelsea's younger brother in after their mother died, has not reached out. In a culture where children also call their aunts "mother" and view them almost as parents, her absence is particularly disappointing.

"I guess they're still not happy with the idea of me having a baby right now," Chelsea explains quietly. She suspects it's because she had the baby out of wedlock but tries not to dwell on it. "It's just going to stress me out for no reason, so I want to focus on raising the child and building a career and if they choose to be part of it, that's well and good, if not, pia iko sawa, it's still okay."

Perhaps more painfully, Joseph also has not come to see his daughter, or suggested a name from his side of the family, which he'll need to do soon for it to be listed on the birth certificate. They do still exchange videos though, so he knows the intimate details of their life: One day Ada was thrusting her tiny fists in the air with excitement, and the next, practicing a furrowed brow. "Every day is something new, so seeing these little changes is exciting, I like it," Chelsea says contentedly. And Joseph is helping them financially at least. Between that and Chelsea's full salary, which she still receives during her three-month maternity leave, they remain financially secure.

Still, there's no guarantee that Joseph will continue to help. Chelsea could petition for formal child support, but she says she might not be entitled to much because they're unmarried and, she adds with some apprehension, it would be an irreversible step into the unknown. "Once you go to court, there's no going back." She could burn bridges with Joseph, she says, and Ada might lose her relationship with him forever. "I want the conviction to care for her to come from his heart, not because he was forced by someone to do it."

She knows intimately what it feels like for a daughter to realize her father supported her out of obligation rather than love. When she was in primary school, before her stepfather entered the picture, Chelsea's father never paid for her schooling, except in class five when he bought her uniform. That small generosity was so unusual that she still remembers it. Then everything changed in secondary school. "He started paying my school fees and I got a medical card from him, so I felt like, maybe my dad is coming back into my life." For years, he'd seemed almost like a figment of her imagination, but now here he was, ensuring she was well cared for and getting a good education; finally expressing his love.

As soon as she graduated, though, his financial support stopped, and the medical card soon expired. Years later, after her mother died, Chelsea found a letter among her things. It was a summons for her father from the Federation of Women Lawyers, an organization that offers free legal aid to women. That was the first time she understood clearly, heartbreakingly, that her mother had sued her father for child support. "It was not a good thing to find out someone only supported you because they were forced by a court to do so," she says ruefully. "I don't want the same thing to happen to Ada, so if the father decides to support her, fine, and if he doesn't, at least she knows he made that choice, rather than that he was being forced, which is worse."

Jane Achieng, a Luo historian at the University of Nairobi, says that before colonialism upended centuries-old traditions, Chelsea's Luo community would have helped her, likely even forced Joseph to take some responsibility for his child. "The social protections were very strong and there were no outsiders as there are today, people with no community, just floating." The extended family clan was the primary economic unit, and communities shared child-rearing resources, unlike today's nuclear families that conserve assets to pay school fees, for example. And the very concept of wealth was different. Historically, Kenyan families measured their fortunes in terms of cattle, land, and children. "Children were the most important part of the wealth," says Achieng. She argues that modern expressions of affluence—like expensive cars that sit unused in gated compounds—don't produce the same social benefits. In Chelsea's case, Joseph might have taken more interest in Ada if the culture still ascribed such high value to children.

While today single motherhood is relatively common—six of every ten Kenyan women will have at least one episode of single motherhood by forty-five—historically it was rare. That's in part because today women are more economically empowered and can leave bad or abusive relationships. But it's also because of a traditional practice called tero or "wife inheritance," in which the community organized marriages for women who'd lost husbands. Asande Bonyo, the ninety-one-year-old Luo women who described giving birth at home, explains that when her first husband died, she was still quite young and so she married another man from the same family, Nyangoro, and they had several children. When Nyangoro later died in a tractor accident, she married a third member of the family, Oketch. "That was the tradition back then, but if you refused the next marriage, that was also fine."

The tero system was also polygamous, and when she married Oketch, he already had two wives, each of whom had their own shamba, a plot of farmland in the family settlement. Bonyo says she and her co-wives formed a tight familial unit. "We loved each other; my co-wives loved me so much that they would even wipe me with water," she says using an expression that connotes deep, unconditional love. Six decades later, she still lives on that same plot of land, next to her co-wives.

Bonyo gave birth to eight children, six of whom survived to adulthood. After the birth of each child, her co-wives and others in her community brought food and gifts. "Those were very good days," she smiles; "you would be cooked for and would just eat." She recalls filling up on fish and arrowroot, a starchy vegetable thought to have medicinal properties, and not returning to her farmwork for over a month. The traditional rest period was forty days, at which point she celebrated with a ritual bath, similar to the Japanese practice of "raising the floor"—a kind of cultural convergence in which groups on different sides of the globe landed on almost identical postpartum traditions of rest and community support, to address the same biological reality.

Much has changed since then, but polygamy still exists in Kenya, says Gloria Kenyatta, deputy clerk of a county legislature in the Rift Valley. "Polygamy is very legal; it's one of the traditional marriages we have in the African setting, so it's allowed, it's there, it's very alive and it's happening." At independence in 1963, many Kenyans were still polygamous, and while the so-called Marriage Bill in the late 1970s would have criminalized adultery, there was little parliamentary support for such "un-African changes." Today, polygamy is more common in rural areas, like the one where Kenyatta works, but there is an urban variant: Mubaba is Swahili slang for a wealthy older man who dates younger women, sometimes with his wife's consent. Often there is a financial component, but, unlike in traditional arrangements, there is no social obligation to provide for the women.

In Chelsea's case, she says Joseph's wife knew about their relationship, but it wasn't clear if she knew about the baby. There was one time, before Ada was born, that his wife called her. When Chelsea realized who it was, she hung up the phone. She never heard from her again.

That episode seems far away now, from a time when she took an interest in anything outside the pale green walls of her flat and the tiny space within them that Ada occupies. It is just Chelsea and Ada now and, of course, her friend Vee, who has been by her side since pregnancy. Another friend, Jen, visits frequently too. Chelsea helped Jen when her son was born four years ago, so Jen is happy to return the kindness now. The two women make up Chelsea's own small community of support.

Vee stands in the kitchenette cooking sweet potatoes—the

steaming pot adding moisture to the already humid air—as Chelsea looks on appreciatively from across the room. "She's really helping me out with the meals and the laundry, and also with the baby; she's been very supportive."

Chelsea needs that help as she recovers, the stitches healing, pain slowly receding. And as it does, she is grateful her body can also nourish Ada. "I have a lot of milk, which is a good thing because some of my friends told me their milk took a day or so to come, so I feel like that was a lucky thing on my path." After she nurses Ada, she takes the tiny baby in her arms and expertly burps her. In some ways, motherhood has come naturally.

Then, at two weeks, Chelsea's postpartum support ends when Vee and Jen return to nursing school. Chelsea was fortunate her baby came during their holiday break, but classes have started again, and the flat feels strange and cold without them. In a bustling city of five million people, she is alone with her baby. Bonyo, the Luo woman, reflects solemnly that while her own postpartum days were filled with fish and arrowroot, "things have really changed, these days you can go hungry and no one cares."

As Chelsea feeds Ada one rainy afternoon, she realizes she hasn't eaten all day but there's barely any food in the flat and she's not sure how she'll get more. Bringing Ada to the shops makes it so much harder to carry groceries and she worries about exposing such a young baby to crowds. In the days right after Vee and Jen return to school, there are a few times when she leaves Ada here asleep while she runs errands, but it fills her with dread. Most days she simply doesn't venture outside the house and only sees her old friends when their posts pop up on social media. "Sometimes it can be hard because maybe you see them having fun and you're like, why are they not visiting anymore, but it's okay," she says, her voice breaking. There is a long pause. "They're just busy with their lives and I don't get to see them as much because maybe I'd need to go out of the house, but I'm mostly with the baby."

There is a particular grief that can accompany new motherhood, in which women mourn all they've lost even as they gain a child: autonomy, privacy, time, sexuality, professional identity. Psychologist Paula Nicolson writes that women often won't admit even to themselves they feel that loss because there is such strong social pressure to exude joy. And she argues that if women were instead encouraged to grieve their old lives, "postpartum depression would be seen . . . as a potentially healthy process toward psychological reintegration and personal growth, rather than a pathological response to a 'happy event.'"

For Chelsea, this lonely time also surfaces fresh feelings of grief at the loss of her own mother. And later that same week, she gets another reminder, when Ada is due for her first checkup and round of vaccines. Public facilities are known to provide the best postnatal care, which has been free since 2013, so most everyone—from wealthy citizens to refugees—uses the public system. Jen suggests the big, national hospital downtown, but Chelsea recoils at the thought of going there. It was where both her parents died and she knows she won't be able to get past its familiar concrete exterior. Her cousin, who has newly reentered her life, offers another idea: Westlands Health Center, a little over an hour away by bus.

When Chelsea arrives at the clinic, a small facility inside a concrete barrier and looped razor wire, she drops off Ada's vaccination booklet then sits on a bench outside next to another mother. They both hold their babies in big, soft blankets and wait for instruction. Eventually, a nurse wearing a hijab and scrubs ushers Chelsea into a sunlit room, where she lays Ada on a long mattress, alongside another baby in a collared shirt. Their four spindly legs kick the air. Ada blows bubbles as Chelsea removes her onesie and then the nurse transfers her to a small plastic scale under a UNICEF poster: *Breast milk is best.*

Four and a half kilograms, the nurse reports and makes a note on Ada's chart.

Chelsea looks stricken.

Ada was four kilos last time, and Chelsea had expected her to be up to five today. *I don't know, maybe I should breastfeed more,* she thinks. Normally Ada just wakes for a minute to feed then falls back asleep, but perhaps she should encourage her to stay awake for longer and feed more. *I feel like she really should weigh more,* she thinks. It is a new concern, on top of others: Ada has been congested and Chelsea blames herself for not dressing her more warmly. She is also concerned Ada's navel is not healing quickly enough, so she applies surgical spirit and checks it frequently for any sign of infection.

"Anxiety is like a switch that turns on," Chelsea says. And she can't turn it off.

Postpartum anxiety is estimated to be more common than postpartum depression, but it is not as well studied or treated because it does not seem to pose the same threat to children—they're not at risk of neglect, for example. And while a clinically anxious mother might appear to be simply providing extra care and attention, what the mother herself experiences is crippling fear. Researchers think it is caused by postpartum hormones that reshape the female brain in areas that control memory, learning, fear response, and stress. Evolutionarily, it made sense for mothers to be sensitive to the slightest danger, because until the twentieth century, only about a quarter of infants survived their first year and only half made it to puberty. But in overdrive this instinct can become debilitating.

Chelsea doesn't have to worry, the nurse calmly assures her. Ada is just fine, she has gained enough weight and is developing well. Still, Chelsea makes a mental note to feed her more.

Ada then gets four vaccines; and Chelsea gets family planning counseling and an HIV test. Chelsea was born at the peak of the AIDS crisis that ravaged western Kenya and especially her Luo community. An estimated one person in every Luo household died or was infected by HIV at the height of the epidemic in the late nineties and early 2000s. It was fueled in part by traditional practices like polygamy, and made worse by Western religious organizations' opposition to condom distribution at church-funded medical centers. In her lifetime though, family planning and condoms have become standard at maternity clinics.

Chelsea is relieved when the visit it over. She walks Ada to an open green space behind the clinic, where she asks a woman to take pictures of the two of them, posing in the shade of a tree. Chelsea looks effortlessly lovely in a gray V-neck sweater, eyes cast softly over her shoulder. Later, she'll post the pictures on Instagram, where she will appear to the world as a joyful, carefree young mother.

Shortly after the clinic visit, something happens that does allay some of her worries: Joseph calls and suggests they give Ada his last name.

Okay sure, why not? Chelsea responds breezily.

Her casual response barely conceals the truth that for her, his suggestion is a meaningful declaration of kinship, something she has craved since Ada was born, though it doesn't confer any practical benefits for the baby. Chelsea hopes it might also portend more contact between the two of them. But weeks slip by, and he still doesn't come to meet the baby. Then one day he messages her to say he has a work event not far from her. They decide to meet halfway and she thrills at the thought of him finally holding their daughter. Just hours before their planned meeting, her phone buzzes again, ominously this time, with a message that seems to fill the room with acrid disappointment. She tries to assure herself that he does care for Ada and while he couldn't come this time, he'll visit when he can.

There are moments though, when a wave of melancholy crashes on her. Sometimes it hits with such force that it strips her of hope and forces her to reckon with the pain buried beneath. And in those moments, she can't bear to hold Ada; can't even look at her. The feeling strikes unpredictably, sometimes in the middle of a warm evening with Vee and Jen. She greets them kindly, smiles, and offers food. Then after making their plates, she disappears to her bedroom where she sits quietly, alone and overcome.

"I don't want to sound too bad, but there are points I feel like maybe I should not have given birth. Because I feel like maybe I should have maybe settled into a traditional family first." At other times though, Ada is the only thing that keeps her afloat—the feel of her downy skin; the warmth she radiates when she naps in Chelsea's arms; the ineffable beauty of her full lips and delicate ears. Her very being draws Chelsea in and relieves some of her pain. "At the same time, I feel like it was really what stabilized me, she's made my mind more mature. You know, I got depressed because I lost my parents, so she came to save me. She gives me a reason to wake up every day and, you know, just be someone in life."

There are studies that show "maternal desire," the feeling of wanting to be close to one's baby, has real psychological benefits. "I see lots of mothers who say their children have given them new hope," explains Mukami Munyoki, a psychologist at Mental 360, an organization that provides counseling to Kenyan youth. "It changes you and literally opens you up in a way that only childbirth can do. You're learning so many things fresh and as you do, you're learning about yourself, so it allows you to articulate your life how you want and in that way, motherhood can heal some trauma."

As the weeks pass, Chelsea relies less on Joseph for her own emotional stability and finds joy in her time with Ada. "It's not the easiest job but it's very rewarding," she says as she gazes down at her infant thoughtfully. "Like when you see those little milestones, when she starts smiling, when you see her grow. It's a beautiful thing, I like it," she says, lightness returning to her voice.

When the baby is about two months, Chelsea decides it's time for her to have her ears pierced. So she dresses her in a pink polka-dot dress and wraps her in a blanket then heads out. A warm breeze drifts across her building's courtyard as she descends the stairs, past rows of vermillion doors on each level and laundry hung to dry in the bright sun. The sound of children playing mixes with propulsive Afrobeat music coming from her neighbor's flat. She pushes open the green steel front door of her building and steps onto the muddy red street, into the colorful spill of life.

A young man selling sugarcane from a cart gives her a smile and a fist bump, then picks up another stalk and thwacks it with a glinting machete. Along the main street, she waves to other vendors in wood and corrugated metal stalls: A woman selling legumes out of squat plastic sacks; a teenage boy in a knit hat bagging potatoes; a butcher selling fresh goat meat, entrails hanging in the window. They all greet her by name. She's lived in this neighborhood most of her life and has a community here. It is good to be reminded.

She reaches the chemist, a storefront with blue trim that advertises medications, banking services, and ear piercing. The pharmacist, a woman in a lab coat with long braids like Chelsea's, greets her from behind metal bars and asks how Ada's navel is healing.

It's gotten better, Chelsea responds. She tells her she's here today to get Ada's ears pierced.

The pharmacist instructs Chelsea to sit on a low bench, next to a shelf stocked with antiseptic solution and scabies ointment.

Chelsea lowers herself carefully, then lifts her T-shirt to nurse Ada before the big event. The pharmacist swabs Ada's earlobes with alcohol and—just as the baby begins to doze off—lifts the plastic piercing gun. Chelsea looks away and readies herself. Suddenly, Ada wails, awakened by the pain, and is freshly angry when the pharmacist sticks the other ear. Chelsea quickly nurses her again, and the baby goes quiet, tears still fresh in her eyes. Chelsea herself is flooded with pure relief.

It sometimes feels as if Ada's feelings are Chelsea's own. They haven't spent a moment apart since she was born. Chelsea is entitled to a three-month guaranteed paid maternity leave, which was introduced here by a woman from her own Luo community: Grace Onyango, the first female Member of Parliament. Onyango was a widowed mother of six and true force of nature. "I was the minority in Parliament, standing up against 158 male MPs," she told *The Standard* in 2018. "But I dominated the debates." One particularly contentious dispute was over paid maternity leave, which Onyango started pushing for as early as 1970.

One of her chief opponents was Labor Minister Ngala Mwendwa, who didn't even think she should be in government. Married women should be home with children and single women were unsuitable for leadership, he argued. "The first duty of a woman is to get a husband. If she fails to get a husband, she has failed her first examination and she is not worthy to represent anybody," Mwendwa said in 1966. Yet on the issue of paid leave, he suddenly professed to care about female employment and argued it would make employers less likely to hire women. But Onyango fired back that women were already taking sick leave when they had babies, so there should just be a formal system. It took two decades for Parliament to come around to her way of thinking, but in 1994 the country enacted two months' paid leave that was later extended to three. As the labor minister had warned, employers were initially reluctant to keep hiring women, but that faded over the next few years. Chelsea's cohort of mothers is entitled to three months' paid leave and some companies offer more as a way to recruit top talent. Most countries provide at least three and a half, and the average for developed countries is about five months paid leave. Now, Kenyan advocates are pushing for six months, proving that the emancipation of women and the will of a new generation can reshape society.

As Chelsea nears the end of her own leave, she starts making preparations to return to work. She pumps and freezes as much milk as she can and tries to sleep train Ada by limiting her naps. "I don't want a scenario whereby we are awake all night and then I have to go to work and I'm awake all day again." Despite her efforts, Ada still wakes up out of hunger or habit several times each night.

Her friend Jen recommends a nanny agency, which sends Florence, a kind and capable woman from the western part of the country. She'll live with them, and sleep on a mattress in the living room. Here in Nairobi, almost all households except the very poorest employ domestic help such as nannies, cooks, and maids, many of whom are female immigrants from poorer neighboring countries, willing to work for below minimum wage.

For Chelsea, it's a relief to have another set of hands and the freedom to leave the flat on her own. "Sometimes you just need a break to get outside and maybe take a walk for thirty minutes." One mild evening, she goes to the nearby agriculture school campus and sits on a bench under a flowering purple jacaranda tree, listening to the roosters crow. She knows this calm won't last. And as she considers what's coming, she can't quite imagine how she is going to manage being separated from her daughter twelve hours a day. "I'm very anxious; I wish the timetable could be a bit slower, or maybe I could get like another month, but I know then I'll want another month and another one."

Then, suddenly, it is time. "The ninety days have passed very fast," she says as she hurries around her apartment to get ready. Motherhood seems to validate Einstein's theory that the perception of time is entirely subjective, based on one's frame of reference. Because while it had seemed inconceivable that the endless days would ever aggregate to months, here she is, in the bright light of early morning, expected to get herself ready for work again. But nothing feels right. Her work clothes still don't fit, and she just doesn't feel mentally ready. She sends her boss a message to ask for a few more days off, and when her request is approved, she exhales deeply. Then she dresses Ada in pink and returns to the clinic for her next round of vaccines.

But a few days later, she can't put it off anymore and boards a matatu minibus to get to the local branch of the large commercial bank where she works. Like most matatus, this one is painted with a colorful mural to appeal to young customers who can't afford taxis or personal cars. When Chelsea climbs off it, she feels a swell of anxiety at the sight of the bank's familiar beige façade sandwiched between a medical clinic and a grocery store.

She finally rouses the courage to go inside. One of the managers greets her and tells her that her desk has been reassigned to a new employee.

We'll give you a new one next month, he says, *so just use this month to get settled back in. You'll be at the customer service center for now.*

From the moment she sits down at eight a.m. she has back-to-back customers, but her mind keeps returning to Ada. She can't shake the feeling that something has gone terribly wrong. "I'm wondering if I could go home and find that my baby's not there." Chelsea has seen the news reports about child trafficking and kidnapping, an alarmingly common occurrence here. An estimated six thousand children are reported missing each year, an average of eighteen a day, and some are even trafficked out of the country. There is a black market for infants, driven by a stigma around infertility; women can be kicked out of their home for not bearing children, so they might pay traffickers for a baby they are told was given up willingly.

Caught in a cycle of catastrophic thinking, the only way out is to video-chat Florence, her nanny, to see for herself that Ada is fine.

Her breasts swell at the sight of her gurgling baby, and she waits impatiently for her lunch break so she can pump. When it finally comes, she discovers that, as she'd suspected, there is no dedicated lactation room, even though the 2017 Health Act requires companies with more than fifty employees to have a space for women to express milk and a refrigerator in which to store it— part of the country's push for mothers to breastfeed exclusively for six months. The bank where she works has considerably more than fifty employees, with branches across the country. But at this branch, at least, employees do not have lactation rooms.

Chelsea knows her office is noncompliant but feels little agency to do anything about it. She'd expected other women to have already come up with solutions, but incredibly, she seems to be the first nursing mother in the office. Or maybe just the only one still there.

She scours the facility for a concealed corner where she can pump. Finally, she settles for the book room, a storage area for documents and other miscellany. It's relatively private, but the air is dank and the stench of old paper turns her stomach.

As she unpacks her pump, she can already hear coworkers calling for her: *Chelsea? Chelsea! A customer needs help!*

She's on her lunch break, though, off duty for the moment, so she stays quiet and continues to fiddle with the flange until she gets it in position, then squeezes with her other hand and immediately feels the pressure in her chest release.

Suddenly, there is a slash of light and before she knows what's happened, she sees one of her coworkers silhouetted in the doorway. He is looking for a file but instead finds Chelsea, wide-eyed and half naked. He turns as quickly as he came and leaves the room, a flurry of frantic apologies trailing in his wake. Chelsea is stunned, then mortified. But she decides there isn't much she can do—Ada still needs to eat.

When she's done, she sheepishly emerges from the room, now ravenous herself. She'd had to use both hands to operate the manual pump and couldn't eat at the same time. But she only gets one break a day, and now it's over.

An hour later, her phone buzzes with a message from Florence that fills her with panic: Ada has finished all the milk Chelsea left and is crying for more. Chelsea hasn't yet received her paycheck so she can't send the nanny money for formula. She knows the only solution is to ask her manager if she can leave early on her first day back. "From the reaction, it felt like an inconvenience to her. You know, they don't really consider the fact that you just gave birth, you have a small child, you are readjusting. Things have changed for you as well, you're no longer independent and able to come and go as you please, because you have to think of someone else who is totally dependent on you. They don't really put that into consideration." Eventually she convinces him she simply has to go and, flooded with both guilt and relief, she returns home to feed her baby.

The issue of working conditions for mothers got national attention in 2019 when MP Zuleikha Hassan brought her five-month-old to Parliament after her own childcare fell through. Hassan was frustrated because six years before, the Parliamentary Service Commission had mandated that a daycare be constructed in the building, but it never happened. "I thought, if they don't want to build a room for babies then I'm going with my baby inside the chambers," she recalls from her office in Kwale county, wearing a hijab and gesturing emphatically. "Traditionally, women took their children with them as they worked on farms or at markets because it was important they be together, so why not in modern workplaces?"

Hassan knew she would not be welcome in parliament with a child, so rather than go in the front door, she used a side entrance that members usually use to access the bathroom. But a security guard spotted her with the infant and shouted at her not to go inside. "So I just grabbed the door and ran in," she says conspiratorially. "I'm pretty big so he would have caught me if he was close." Once she was in the chamber, though, only the speaker could remove her, and at the time, he was at the lectern arguing that Kenya should take military action against Somalia. "When he saw me, he just lost it because here's this macho man with the testosterone, I mean, how much more manly can it get than war? And then there's a woman and baby interrupting that very important, masculine time," she laughs.

The chamber erupted in shouting and pushing with Hassan at the center of the fracas, holding her infant daughter in a pale pink blanket. One MP asked her pointedly, what if the baby vomits on me? "Well, how do you know that you didn't vomit on people?" she remembers thinking. "Maybe your mom went to an important meeting, so if you vomited and you pooped on someone, why can't someone else? This being is another Kenyan, a person who's coming up and you'll depend on *them* in future."

The incident made international news. "And by five that evening, there was a crèche in Parliament," she recalls. Some of her critics claimed the facility had already existed but she laughs that off. "They are really big, fat liars because I went with them to that room and said, These are all new things, they're spotless and there's no staff member manning the room. Why can't you just admit it didn't exist before today and say sorry?" For her, the issue is bigger than just getting childcare in Parliament. She is now pushing the Breastfeeding Mothers Bill, which would require employers to provide facilities for infants. "If as an MP I'm suffering, how about if you're just an ordinary Kenyan who is not privileged? Obviously, they're going to be suffering much, much more."

As for Chelsea, the morning after she'd left work early to feed her own baby, she readies herself to return to the office once again. A little before seven, she pulls on a fitted black dress over a white button-down with puffed sleeves. She looks the part of a confident professional but is still deeply uncomfortable leaving Ada. And as she comes out of her bedroom, her fears are confirmed: Ada is lying unattended on the floor and Chelsea finds Florence in the bathroom, doing laundry and wearing earphones. Chelsea is upset. Ada already knows how to roll, so someone needs to monitor her at all times.

So long as the baby's awake, you should be with her and not wearing earphones, Chelsea tells Florence firmly. *No one is going to scold you for not doing laundry, but you can't just leave the baby alone like that.*

The nanny nods and hurries from the bathroom.

Chelsea is still worried, but it's time to leave. So she takes one last look at Ada on the floor, tiny in an oversized Christmas-themed onesie, and tells herself the baby will still be there, just as happy, when she gets back. Then she gently closes the front door, stops briefly in the hallway to put on a pair of round, white earrings, and walks to the bus stop.

As she waits, her mind takes the opportunity to dwell on another source of stress; Ada needs diapers, but Chelsea isn't sure how she'll afford them. Joseph hasn't sent money this month and it's hard to get by on her salary alone.

"I mean, I do what I can. Like emotionally, mentally, I'm trying," her voice trembles.

That evening when she gets home, she scoops Ada in her arms

then sits on the couch to breastfeed her. They both immediately seem happier.

For the next few weeks, Chelsea goes to work then rushes home to spend as much time with Ada as she can. But she can feel the toll that the schedule, and the stress, is taking on her body. Sharp stomach pains keep her up at night and during the day, she feels nauseous and weak. Ada also has a raspy cough and one of her eyes begins to look inflamed. Chelsea decides they need to see a doctor, so one evening after work, she takes Ada to Melchizedek Hospital, a small, family-owned facility she has visited before.

It is dark by the time they arrive, and she's comforted to see the familiar glow of its blue and white sign. The doctor diagnoses Chelsea with ulcers and an *H. pylori* infection, and Ada with an eye infection, and sends them both home with antibiotics. But later that night, Chelsea feels worse still. She's so uncomfortable that can't sleep even when Ada does. So she returns to the doctor a few days later for more tests, which reveal she also has low blood sugar and a sinus infection, for which the doctor prescribes hydrating salts and more antibiotics. He recommends she stay in the clinic overnight to recuperate, but Chelsea doesn't want to keep Ada there longer than necessary; who knows what she might be exposed to. She asks the doctor if, instead, she can get the IV infusion there and have the rest of the medicine to take home. He reluctantly agrees and she leaves the hospital in the early hours.

The next day, after Chelsea has called off work, one of her managers, an officious woman named Grace, visits the hospital to investigate whether Chelsea is truly sick. "And I don't know why," Chelsea recalls, "but the hospital revealed my information to her." The medical staff tell her boss that Chelsea is no longer there. Grace calls Chelsea and accuses her of lying about being sick then demands an explanation for why she has taken the day off.

Chelsea tells her she was at the hospital until very late and is still sick, but she's now convalescing at home.

"I left because I didn't want to stay longer with the baby in the hospital," she says, expecting some sympathy. But she doesn't get any. Grace tells Chelsea she has no excuse for not returning to work.

The phone call only makes Chelsea more nervous to go back to the office when she's feeling better. "I'm not looking forward to it honestly, it's just that I need the job. And otherwise, if I had a choice, I wouldn't even be working there. I think she's just too much to . . ." Her voice breaks as she begins to cry. Then she draws a breath, wipes the tears from her eyes, and tries to steady herself. "But anyway, we'll see, we'll see how things go." She knows that she is all Ada has. Joseph is no longer sending money, though the two of them still video chat sometimes and have the same easy chemistry. "He has not been well off financially for the last few months so I've been taking care of the bills, but it's been hard."

All of Chelsea's work caring for Ada—the late nights, the hospital trips, the breastfeeding and diaper changes—has no monetary value. And after she puts her salary toward Ada's needs, Chelsea is sometimes unable to feed herself. She knows she is not eating as a nursing mother should, and it's probably affecting her health. Smith College Professor Loretta J. Ross writes that, "mothering, radically defined, is the glad gifting of one's talents, ideas, intellect, and creativity to the universe without recompense." But Chelsea cannot survive that way. With Joseph unreliable and her family unwilling, there's only one more person whose help she can seek—her own mother.

"When my mom was sick and it was looking like she wasn't going to make it, her best friend told me she had some money in this account and I should follow up," she says, holding the ATM cards that bear her mother Ada's name. At the time, Chelsea was so overcome with grief she didn't think much about it, but later, as she was going through her mother's belongings, "I happened to find the final receipts when she had used the account last . . ." She trails off as tears fill eyes. Now, for the sake of her own daughter, she is finally willing to navigate this sensitive terrain.

So on the afternoon after her hospital visit, when the medicine begins to kick in and Chelsea starts to feel somewhat better, she decides to use the remainder of her sick day to visit Co-operative Bank, where her mom held an account. She puts on a peach shift dress and sweeps her long braids into a ponytail. Going to the bank is one step in a logistical gauntlet: She has already gone to the Huduma center for a death certificate; a public trustee for an indemnity; a lawyer for certification; and, after she gets a letter from this bank, will still need to go to a regional chief upcountry for his sign-off. "It's a very long process," she sighs as she opens the heavy bank door. "And having to find the death certificate, it takes me back a bit. I mean, it's not a good feeling but anyway, it's something that I just want to be done with and forget about it."

The branch is already crowded so she takes a number and settles into a grey vinyl chair to wait. But before her number is called, her phone rings. She's not pleased to see who it is but answers anyway. A female voice speaks in angry Swahili; it's Grace again, asking for proof that she had been sick.

"I was ill, I got medicine at the hospital. Plus, I had sick-off time . . ." Chelsea tries to explain.

But Grace interrupts. "Why didn't you send me the paperwork then?"

"Send it at three a.m.?" Chelsea responds sharply. "I got home and slept because I also had the baby; I sent it in the morning when I woke up."

"Yeah, because to you this job is not a priority," Grace says, her voice rising.

"No but see, I had already— Grace, I had already told you I was in the hospital."

"The thing is, this case is now with HR," Grace cuts Chelsea off. "Me, I'm just collecting facts so I can write everything down and submit it—that's why I went to the hospital to confirm what was happening, because it's not for me to handle this now. Honestly, I want it handled by HR."

"Sawa," Chelsea says softly: *Okay.*

The call drops and Chelsea stares at her phone, unsure what to do next. Soon enough, the decision is made for her. She receives an email from human resources that lists "several incidences of professional misconduct" including: "You lied to the management that you had been admitted to Melchizedek Hospital, which was later found not to be true." All her protestations had come to nothing because here in writing, the chief human resources officer is calling her a liar. It is gutting.

Two days later she receives an ominous follow-up email with the subject line: Invitation to Attend a Disciplinary Hearing. In it, the human resources officer instructs her to report at eleven the next morning to a hearing in which she will be asked to respond to the allegations of misconduct. "I had less than twenty-four hours to prepare my case," Chelsea recalls.

She sleeps fitfully and wakes early. She's too nervous to eat much before she leaves her flat to board a matatu for the hour-and-a-half trip to the central business district, where the bank is headquartered in a silvery office tower. As instructed, she takes the elevator to the tenth floor. Then, she waits. An hour passes, and finally an administrative assistant leads her to a conference room where four men—three HR representatives and a lawyer—sit ready for her. She nervously takes her seat across from them. As soon as she does, they begin to grill her about what happened at the hospital and whether she refutes Grace's allegation that she lied.

"I was overwhelmed because it was four against one and I didn't know what information they had from the manager. So let's just say, I was blindsided," she recalls, and swallows hard as if trying to suppress a surge of emotion. She tells them she is a new mom, the sole provider for her baby, and had been doing her best to fulfill her professional responsibilities. The men seem unmoved. At the end of the meeting, the HR manager issues her the termination letter he already had prepared.

Chelsea's firing is highly concerning, says Kenyatta, the deputy clerk in the Rift Valley. The county government where Kenyatta works makes sure local businesses are in compliance with the 2017 Health Act that requires nursing mothers get certain supports, and businesses that don't follow the law need to be reported, she says. "That is not right, it's not acceptable. You cannot fire nursing mothers just because they are mothers—because she did not have a lactation room and so on—she probably needs legal action."

Chelsea does suspect her dismissal was not entirely proper, that perhaps she should have had a lawyer with her. There seems to be a disconnect between the policy's intention and its implementation but for now, Chelsea doesn't have time or resources to explore legal remedies. She is singularly concerned with how she'll provide for Ada.

On the bumpy matatu ride home, she swings between a feeling of devastation and a kind of "absentminded" disbelief that she no longer has a job. She knows she needs to try to stay calm. "Right now I'm focused on just centering myself because I don't want to like, fall into a depression or get stressed because it will make my situation worse. I just want to have a level mind so I can figure out how I'm going to pay the bills."

Ruth Mumbi, an activist who grew up in Nairobi's informal settlements and now advocates for women there, says the capitalism that replaced traditional systems treats human beings, particularly women, as labor to be exploited. "But women take care of the labor that's going to come tomorrow and produce more profit, so there should be support for them to work and also maintain mental stability. It's really traumatizing the way we torture women for being mothers."

When Chelsea finally opens the door to her flat after the disastrous morning, Ada turns and smiles broadly at the sound of her mother's voice. She is old enough now to sit mostly unassisted, and she eagerly, somewhat clumsily, stretches her arms to welcome her home. Chelsea hugs the baby and gets down on the floor to play. Ada's burbling presence is so soothing compared to the plate-glass brutality of modern professional life. "After all the stress, you come back to the baby and just forget about everything."

In this moment of relative calm, she can see that trying to succeed in an environment so uninterested in acknowledging her humanity was not sustainable. "Working there really wasn't conducive to having a baby. Mothers, once they leave work it's not like they're going to rest, they're going to start another shift and sleep with someone who wakes up like ten times in a night; they should understand mothers have like two jobs, or even three." So while being fired is a blow to her ego and her financial security, part of her is at peace. "I feel like I've left something very toxic, like a burden was lifted."

ANNA
FINLAND

IT IS THE DARK season in Turku. Rows of birch trees wilt in the freezing rain, remnants of their once brilliant yellow leaves lay soggy at their roots. In Anna's neighborhood by the harbor, wet wind blows in from the Baltic Sea and beats against the apartment blocks. The anemic sun is no match for it, can only hoist itself into the sky a few hours a day and not even high enough to hit some stretches of Anna's street, which remain in continuous shadow for weeks. The sidewalks are quiet save for a few intrepid pedestrians in all-weather gear. One of the few bustling spots is the nearby indoor market, where vendors at wood-paneled stalls sell malty rye bread and rich shrimp salad—comfort food made for this season of hunkering down.

Anna and the baby are confined mostly to her bedroom, where she shuttles the newborn between her bed to feed and his adjacent cot to sleep; and so the first days of his life pass in a haze. He still doesn't have a name, so they call him hän, a gender-neutral word for both "he" and "she," or else by his nickname, Paavo. And they exult in the contours of his tiny face, his fine black hair that stands up in patches as if electrified. Normally, a public health nurse would visit Anna's flat a week after she left the clinic to help with baby care and feeding—one reason the country has some of the highest rates of breastfeeding—but the home visit program has been suspended since the start of the pandemic.

Anna could have used the support, because a few days after they get home, things take a turn: Anna notices the baby seems uninterested in eating and is somewhat listless, even for this melancholic season. There is a yellow cast to his skin that makes her think perhaps he is jaundiced, as her daughter Liv was at birth. So she and Masa bundle him up and trudge across the slushy city and into the light wood warmth of the maternity clinic. During the examination, the doctor confirms that the baby has developed jaundice, as she had suspected, and also mild anemia. That means he can tire easily and may not feed well. It shouldn't last long, the doctor assures them, but he advises Anna to nurse as much as possible so the baby gets enough liquid and nutrients.

Back home, Anna feels responsible for pulling her newborn from his lethargy and feeds him even more than before. They sit in the pale winter light of the living room, its walls covered in art she made years ago, relics of a time when she could do anything beyond caregiving. Now, she thinks, she can hardly find a moment for even the most basic elements of her own survival: eating, sleeping, bathing. Feeding the baby takes hours each day and in the chopped-up remaining time, she only wants to rest. She had insomnia for several nights before she went into labor and now can't seem to make up the deficit, though her body craves it. Still, she's surviving thanks to hormones that, as she says, give her energy that club kids would need substances to replicate. "In a way, I wish that part would continue after this baby phase is over," she laughs.

It helps her get through life now as a mother of two. Liv, who stays with them half the week, has embraced her role as big sister.

She sits on the couch next to the baby and gently strokes his arm. She is used to having younger siblings because she has several at her dad's house, from his relationship with his current partner. Still, it's an adjustment, and Anna is proud of how welcoming Liv has been.

Slowly, the infant begins to feed better as his body learns to digest milk. And a week later, Anna and Masa return to the clinic, where they learn that he is now above his birth weight. They are relieved; the nurse who delivers the news, a blonde woman in blue scrubs, gives them a smile. She also saw them at their last visit so she knows how meaningful it is that he's gained weight. The way the system works, this same nurse will see him at all fifteen regular checkups he'll have from now until he enters primary school, and a doctor will join only a third of the time, an indication of the primary role nurses play.

The nurse understands how hard breastfeeding can be and tells Anna not to worry too much about giving him formula instead. It's part of a Finnish philosophy that reducing maternal stress is also beneficial for the baby.

Take care of yourself so you can take care of the child, she tells Anna gently; *as long as he's growing, it's fine*. Then she asks if they plan to follow the standard inoculation schedule. Masa isn't sure; he's particularly skeptical of newer vaccines, in keeping with what he describes as a philosophy of minimal intervention.

Eastern medicine says you don't try to save a life that cannot be saved; Western medicine would say to keep trying, to prolong a life that was going to die, he explains.

That is a bridge too far for Anna. *I just can't imagine this new life would be left out there and we would do nothing ...* she trails off.

Masa defers to her expertise. She routinely takes the lead on parenting and so, as Masa explains, "In some ways I'm just a spectator going through all these big changes and the whole pro-cess from the outside." The mother's role is clear immediately, particularly for those who breastfeed, he thinks, but what is his? He has no one to help him work through these big questions; doesn't even remember his own dad. "I haven't had a father figure or role model, it is completely from scratch."

As part of public prenatal care, expectant mothers have a one-on-one session with a public health nurse in which they can reflect on their own childhood and consider what they might want to do differently with their children, a powerful exercise meant to break intergenerational trauma. "It is very important to discuss these things with them," says Tuovi Hakulinen, the head of research at the Finnish Institute for Health and Welfare, who helped design the program. "If a mother witnessed domestic violence in her childhood, for example, talking about it can help her understand that it's not her fault and she can select her own way to be a par-ent." It's a program that might have benefited Tsukasa, had it existed in Japan.

Hakulinen is working to create a pilot program that will provide the same kind of counseling to fathers and non-birthing partners. Right now, fathers only attend prenatal appointments along with mothers. "They might be more comfortable sharing their experi-ence with a public health nurse but not a partner, so they need that privacy," says Hakulinen. During the sessions, nurses will also provide parenting advice, which Hakulinen says many fathers receive better from a professional than a spouse.

That might have helped Masa learn to be a better parent and not resent Anna for offering suggestions. Her shift to the lead par-ent role is one way he can feel their relationship changing. He isn't sure where it's headed and, Anna professes, neither is she. "We'll find out down the line if there's still something between us as grown-ups as well," she laughs.

A few weeks later, Anna's early surge of amphetamine-like energy begins to subside and getting up every few hours is harder. But Masa still doesn't wake when the baby cries from his little cot next to their bed. He sleeps so soundly, he isn't even sure how many times the baby is up at night, whimpering to be fed or changed or held: "Three? Two? Depends on how hungry he is, I guess."

Masa wants to be more helpful, and asks Anna to wake him.

I can imagine how tiring it must be to do it all alone, he tells her.

Still, she finds that it's often just as exhausting to try to rouse him and wishes he would be more proactive about getting involved; to figure out ways to help that she doesn't need to manage. As the days wear on, the brutal brew of hormones and sleep deprivation takes a toll, and she begins to resent him for not doing more.

Her daytime chores bleed into overnight feeds, and she develops a chronic headache that only worsens as she falls further behind on sleep. She becomes so exhausted she doesn't bathe, can barely eat.

Would you like to shower? Masa suggests one quiet morning as she sits with the baby on the bed.

She gratefully accepts and begins to ready herself. Then five minutes later, she realizes Masa still hasn't returned to collect the baby. In fact, she realizes, he's gone off to do something else entirely. The casual way she perceives him as having abandoned her pushes her over the edge and she goes to find him.

Here, why don't you take the baby so I can at least eat, she says sharply. *You know, in Finland, society is very equal, there is not this idea that the woman is the only one taking care of the child and it's her problem.*

A MONTH AFTER THE baby is born, Anna and Masa decide on his name.

"It's Luka," Anna says, looking down at their round-faced infant with a smile. They wanted a name that was gender neutral and easy for the Finnish speakers on her side and the Japanese speakers on his to pronounce, she explains. She sounds relieved to have finally settled on it.

Still, they continue disagree on other things and frequently bicker. One evening in early March, as Anna is struggling to get Luka to nurse, Masa tells her he thinks the baby isn't getting enough to eat. She finds his remark particularly cutting given the difficulty she's had and the concern they share about him gaining enough weight. Anna feels trapped in a constant cycle of feeding, in order to keep her milk supply up, and it seems to her that Masa doesn't understand how hard that has been, or why it's so important.

Masa takes the infant from Anna's arms and, as she recalls, grumbles, *You're starving this baby to death.*

Then he carries Luka to the kitchen and calls to Anna that he is going to give him the milk she had pumped earlier.

Anna is suddenly furious. She'd worked hard for that milk, and Masa shouldn't be using it so recklessly. It's a precious resource that signifies the possibility of her future freedom, a time when someone else will take responsibility for feeding the baby so she can get a break.

No Masa! It's not yours and he doesn't need it because I'm here—and I should be nursing to keep my supply up anyway!

Masa instead finds a box of formula. Hands full, he sets Luka down on the counter and cuts open the package with an unsterilized kitchen knife. Anna rushes in to find Luka squirming unhappily next to Masa.

You can't do that, Masa! she cries and grabs the baby.

Masa realizes what he's done and puts the knife down then sighs sharply and leaves the room. Anna stands in shocked silence, but as she watches him go, feels a stirring of compassion. She knows the demands of parenthood are new to him.

Still, Masa is upset that she's painted him as uncaring. He's just trying to help feed the baby, and *has* been worried Luka isn't getting enough nutrition.

Okay, now I'm actually going to be the asshole who would just leave, she remembers him saying, as he angrily begins to pack his things.

Anna flushes with rage. She puts down the baby, grabs a stack of Masa's clothes, and hurls them in his direction.

You can take these with you as you go! she yells.

He shoves the garments into his bag and strides toward the front door.

But Anna realizes in that moment that once he's gone, she'll be alone again. So she follows him into the bright white hallway and pleads with him to let her go outside for a moment to cool off before he leaves. Instead, things only intensify as Anna tries to wrest Masa's bag from him so he'll stay. Then, as Anna later remembers it, he shoves her. Masa says he was just protecting his bag and describes it as a mutual altercation. "It was a very charged situation," he says, "very charged." Neither of them feels good about it, and the episode ends as quickly as it began. Masa hurries down the stairs and she is alone again.

In the heavy stillness of her flat afterward, Anna debates whether to notify the police. She doesn't do it immediately, but eventually decides the incident does need to be clearly documented. The resulting court documents describe it as a "petty assault" they both took part in.

Masa acknowledges he should have been more careful with Luka. "The knife was nowhere near him but I can understand how Anna saw it, there's this knife flashing next to the baby, so I agree with her that it was not okay." But he also says that he and Anna had been bickering so much even before their big blow up that he thinks it's best if he stays with a friend for a while. "It's clearly not okay for baby to be brought up like this and I can't see any way the tension will get lower, I only see it getting worse."

Anna also thinks they need a break. "We have things to discuss really seriously, like how to go on as a family."

A few weeks later, Anna writes Masa a long message apologizing for her part in the situation, hoping that will smooth things over, but it doesn't. Instead, she says he tells her she's made him feel worthless as a father, and that he hadn't said anything because he hadn't wanted to anger her, but he had finally reached his breaking point. Anna thinks perhaps she could have anticipated their blowup and done more to prevent it. "I didn't see his needs or his fragility enough, and I think it surprised him as well." She feels responsible to help him through the turbulence of new parenthood. But as author Gemma Hartley writes, managing a partner's emotional state can exact a psychic toll. "Women are, in many unpaid ways, expected to keep those around us comfortable at all costs—including the cost to self."

In the next few days, Anna reflects on the episode and considers how much of it was precipitated by their different views on gender roles. She is surprised that Masa seems to be falling back on the traditional division of labor he saw as a child, like a default to his factory settings. He seems to expect that because she is a woman, she'll do the caregiving work. "I don't know if his ideas are changing or if they're just coming out now," Anna says. It's surprising because in most other aspects of his life, he's so eager to defy convention. That was one of the things that drew her to him, his unusual way of looking at the world. Even now, between his shifts cleaning boats, he has started to conceive a performance art piece about death, so he is clearly willing to engage with big, thorny topics in nontraditional ways. But it seems that kind of norm bending hasn't extended to the work of parenthood.

It's not just that she would like relief from the drudgery, or to admire Masa as she once did. It's that there are larger implications: She wants to model equality for her kids and preserve the country's egalitarian culture for the next generation. "I don't want Luka to learn that women should stay at home, that they're the ones who will take care of all the world's population when babies are born."

Finland's feminist heritage can be traced to legends of "Terra Feminarum, the mysterious Northern Land of Women," which Roman texts describe as a land between Sweden and Russia that was home to powerful, nature-worshipping female leaders. And Finland's national epic, *Kalevala*, goes further, referring to the North Land as a "man-eating village." Historians think that colorful mythology might actually be based on early Finns' interactions with the Sámi people, an ethnic minority whose society was led by female shamans.

In 1906, Finland made history by allowing all adult citizens to vote, and then the next year, in the first election where women had a say, it promptly elected the world's first female parliamentarians. (When Riitta Uosukainen became its first female Speaker in 1994 after serving as education minister, she oversaw Finland's public school system, which ranked at the top worldwide and also, in the tradition of those ancient man eaters, talked openly about how much she enjoyed sex.)

Some of those first female parliamentarians were labor leaders who pushed for equal rights for female workers, but it wasn't until the country was devastated by war that it finally enshrined those supports into law. Finland entered World War II in 1939 when the Soviet Union invaded it with a combat force five times the size of Finland's, and a year later, looking for a partner in their fight, Finland entered an informal alliance with Nazi Germany. By the end of the war, Finland had lost almost a tenth of its territory and two percent of its population. The country's economy was already enfeebled before a postwar peace treaty compelled Finland to pay steep reparations to compensate the Soviet Union for damage.

Finland plunged into poverty. Sandwiched between Russian communism and Western free markets, the country blazed its own "welfare capitalist" middle path, to claw its way back to prosperity. Capitalists worked with the government to map out a business-friendly environment—that has since produced successful international companies like Nokia—and got labor unions on board. Those unions advocated for strong worker protections, and the Finnish government adopted them in the 1960s as a way to make the workforce more productive. Business interests agreed to tax hikes that would keep workers healthy and productive, which set the stage for today's public health system, day care, and paid parental leave. In that postwar period, there was a sense of optimism; the country had suffered deadly losses but had never actually been occupied. Finns saw a brighter future ahead and began to have more babies—there was even a saying, "the third for the fatherland"—though the government did not explicitly encourage fertility.

In 1964, the country implemented a nine-week maternity leave, which was soon extended to three months. And in 1978, fathers also got a two-week paid paternity leave. Today, birthing parents get forty days paid pregnancy leave before the child is born, then parents get almost a year of paid leave after the baby is born, which they can split as they like. It's funded mainly by contributions from employers and employees, and topped off by the Finnish government. The country spends a little over one percent of its overall budget on parental leave, slightly more than Japan by percentage and on the higher side in general, compared to other countries.

Finnish economists argue it's worth it because generous maternal supports have helped keep women in the workforce at higher rates than most other countries, while also having children. Over time, the expectation became that, with such generous leave policies, all women would work. That was notably different from how Japan rebuilt its own postwar economy, with women in the role of professional housewife.

As Prime Minister Sanna Marin put it in a speech nine months before Luka was born, "Women's full and equal participation in society has made Finland's development possible. A hundred years ago, Finland was a poor and conflict-torn society. It was not possible for us to ignore the potential of half of our population."

Anna learned all this history in school. "After the Second World War there was no such thing as housewives anymore—so that's something that's very rooted in our upbringing and in this society, that women have the right to do the same thing as men. In Finland, men and women are very, very equal." It's so fundamental that she takes it for granted, which helps explain why she has had such a hard time navigating homelife with Masa, whose upbringing in Japan was so different from hers. Before now, Anna had never needed to explain it. "I don't see many of these daily basic things as feminist, but of course they are."

Getting to the point where equality is normalized takes time, though. Japan is still trying to convince fathers to take parental leave, but many are reluctant because they worry it could hold them back professionally. Finland, on the other hand, has had some form of paternity leave for nearly half a century, so society has become more accepting—though it is still true that lower-income men and immigrants take *slightly* less parental leave, as do men in managerial roles and entrepreneurs.

Anna can see that inclusion of fathers in domestic life when she goes for a walk one late winter day with Luka, after dropping Liv at school. Anna is stylish in a black winter coat and hexagonal wire-rimmed glasses. There is a dusting of snow on the ground as they stroll through their neighborhood, past various markers of modern urbanity: trattorias, bike shops, vintage-clothing stores, and young fathers out with their own small children. First, a man in a dark peacoat and olive beanie, his black jeans rolled up to reveal colorful New Balance sneakers, glides by with a stroller. A block later, a bearded man in workpants lifts his pigtailed daughter onto his shoulders. The men project an ease in their fatherhood, and a kind of confident independence.

Anna remarks that on these walks she often sees more fathers than mothers pushing strollers.

Finland is the only country in the industrialized world where fathers spend more time with school-aged children than mothers. The difference is only eight minutes; about as even as it can be. Local blogs enthuse over these men they've dubbed "latte pappas," young fathers who take advantage of generous parental leave to spend time with their children in cafés and city parks. (The term came from Sweden, and some Finnish speakers have invented the related expression sumppi-isukki, or "stale coffee dad," for the less fashionable set.)

Research has shown this kind of extended time together can actually produce neurological changes that make men and non-birthing parents more effective caregivers; one study that compared brain scans of first-time fathers found that those in countries with longer paternity leave had changes in regions associated with sustained attention. Here in Finland, local parenting blogs have observed that fathers who spend extended time with their children are more competent caregivers and, because they develop an appreciation for the difficulty of traditional "women's work," more respectful of their partners.

That has turned them into something of a romantic archetype: Latte papa characters now appear frequently in Nordic romance novels. Elin Abrahamsson, a researcher at Stockholm University, writes that these characters are different from typical swaggering male leads. They are instead "'gender-equal' middle-class men who are often represented as already responsible for family and household commitments" and whose, "gentle and grounded qualities make them accessible as equal life partners."

As for Anna and Masa, there isn't much holding them together anymore. So as the weeks go by, and the tension over the division of caregiving roles continues to poison their relationship, they finally decide that their problems are so intractable, Masa's move from their flat should be permanent.

APRIL FINALLY COMES, WITH its promise of lighter, longer days, an emergence from the gloom. Birds return, red squirrels bound bright-eyed from their nests, and the ice on the Aura River loosens its grip. Perhaps most importantly, at three months old, Luka has begun to sleep better, so Anna feels increasingly restored. She even brings him to stay overnight at her parents' house and is surprised by how soundly she can sleep with him in another room. "With Liv, I would have been in there every two minutes, checking: Is the baby inhaling? Okay. Exhaling?"

She allows herself to relax and sits quietly in the soft evening air, a nonalcoholic beer in her hand. It's supposed to increase milk production, she explains with a smile. In the bassinet next to her, Luka wriggles himself awake and begins to coo. "Here he is!" she enthuses as she lifts him to her chest. He's more engaged with the outside world now; he plays with toys and giggles when he's pleased. Anna can communicate with him better too. She reads his subtle cues in a way she never learned to do when Liv was small. And he looks older: his limbs more filled out, hair flatter at the crown of his head. "I have to say, to me he gets cuter every day," Anna smiles.

As Luka develops, so does she, and at three months postpartum, Anna feels ready to reclaim some of her professional identity.

So she accepts a short, contract job—just a few days long—with a former employer as an event supervisor at a conference. She kisses Luka goodbye at her parents' house, then excitedly heads to Logomo, a converted factory that is now one of Turku's largest venues. She is glad to see its familiar brick façade and inside, the modern, glass-walled convention hall, humming with activity. Being back here inspires a surge of creativity that she's grateful to feel again.

Anna is allowed to do five hours of paid work a day, and still get half her daily parental leave pay. Mostly she does it for the intellectual stimulation and to stay professionally relevant. "It's really more like a hobby but it's nice to get a little paycheck too," she says. A few weeks later, her company asks if she's up for a more complex design project that involves putting together a client proposal. She considers it—she had enjoyed being back in the land of adults—but in the end decides not to do it. She's not ready for such a big assignment, and she also needs time to deal with the instability in her personal life.

Her relationship with Masa has broken down entirely, she says, and he has started to express to her family and friends that their separation is making it hard for him to bond with his son. Anna says she'd like to work through their issues with him directly, but it's hard. "We cannot communicate," Anna says, "we can't deal with things." She knows he's struggling and worries about what the stress is doing to his mental health.

Masa acknowledges he is in a "a really bad place, just really on edge." Even without such extenuating circumstances, an estimated thirteen percent of fathers become depressed around the time their baby is born. Hakulinen, the researcher at the Finnish Institute for Health and Welfare, who authored that study on new fathers, says she suspects the rate is actually higher but that men often don't seek help because of stigma.

Masa begins seeing a counselor at a local church that offers free family therapy. Anna goes with him and then together they transfer to a therapist in the public system. In those sessions, Anna recounts, Masa expresses feelings of inadequacy and rage at her for making him feel powerless as a parent. Anna is sympathetic but has her own resentment that, though he says he wants to be more involved, he has stopped contributing to the daily expenses of raising Luka.

"Everything fell on me," she explains later, back at her flat. "The parental leave pay is nice to have, but it's way less than my paycheck was when I was working."

She only stays afloat because of public supports like the standard child benefit, slightly more than two hundred euros a month for both children that she'll get until they turn seventeen. She spends it mostly on diapers and clothes for Luka. "He's very expensive at the moment," she says, smiling as she lifts the baby to her lap. She's the only adult living in the flat now, so she should also get the single parent benefit, a roughly seventy-euro monthly supplement to the regular child benefit, but because Masa has not changed his official address, she doesn't qualify. It's not that he is trying to spite her, he says. He's been staying with a friend he only just met but who was generous enough to take him in, and once he gets his work visa and can earn more income, he says, he plans to get his own place and contribute financially.

As things stand though, it seems clear that their only path forward is through the legal system, so they begin a formal custody proceeding and communicate exclusively through lawyers. But they need an arrangement until the court makes its final ruling, and so their case worker recommends, and they agree in writing, that Luka will live with Anna and see Masa twice a month for two to three hours at "supported meetings" in the presence of a professional facilitator. Anna says she's happy with the arrangement and relieved not to have to host their get-togethers in her home anymore: "It's a neutral location with a time limit and there are professionals involved, so it's not just me trying to keep some distance."

And there is a secondary benefit: To register for the meetings with Luka, Masa must use his new address, and that means Anna is now officially a single mother and entitled to the single-parent benefit. She's also now eligible for child support from Masa. That starts at about two hundred euros a month, and the state determines that Masa's income is low enough that the social welfare system will cover the whole thing. "At least I know the minimum amount is coming," Anna says.

Their situation is relatively rare because only about thirteen percent of Finnish mothers are single. While the marriage rate is declining, many couples cohabitate, as Anna and Masa had been doing. These couples get virtually the same rights as married people, with the exception of inheritance, even as the relationships are often shorter than marriages, and people change partners more times throughout adulthood.

Anna doesn't feel any stigma in single motherhood. In some ways it's a relief. That's reaffirmed when a few days later, she meets a friend at Café Art. It's a sweet little spot by the river that smells like cinnamon and has a grand piano in the corner but no ambient music, so it's conducive to real conversation. As Luka sleeps in his stroller beside her, Anna pours tea from a yellow kettle and listens to her friend describe a recent relationship that fell apart after a series of romantic mishaps and complications. Anna is sympathetic, but also feels grateful not to be fretting anymore about her relationship with Masa; it's over, and she can relax into just being a mom. "I kind of realized this is not the moment to focus on myself and that's actually quite liberating."

Freed from the fuss of romance, she throws herself into the straightforward salve of scheduling. She arrives for the first supervised meeting between Masa and Luka at the address the caseworker has given her. It turns out to be a charming nineteenth-century building in the city center with a well-kept playground outside. It's mostly residential and there's no indication it also functions as a meeting place for families that need support. Inside, the center itself is well-kept and bright. Masa eagerly awaits his son in one of its colorful rooms. There is an assortment of toys on the shelves and a big window bathes the space in natural light. Anna arrives at the front and gently hands Luka to the supervisor so she can bring him to Masa. Then, as directed, Anna leaves. But things quickly take a turn: Fifteen minutes into their two-hour session, Luka cries so hard the supervisor has to call Anna to ask her to return. She isn't surprised; Luka hasn't seen Masa for some time so he's not comfortable alone with him. Anna stays the rest of the session, playing with the baby on the floor as Masa, seemingly unsure what else to do, takes photos. Still, Luka sobs whenever he comes near.

Oh, darling little one, the supervisor says, *you should be making eye contact with your father.*

It hurts Anna to see how hard it is for Luka to connect with his dad, and Masa becomes increasingly frustrated, at the immediate situation and what it indicates more broadly: that he's become estranged from his own son. He and Anna snipe at each other, until finally the supervisor has to intervene. The whole episode is so difficult, Anna isn't sure how they'll make it work going forward but hopes the supervisor can help.

She wants Luka to have a relationship with his father; they both deserve it and are entitled to see each other regularly, she says, in keeping with Finnish law that prioritizes the rights of the child. Finland signed a UN convention to that effect in 1991, and on top of that, the country has several laws that enshrine children's rights and state they must be treated equally as individuals.

It's part of the same philosophy that created Latte Pappas, the idea that children have a right to spend time with their fathers and that those fathers also have the right to time with their children. Anna is glad the framework exists to help them try to forge that relationship. "I have to admit I was a bit prejudiced before when I thought about these kinds of public services," she says, "I'd always assumed they were only for 'certain kind of families,' but now that we're in this situation, I can see how much help it provides and they're genuinely doing a good job."

As they try to chart a better path, the weather turns emphatically beautiful. Turku empties out as residents go to mökki, traditional wooden cabins in the forest, for Midsummer, a late June holiday that celebrates the "nightless night" when the sun never sets in Northern Finland. As far back as the eleventh century, people would light bonfires for Ukko, the Finnish god of weather and crops, and host loud celebrations to drive away evil spirits. The magic of nature was believed to be in full force, as the country's giant conifer forests became sun-dappled sanctuaries of green and brown, filled with wild edibles and bushes heavy with berries. People were thought to follow the same natural rhythm, so Midsummer was also seen as the best time to find a spouse: Girls cast love spells and tucked flowers under their pillows to invite dreams of future husbands. When Christianity arrived in the twelfth century, the festival was rebranded as the feast day of John the Baptist, but celebrations of the natural world continued. Today, Midsummer is greeted with bonfires, summer saunas, and drinking late into the bright night.

Though there is almost no darkness, Anna still doesn't put blackout shades on Luka's windows; he has to learn to sleep through it like everyone else. And for the most part, he does; he still wakes up once or twice, but it's much better than it was just a few months ago. It probably helps, too, that he's begun to eat some solids, starting with mashed potatoes. One afternoon after Anna has fed him, he lies on his back on the couch next to her, his small bare feet kicking gently at her outstretched hands. She gives them a playful shake and he squeals in delight.

On the wall behind them is a charcoal portrait of Liv as a toddler that Anna drew almost a decade ago. Back then, she'd felt differently about her confinement, a mix of stifled professional ambition and panic about whether she could even survive parenthood. "I was still eagerly waiting for my future to happen, I guess." Now, with her second baby, she just enjoys watching him grow and reminds herself each phase is temporary. "I know new worries and joys will replace these," she says. She's careful not to torment herself with thoughts of the things she can't do, all the lovely weekend trips she isn't taking now that the weather's improved, the professional goals she has yet to achieve. She knows those days will come and has learned to comfort herself, as she would her children—now by recognizing the importance of motherhood itself.

A few days later, she gets a message from Masa saying that from his new flat just across the railway tracks from hers, he can see into that room where she and Luka had been sitting. She knew his balcony faced her window because he'd pointed out to her generally where his apartment was, but the message is still unsettling. Masa says he had chosen to live so close because he thought it would make coparenting easier. But Anna decides it might be time to put some real space between them.

SARAH

US

THE DAY AFTER SARAH leaves the hospital, three days after she gave birth and still sore from delivery, she makes her first visit to the pediatrician. Vivian is jaundiced and the hospital doctors had warned that if her bilirubin levels continued to climb, she would have to go in something called a BiliBed, a simultaneously cute- and ominous-sounding fate.

So that morning, Sarah and Brian take her for follow-up at the pediatrician's office, a modular building that sits just next to the towering Jordan River Utah Temple. As they pull into the parking lot, its trumpeting golden angel hovers above them. Sarah hardly notices as she climbs out of the SUV and carries her tiny newborn inside. This office is one of several locations of the same practice and has the feel of a well-run franchise: gray walls with exuberant orange accents, a fish tank on one wall. Sarah navigates through a kinetic knot of children clustered around a ball dispenser to reach the front desk. The receptionist tells her their regular doctor isn't in, so they'll see the physician on call.

In the exam room, the doctor gently lifts the baby onto a scale beneath a Winnie-the-Pooh wall mural. Then she compares her weight to the one listed in her record and reports that Vivian has lost seventeen percent of her bodyweight since birth.

That's a significant difference, she tells them soberly, and she thinks it would be best to supplement breastmilk with formula.

Before Sarah has time to absorb that, the doctor asks a nurse to demonstrate a "paced feed" for them. But just the sight of the plastic bottle in the nurse's hand feels like an affront. Sarah had intended to breastfeed Vivian exclusively for six months. Introducing formula in the first week was not part of the plan. Terms she has read like "nipple confusion" and "supply drop" flash in her mind. She watches as the nurse sits their wobbling baby upright and brushes the rubber nipple against her lips to coax her to feed. The baby's tiny cheeks draw in and out, but she soon tires and the nurse explains cheerfully that it's important to take frequent breaks.

Sarah nods and holds her breath. As soon as they're back in the car, she exhales in big, disappointed sobs. Brian comforts her, tells her he supports her desire to breastfeed, but that it will be okay no matter what happens. His son, Mason, was formula-fed and he turned out all right. *Why don't you text Jess?* he suggests.

Sarah nods and takes out her phone to message her sister, the lactation specialist: *I was feeling so confident, like we were getting breastfeeding down. Now this!*

Her sister quickly responds. *DO NOT give her formula. We'll save that as a very last resort.* Then she adds: When you have a chance, FaceTime me.

They pull into their cul-de-sac and Sarah can't get inside fast enough. The sight of Jess's face calms her.

Let's try a finger feed, her sister suggests, and explains to Sarah how she should insert her finger into Vivian's mouth, along with a syringe of pumped milk. As the baby sucks her finger, she'll also pull in milk.

Vivian still has trouble latching, but does better than before. Sarah is encouraged. Then she realizes that to keep this up, she'll have to constantly pump or nurse. It's a slog. And a few hours later when Vivian cries inconsolably, she breaks down as well.

Sarah was always an overachiever. In college, her grades were so exceptional she received an academic scholarship, which, combined with the tuition waiver she received because her father had worked for BYU, meant the university actually paid her to attend. She graduated with honors, then excelled in her master's program. She's used to wielding her intellectual power like a weapon. And she tries to apply that same ability here; to beat back the difficulty of early motherhood with rationality and diligence. Get the syringe. Pump the milk. Give her baby the nutrient-dense ambrosia she's read so much about.

Why is it so hard?

I can't do this, my baby's upset and I can't calm her down, she wails to Brian. *Why can't I just be back in the hospital where somebody else can help take care of her?*

Brian is desperate to make things better, but also keenly aware he can't do much besides wake up every few hours to help, dutifully holding the syringe while Sarah puts her finger in Vivian's pinhole mouth, a two-person job. It's not his first experience with a newborn, and his assuredness is comforting. By the next afternoon, the baby is feeding better and Sarah wonders whether she still needs to worry about her weight. Then she wonders if there's anything else she should worry about. It's all so new, maybe she's missed something critical. Her brain jumps wildly in search of the source of her anxiety.

Such vague concerns don't seem worth bringing to Brian, so instead she turns to Facebook. Its cobalt glow fills her corner of the bedroom as she relaxes into the pillow to read posts from other mothers about feeding, sleep, and what's typical for newborns. She knows it's not the ideal source. "You do end up with some people spreading really bad information because anecdotal information is not research, and that's why you have all these people who swear by things like essential oils to cure everything."

Still, there is some useful information in the mix. Like scattered posts about community centers with programs for new parents. That sounds promising. There are also nurse home visits, funded through Obamacare and modeled on the Nurse-Family Partnership that cut child abuse and neglect almost in half. But, Sarah learns upon deeper internet investigation, all those services are only available to low-income families. "I'm glad they have those programs," she says. "Now if only they'd help middle-class families that may also be struggling but don't qualify." That's different from a country like Finland. It created its own nurse home visit program using the American Nurse-Family Partnership model but, unlike the US, extended it to all families. The US is often a leader on research, if not always implementation.

Some women Sarah knows have used postnatal doulas but she soon discovers they cost more than she can afford, especially since Brian is losing a week's salary to be here with her and Vivian. And their insurance, for which they pay a five hundred dollar monthly premium, doesn't cover that kind of postnatal care. It certainly wouldn't pay for the "confinement hotels" she's seen advertised. They're based on the Asian system of care, but unlike Japan's public postpartum centers, the American version is private and luxurious: At the Utah Postpartum Retreat in downtown Salt Lake, new mothers receive both lactation services and in-room pedicures. "Through endless pampering, personalized meals, sumptuous accommodations, and expert support, we aim to empower parents to embrace their postpartum journey," its website reads. The cost of entry is over a thousand dollars a night.

In a particularly American twist, high-end postpartum care is often marketed as a way for women to return to work faster and not let childbirth slow down their careers. That culture starts at the top. Yahoo CEO Marissa Mayer famously took a two-week working parental leave. She also had a nursery built next to her office where her newborn was attended by a nanny. That same year, 2012, PBS named Mayer a "Woman Remaking America." In her interview with the network, she said she didn't consider herself a feminist because she lacked the "militant drive and sort of the chip on the shoulder that sometimes comes with that." Through curtains of blond hair, she went on: "It's too bad but I do think feminism has become, in many ways, a negative word and there are amazing opportunities all over the world for women and I think that more good comes out of positive energy around that than negative energy."

In fact, as many as a quarter of American mothers go back to work after two weeks as Mayer did, but the vast majority are in low-wage jobs without any maternity leave—or office nurseries for that matter—and many are women of color. Black women receive, on average, almost a month less paid leave than white women. And numerous studies suggest that's one reason Black women have lower breastfeeding rates: they're separated from their babies earlier.

Disparities in American motherhood might help explain why there has not been a unified push for better protections and support: More privileged women already have them. But affluence isn't always protective. White Americans in the wealthiest one percent of counties still have higher infant and maternal mortality rates than the Finnish average, according to a study by Dr. Ezekiel Emanuel, vice provost at the University of Pennsylvania. That disparity is likely because even wealthy Americans can't simply "buy out" of the uneven quality of the American healthcare system as a whole, Emanuel writes. Improving outcomes, even for the wealthiest, would "require improving care systematically, for all people at all facilities."

Sarah can't afford private postpartum care, so she does the best she can with advice she gleans from online mothers' groups. Brian wants to be more involved, but he has to go back to work a week after Sarah comes home from the hospital; they can't afford for him to take any more days off. That's put him squarely in a supporting role. "Sarah pretty much takes care of the baby, mostly by herself, and I just kind of get her things when she needs things and get stuff done when she needs stuff done." They had both sought a nontraditional life, outside the strict gender roles of the church, but the economic reality seems to be working against them.

Even fathers who do have the financial and professional flexibility to be more involved parents can feel social pressure not to take time off work, just as Kaz did in Japan. "I think there's still this sort of antiquated fantasy that dads don't want to be around their kids," *New York Times* opinion writer Jessica Grose says, as she drives through the Brooklyn neighborhood where she is raising two children of her own. "I think it's in some ways harder for working dads who want to be really involved parents because they get less flexibility at work, whether implied or outright; it's still sort of going against the gender norm, like of course moms will want to be with their kids but if guys want to be with their kids, that's unmanly or there's a lot of baggage about that."

There are now men in leadership trying to change that culture by example. US Rep. Jimmy Gomez, the California Democrat, has made parenthood central to his public identity since the start of his fourth term in Congress in 2023, when he wore his four-month-old son Hodge in a baby carrier as he cast his vote for House minority leader. Pictures of the pair went viral: Gomez, with his thick dark hair perfectly combed, wears a Congressional pin and holds a half-full bottle as Hodge playfully kicks his bare feet. Online commenters and some of his colleagues suggested Gomez start a "Dads Caucus," he recalls in his laid-back California lilt from his Congressional office, which has, along with an LA

Dodgers' insignia on the door, a bassinet in one corner and a play-pen in another.

There had been attempts to form a Dads Caucus before—a bipartisan, bicameral group of fathers in Congress. "And the Republicans would always back out," he laughs. This time, he decided to invite only Democrats to show the idea could work, even with just one party.

Now there are thirty-eight members, including Reps. Joaquin Castro (TX), Seth Moulton (MA), Eric Swalwell (CA), Adam Schiff (CA), and Rashida Tlaib (MI), one of two female mem-bers. They have a group chat, he says, where they discuss typical dad stuff like daycare or whether to worry if a child hasn't hit a developmental milestone. There was a particularly long back-and-forth about how much leave to take after the birth of a child. Congressmembers are entitled to twelve weeks paid and Gomez encouraged his fellow dads to take it all, eight at the very least. "You want to reflect that you're living up to the policies you're pushing," he says.

He ran for Congress on his record of expanding paid parental leave in California as a state legislator. And he says he saw how successful policy was in leading culture there: Once paid leave was legally guaranteed, it became more acceptable for men to take it. That's similar to the way in which Finnish society grew to accept—and then admire—men who took parental leave. Since California's policy went into effect in 2004, the number of parents who took time off has doubled, and fathers have accounted for most of that growth. Four out of five new fathers in California now take some paternity leave, about the same as in Finland, though Finnish leave is longer. That will have far-reaching effects: When fathers and non-birthing partners take leave, mothers are more likely to breastfeed and less likely to require antianxiety medication, anti-biotics, and even hospitalization. Those fathers who take parental leave are less likely to get divorced and more likely to report that they have good communication with their children as they grow. And children whose fathers who are more involved starting in infancy have been shown to have slightly better social-emotional skills later in life.

Before Gomez became a father, he and his wife had a conversation in which they agreed he would take an active role and she would not be the "default parent," or primary caregiver to their children. Now as a member of Congress, he has tried to make a similar commitment in the way he governs. "There's a sense of default legislating," Gomez says, "the women of the House are going to work on these issues and men, we're just there to vote yes when the time comes." As dads and non-birthing partners play a bigger part in American home life, he hopes his Dads Caucus will encourage male legislators to play a role in getting more family-friendly policies passed.

As for Sarah, she is mostly alone after Brian goes back to work. Sarah misses his companionship more than anything, and eagerly waits for him to come home at the end of the day so they can pick up their conversation where they left off. It would also be nice if he was around more to tell her she's doing a good job and that Vivian seems to be developing well, especially after their bumpy first few days. Facebook groups just can't offer the same kind of reassurance. Finally they have their two-month visit with Vivian's pediatrician, but it doesn't go particularly well. The doctor tells Sarah he's concerned Vivian hasn't gained enough weight and schedules a return visit a week later to see if she's made progress. Sarah tries not to let her worries consume her, and when she brings Vivian back again, the doctor says he thinks the baby is probably fine but can't be sure because not much time has elapsed. He asks them to come back in another two weeks.

At that point, Sarah takes matters into her own hands. She buys a baby scale so she can keep constant track of Vivian's weight. "I just decided to do it," she says conspiratorially.

What do you think? she messages her sister, with a link to the scale.

Her sister responds: *Well, we don't normally weigh babies every day, the idea is just to make sure they're trending up. And,* she cautions, *over-checking can make you neurotic, so just keep that in mind.*

Neuroticism is of course a flexible term. Sarah watches as Vivian drops a few ounces one day—usually when she's spit up more—then gains it back the next. It seems like she's trending up but Sarah is now too deep in decimal-level variance to draw any meaningful conclusions. Like Chelsea, nine thousand miles away, she's developed an almost compulsive concern about her baby's weight, perhaps because it seems like something she can control as she navigates postpartum life without the support of the community in which she was raised.

Sarah knows how much help her neighbors in Happy Valley could have provided because she saw the way they showed up for her mom. When women had babies, mothers rallied around them and took over housework. There was a feeling they were all in it together. Still, Sarah is steadfast in her decision to leave the LDS community. To her, the support isn't worth the sacrifice. Sometimes she has to remind Brian, though. One day in the kitchen as she stirs mac 'n' cheese, he gets wistful about their old church congregation—the events they no longer attend, the people they no longer see. And though it's been about two years since he attended a church service, it's still hard to shake the idea that he should be going.

Church is one of those things where it's like, you're supposed to do it, it's kind of like an expectation, he says. *I don't know, like part of me still wants to be, you know, going to church and doing that kind of stuff.*

Sarah looks skeptical. *But if you were to go back and you were honest with your bishop, you'd get excommunicated anyway. So . . .* she trails off emphatically.

They are so busy now that it's hard to find time to build a community to replace the congregation, though. They haven't gone to any more polyamory events, and Brian hasn't even seen Nick since Vivian was born. So one weekend, he invites Nick and his female partner Amanda to come over. It's easier than leaving the house and Sarah likes hanging out with them. "Nick and my wife get along really, really well and I feel like they have a lot to talk about and they hit it off really well, at least as friends," Brian says.

When they arrive, Brian and Sarah's dogs—Maggie, a big Bernese mountain dog and Aria, a slightly smaller pit mix—bound over to greet them, sniffing loudly and angling to be pet. Brian shouts at the dogs to get down but Nick isn't bothered, greeting the frenzy with an easy laugh. Sarah likes that about him, he has an equanimity that puts her at ease, and takes the sting out of what could be an awkward situation. The four of them move into the sunken living room and arrange themselves on the soft black couch as the dogs follow closely underfoot. Nick and Brian quickly fall into a conversation about gaming as Sarah goes to the kitchen with Amanda to get food for everyone. The house feels warm and full. The only person missing is Mason, Sarah's stepson. He's met Nick, seen him kiss his father. But when Brian tries to explain their relationship, Mason seems uninterested in learning more, so Brian doesn't push it. Mostly, Brian sees Nick on weeks like this one when Mason is at his mom's.

There's limited research about the impact of polyamory on children. One of the leading scholars is Elisabeth Sheff, a therapist who also serves as an expert witness in child custody cases related to consensual non-monogamy. She writes that children's attitudes about living in a polyamorous household change as they grow. Young children are simply happy to have additional adult attention; tweens, like Mason, are more aware but prefer not to know too much about their parents' sex lives, and in the current landscape of blended and nontraditional families, they usually don't see it as problematic. Teenagers are primarily focused on their own independence and social relationships. Overall, Sheff found children in polyamorous homes to be well-adjusted and, "thriving with the plentiful resources and adult attention their families provided."

Sarah wants even more for Vivian and Mason: for their nontraditional household to be a source of liberation. "One of the hardest parts of Mormon culture is that it's really hard for kids to come out, so my hope is that because Mason knows Brian's already part of this group, there's going to be no judgment: You're gay, great. You're bisexual, great."

THE LAST WEEKS OF Sarah's three-month parental leave fall in a strange sort of in-between season. It looks mild and the snow is mostly gone from the ground, but when she takes Vivian for a walk, it doesn't feel like spring yet. She puts Vivian into a stroller and heads out past the "Wild West Park"—a playground complete with a kid-sized sheriff's office and saloon—but the wind is so bitter that Vivian's nose soon turns red and Sarah retreats to the car.

It's hard to have a calm stroll anyway because she is increasingly concerned about going to back to work; specifically, whether she has enough frozen milk stored. "I have a few little bags, but that's about it," she says opening the freezer drawer. She adds another pumping session in the evenings after Vivian goes down, but can't produce much then. At night, she listens to the baby's whispered breathing and wills herself to stop worrying.

It's similar to what Chelsea is feeling, all the way in Nairobi. They both get twelve weeks of leave, though Sarah is only paid for half of it and had to burn through her sick and vacation days first. Still, that's more than many American women get. The US is famously the only country in the world with no national mandated paid maternity leave, with the exception of a few Pacific Island nations.

"We make motherhood harder than it needs to be," Grose says animatedly. "We live in such a wealthy, resourced, safe country, so it's consistently just completely baffling to me that we haven't figured out how to make it better."

It's not as if American women haven't tried to get paid leave, through decades of activism. After World War I, American female labor leaders joined their peers from Western Europe, Asia, and Scandinavia in Washington, DC, for the inaugural International Congress of Working Women in 1919. As the leaves turned crimson along the Potomac, they endorsed a platform that the International Labor Organization soon adopted: Twelve-week paid maternity leave with employment protection. At the time, no country on earth met that standard. But as the postwar world bound itself back together with stronger social fabric, many moved in that direction: Finland was the first, mandating paid leave for some women the very year the recommendations came out; Japan followed after World War II; and seventy-five years after the recommendations were first issued, Kenya used them to create its own program.

Though the US failed to adopt the platform, President Franklin D. Roosevelt pushed for something similar, saying, when he signed the Social Security Act into law in 1935, that it was "by no means complete" in part because he thought it should have also included lost wage insurance, what today would be called "paid leave." Roosevelt pushed Congress to draft such a bill and then asked its sponsor to wait to bring it to a vote until he could give a speech rallying support. But he never got to make his case. Roosevelt's sudden death in 1945 marked a tragic end to that early push for American paid leave.

The powerful feminist movement of the 1960s drove women's rights to the center of political debate and its leaders built on demands of those earlier female labor organizers. They pointed to countries like Finland as proof that parental leave policies could help women thrive, but lawmakers saw little economic incentive to accommodate them. Republicans in particular were more sympathetic to the ascendent "pro-family" counter-movement, a coalition of evangelical Christians, neoconservatives, and Mormons from Sarah's own community that pushed to keep women's work within the home.

Then the economic winds changed, and so did women's position in American society. The 1970s brought high energy prices and inflation, so many families couldn't survive on a single income. Two thirds of all new jobs that decade went to women. With a more female workforce, feminist goals gained traction. And, along with the reproductive rights guaranteed in Roe *v.* Wade, activists argued women also had the "right to bear children" and all the protections that required. Soon after, President Jimmy Carter signed the Pregnancy Discrimination Act into law. The US seemed poised to join its peer countries in maternity leave and supports.

Then business lobbies began to signal concern that companies would have to shoulder the costs, and flexed their considerable political muscle. The National Association of Manufacturers told Congress in 1977 that it opposed employers "subsidizing parenthood." For almost two decades, no parental leave bills could make it into law. Over and over, Congress debated a law that would have granted twelve weeks of unpaid leave. But when it finally passed in 1990, President George H. W. Bush promptly vetoed it. He explained that he *did* support parental leave but *only* if businesses provided it voluntarily. And big corporations had made it pretty clear by that point where they stood. It turned out the American people felt differently though: Bush's opponent in the next election, Bill Clinton, campaigned on the issue of paid leave and won. The first piece of legislation Clinton signed was the 1993 Family Medical Leave Act, which provides up to twelve weeks of job-protected leave. And it's not just for postpartum women; the majority of users are workers with serious health needs. Still, only employees of government agencies and large companies are eligible, which leaves out nearly half of American workers. And the leave is unpaid, a concession to the corporate interests that, once again, made their displeasure known, deriding the new law as a "destroyer of business" that could "lead to discrimination against women."

So Sarah, who had a baby more than a century after those first activists called for national paid leave, still isn't entitled to it under federal law. Her leave is partially paid only because her local union advocated for that, and twelve weeks, though long by US standards, still feels short.

The day before Sarah is scheduled to go back, she hands Vivian to Brian so she can pack her pumping bag. She makes sure she has extra parts and that everything is cleaned and ready. As she does, she watches happily as Brian nibbles Vivian's neck, sending her into fits of cackling laughter. Vivian already seems to distinguish that her mother provides comfort and her father is there for entertainment.

She had always said she didn't want to stay home full-time with her. "But now actually being home, I don't mind it; I'm not running from place to place trying to get a million things done." In this moment, with Vivian's laughter bubbling through the house, she feels a craving to be close to her. It's a familiar feeling that started when she was pregnant: the desire to stay entwined forever.

The next morning, her body thrums with nerves. And as she navigates her black SUV out of the driveway, that same longing returns. It tightens across her chest when she turns from the quiet cul-de-sac into the rush of the main road. Past the Zions Bank branch, the Latin grocery, the small single-family homes, cheaper than those farther east where the mountain views are even better. Everything is as it was in the dark of winter when she last made this drive, Vivian still warm in her belly. But now the aspens are fuzzy with spring and each roadside feature marks the growing distance between them.

She turns onto a one-way street and all at once the brick-and-glass exterior of the school where she works as a technology specialist rises to greet her. Clammy with anticipation, she pulls open the building's heavy steel doors and finds herself back in the main hallway that's filled as always with the sounds and smells of children.

When she arrives at her office, a narrow room off the library, she surveys her desk. It's mostly as she left it, a tall stack of laptops ready for distribution next to a framed card from children she taught. There are thousands of unread emails in her inbox. She scrolls through, happily discarding them in huge batches: All the work that got done even though she wasn't here to do it. A sudden and surprising surge of relief washes over her. It feels good to have a sense of purpose again, to be part of a team. After three months at home with a newborn, her intellect is ravenous for something to chew on, and she savors the mental stimulation.

That evening when she gets home, she knows she should start dinner but all she wants to do is hold Vivian. And so she does. It's unlike her to deviate from routine, but her baby's soft little presence has forced her to loosen her grip on time. "I'm trying to just let it be and go with the flow so I don't get frustrated if it's not a schedule I can count on."

A MONTH LATER THOUGH, she is less sanguine. The novelty of being back at work has worn off but the feeling of wanting to be with Vivian remains. There are times it hits with such force that she stops short, shuts the laptop she's programming, or puts down the tray of little blue robots she uses as a reward for the fourth graders. It can be hard sometimes to find joy in the aspects of her job she'd always liked.

That could be due to sheer sleep deprivation. At night she crawls into bed with a wearable pump to supplement her daytime production, but she can never get comfortable and is also up twice to feed Vivian. Morning comes before she ever reaches deep sleep and it's as if some critical cognitive center has gone dark. At a mid-morning meeting, she can't focus and the right words hover just out of reach.

By late afternoon, exhaustion really sets in. That's when she makes the forty-five-minute drive to her parents' house to pick up Vivian. There are daycares closer but they're unaffordable, even on two incomes. She understands that this was the calculation she made when she decided to have children, and now it's her responsibility to make it work. So with the last of the daylight splashing the peaks with rosy alpenglow, she drives through the blur of exurban sprawl below—fast-food restaurants, office parks, weight loss clinics, and gun ranges.

Like an involuntary mantra, she repeats, "I'm so tired, I'm so tired." She wills herself to stay awake as black pickups and white Teslas barrel past, their license plates alternately declaring, "In God We Trust" and "Ski Utah!" But she can feel herself slipping under. At the next exit, she pulls into a gas station. She scans its bright aisles and finally settles on potato chips and a Slurpee. Back in the car, she puts the drink in the coaster and the open bag on the tan console next to her. Then she pulls back onto the highway, hoping the chips' crunch and the icy jolt of the Slurpee will keep her conscious. "I don't even care if nutrition-wise, this is a bad choice," she confesses, "it's better than falling asleep." She lost over fifty pounds before she got pregnant but to her disappointment, she is quickly regaining it now.

As she pulls off the highway into her parents' neighborhood, the light is gone from the sky. When she opens the door of their house, Vivian is waiting in the front room and wails at the sight of her. Sarah carries the baby to the couch and sits on the end, next to a curio cabinet filled with biblical figurines.

Once Vivian is happily feeding, Sarah's mom tells her about their day:

Oh, she rolled! She hasn't done that before, right?

She's been trying but no, never actually did it.

Yeah, I put her down on her belly and then all of the sudden she was on her back. I tried to get a video, but I missed it, I'm sorry.

That's all right, Sarah says gently.

When Vivian finishes, Sarah sets her back down on the floor and, after some gentle coaxing, the baby rolls again. Sarah feels satisfied: "I'm glad I got to see it, even if it wasn't the first time."

She's not so bothered by missing milestones, just time together. "It's been difficult, I just want to be able to be with her," she says. The ideal situation would be to work part-time, like Anna is doing this month, but Sarah knows that's not realistic. "Financially, it's just not in the cards for us: I'm our primary breadwinner so we could never take that substantial of a pay cut, plus I carry our insurance." Their premium would more than double, to about twelve hundred dollars a month, if she went part-time. In America's shrinking middle class, time with children is a luxury parents like Sarah cannot afford.

Grose says there are a lot of Americans who would welcome the opportunity to spend more time with their young children: "You know, many people would prefer to be the person who cares for their kid in the first year of life, and I don't think that there's anything wrong with that, and so I don't think that's just necessarily social conservatism, that's also, I want to be with my infant."

President Barack Obama tried to give American parents more of that time. He campaigned on the issue of paid family leave and issued an executive order that gave six weeks paid parental leave to federal workers in 2015. Then in his State of the Union Address later that year, he called on Congress to send him a bill that would expand it to all Americans. But he faced significant resistance: A representative from the US Chamber of Commerce warned ominously that the business community planned to wage "all-out-war" against guaranteed paid leave, and no bill made it through the Republican-controlled Congress. Obama recognized the political reality and so he instead encouraged states to set up their own programs and put in his budget proposal two billion dollars in federal incentives. That never got Congressional approval, so the states moved ahead on their own. And by 2026, as new programs go into effect, at least thirteen states and the District of Columbia will have some amount of paid family leave, most about twelve weeks and paid through a payroll contribution.

As it turns out, those programs have not made American businesses less profitable. In fact, paid leave can help companies by lowering turnover costs because fewer women leave the workforce. After Google instituted its eighteen-week paid parental leave policy, for example, the rate at which women left fell by half. And Google now uses paid leave as a perk to recruit talent. But that leaves small businesses—whose employees are ineligible for even unpaid leave through the Family and Medical Leave Act—at a disadvantage. Molly Weston Williamson, a Senior Fellow at the Center for American Progress, said that in state after state over the past few years, she's seen small business owners support paid leave programs as a way to compete with larger corporations. "If you're Google, you can just pay out of pocket for whatever you want to offer to attract people, but if you're a little mom-and-pop, that may not be financially viable without this kind of system," Williamson says.

But some large corporations that now offer generous leave programs don't want to give up their competitive advantage. Rep. Gomez, the California Dads Caucus founder, says he's tried to convince companies to support a national paid leave policy, but it can be tough. "Some of them now don't want a federal program because they use it as a benefit that they can compete for workers with," he says. Those huge, profitable companies are essentially trying to hoard paid leave for their own benefit.

Gomez says despite all the complexity, it's still important to push for a national program, especially because more conservative regions are unlikely to implement state programs. "We don't want the country as a whole to become more imbalanced, that's not good for the stability of our democracy," he explains. Gomez says the challenge is to get bipartisan support. And there are signs there could be some, even if the appetite is limited. Republican Senator Marco Rubio has introduced a paid family leave bill almost every year since 2018 that would have workers borrow from their own Social Security to cover the cost. And Ivanka Trump, as presidential advisor, helped enact a paid leave policy for federal employees in 2019, though it was tucked inside a defense spending bill, so many Republicans who opposed paid leave still voted for it. Then after Rep. Anna Paulina Luna, a Trump acolyte from Florida and self-described "pro-life extremist", gave birth in 2023, she authored a bill to allow Congressional mothers to vote by proxy for six weeks postpartum. Gomez buys the concept but isn't sold on the bill because it doesn't extend the same protections to non-birthing parents. The issue blew up on the Dads Caucus text chain.

IN LATE MAY, THE snow is almost gone from Utah's peaks, replaced by long runs of wildflowers. The valley gets warmer each day, a balmy prelude to the blazing crescendo of summer. The school year is rushing to a close and Sarah is ready for the break. As always happens at midday, her chest begins to tingle and she realizes she needs to get to the "wellness room." Sarah is one of six nursing mothers at this school—five teachers and the school janitor—and they've created a strict schedule for this small space off the main hall, equipped with a chair and sink. Under the 2010 Affordable Care Act, large employers are required to have a space for nursing mothers to pump, "other than a bathroom, that is shielded from view and free from intrusion from coworkers and the public." The 2023 PUMP Act expanded that benefit to an additional nine million working women not covered in the original bill, but even so, an estimated one in three working mothers still lacks reliable access to a lactation space, a situation similar to Chelsea's.

Sarah feels fortunate to have this room, even if she has to share it with so many other women. As she sits down in its soft chair and attaches the pump's tubing, her phone buzzes with messages from a text chain she's on with several other teachers. She secures the flanges to her chest and when she reads what the messages are about, her stomach drops: a horrific school shooting is underway in a nearby state. The pump's motor hums to life as Sarah pulls up a news livestream on her phone. She watches as throngs of children and teachers race from the building, frantic parents line up outside and emergency vehicles arrive—all the familiar players in this now recurrent drama.

Sarah grew up in the wake of Columbine, the 1999 school shooting that set off decades of terror, and she's done active shooter drills since she was a child. She and her classmates learned to move away from windows, keep silent and huddle in the corner to make it seem as if the classroom was empty. She never thought much of it, she says. It was just the reality of growing up in a country where violence is endemic.

Then after she graduated from her master's program, she got a job as a first-grade teacher and that same year, twenty first graders and six adults were killed in the Sandy Hook massacre. She began to play out scenarios in her mind about how she would stay calm and keep her own students safe if something happened in her own school. The threat of violence finally felt real. Now, she leads students through the same drills she did as a child, at least once a schoolyear.

More text messages keep coming, filled with frustration and anger. A school librarian in the group is particularly outraged. She had been battling a group of parents calling for a book ban and the schoolboard recently capitulated to them.

It's really sad that legislators are faster to ban books than they are to ban assault rifles, the librarian messages the group.

Utah is one of thirty states that allows school employees to carry guns. The teachers on this chain want fewer firearms in the community, not more, but Sarah doesn't think that will matter. She's seen how this goes: the cycle of anguish and calls for policy remedies that evaporate into the next news cycle.

She turns her pump off and the motor stills. Then she packs her bag and readies herself to finish the rest of her day, the rest of the school year. What can she do but continue to participate in the drills, and now, as a mother, try to push forward, even while knowing that someday the worst kind of tragedy could befall her or her children, and their community doesn't seem to care enough to prevent it.

IN JUNE, VIVIAN IS nearly six months old and Sarah starts "baby led weaning" by offering her small finger foods. Vivian quickly gets the hang of it and gleefully grabs everything from waffles to green beans. Her pediatrician had recommended they start earlier, around four months, to expose Vivian to a variety of foods, which he suggested could be protective against allergies. *Yeah, I'm not doing that*, Sarah had thought to herself; she'll breastfeed for the full six months as she'd planned. She's become more confident in her own instincts. The same goes for sleep. She still battles to get enough of it, and now one of their dogs has injured her paw and is sleeping with them as well. "I feel like I want to cry, I'm just so tired," Sarah says, with a plaintive laugh. So she bends the "safe sleep" rules she abided for so many months and lets Vivian stay in their bed after she nurses her. "We just have to survive." She's edging closer to the philosophy Anna's public health nurse espoused: that mothers should do what they need to do to stay functional. Care for herself so she can care for the baby.

Sarah also tries to accommodate Brian's needs. June marks his one-year anniversary with Nick, but because of the new baby and everyone's conflicting work schedules, it's been hard to find time for the relationship. "I mean, we're not the most organized polyamorous group," Brian laughs. "I really need to get like a Google calendar or something so we can plan dates more often."

But the stars finally align. Their anniversary falls the same weekend as Pride, so they make a plan to spend the night at a hotel together, then meet Sarah and the family in the morning for the parade.

That evening, Sarah struggles to stay awake past dinnertime.

But she still has to put Vivian and Mason to bed before she can even begin to organize for the next day's events. In the bath, Vivian holds a purple plastic boat and alternates between squeals of delight and shrieks of exhaustion. When she's finally asleep, Sarah shuffles from the darkened room to start the next round: Preparing the diaper bag. Finding the extra clothes. Packing snacks.

She stops suddenly in the middle of the kitchen. *I hate this*, she fumes. *Brian should be here, doing all this organizing stuff with me.*

She leans heavily on the counter and takes off her glasses to rub her eyes. Then, with a concerted inhale, forces herself to remember what she learned in the books she and Brian read about ethical non-monogamy.

Okay, what's driving these feelings? she asks herself. *This is just a break from the norm, it's not that I really need him and he isn't here for me. And I'm glad he's getting this time.*

She has a faint sense that she has her own needs she could do more to indulge. Like the craving she's had since early pregnancy for a cold, salty margarita. But the thought of getting herself out the door to a restaurant feels prohibitively exhausting. "And I already feel like I'm missing out on so much time with Vivian, it's hard to take even more."

She hasn't gone on a date alone with Brian since the baby was born. Recently her sister Julie offered to watch Vivian on Sunday mornings so they could go to the gym together, but aside from that, the only real time they spend alone is the drowsy hour between Vivian's bedtime and theirs. They usually watch TV. "I mean, it might be nice to have a date night every now and again but for the most part, I think it's been okay," Sarah says. And someday they will, she assures herself in the darkened kitchen as she grinds through the rest of her to-do list.

The next morning, her anxiety eases when Brian calls to tell her he's heading home to help her get into the city. As he comes through the door, she feels a rush of excitement. He's back. She'd missed talking to him, as she always does when he's gone. They load the car and drive with Vivian and Mason to the local light rail stop. Purple peaks frame the buzzing parking lot. They finally find a spot and Sarah unstraps Vivian—who's wearing a rainbow tutu that matches her own—and transfers her to a stroller festooned with streamers. Brian wears a shirt in the colors of the bisexual flag and a bisexual flag as a cape. He thuds the trunk shut and leads them to the crowded platform.

Soon, a train glides into the station. They crush on board before the doors chime closed. Inside, it's standing room only and almost everyone is dressed for Pride. Sarah feels a rush of camaraderie.

Isn't she the cutest in that little tutu? a woman enthuses over Vivian.

Oh my gosh, the cutest! a man next to her agrees.

Sarah beams. *This is her first Pride, she's very excited. And it's mine, too.*

Oh really? the woman responds eagerly. *Yeah, it's ours too!*

"It's easy to feel like you're on your own, especially in such a conservative state," Sarah says. "So how cool is it to have this event where you can see there are a whole lot of other people here who are part of this same community?" She knows it's not her community exactly; she's attending as an ally with a shared disdain for religious intolerance. But it feels good just the same.

They disembark at the City Center stop and quickly melt into an even larger crowd. At the end of the block, Sarah's sister Julie waits with her two teenage children, one of whom is non-binary and the other, a lesbian. Julie is the sister who married just after college and struggled when her husband pushed her into a housewife role. After many acrimonious years, they recently divorced and here she is, reinvented, in purple lipstick and a black T-shirt that reads "Love Loud."

Julie's ex-husband doesn't acknowledge their children's identities, but their grandparents, Sarah's parents, are more accepting. Sarah is proud of them for working to understand. "I think they still view it as a sin but also look at it like, it's no different than if my child was drinking alcohol: I don't necessarily agree with their choices but I still love them anyway." It's proof that familial love—and generational renewal—can defy even longstanding prejudice.

Sarah is also grateful that though she has differences with her parents on the subject of religion—and hasn't even broached the topic of Brian's polyamory—they have still stepped up to help raise Vivian. She knows other LDS families might draw a harder line. So while the wider community may not always be welcoming, at least she is close to her parents. Geographically at least, that's true for the majority of Americans. The US is larger than Kenya, Finland, or Japan, but four in ten Americans still live within an hour's drive of extended family, and those who don't tend to be high income and in a better position to pay for domestic support. Living close to family has real economic advantages for women like Sarah: Married mothers of young children are more likely to work if they live near their own mothers or mothers-in-law, because of the challenges American childcare presents. So while living in a conservative place can be challenging, Sarah does what she can to find a likeminded community.

Their group eases into a clearing in the crowd to watch the parade. Sarah takes the opportunity to breastfeed Vivian, the baby's little rainbow headband still in place. She doesn't use a cover or make any attempt to hide her body. She hopes it could help other women, who might not know what a good latch looks like. And fundamentally, for her, it's an act of defiance.

"Sometimes I wish I still went to church because I'd breastfeed in the pews and dare them to tell me to go to another room," she laughs.

Suddenly, a cheer goes up around them as a group marches past—several in colorful platform heels—with a sign that reads, "Know That You Are Loved." Brian looks elated; the transcendent feeling of acceptance.

Then comes a smaller group. The men wear ties and the women are in long skirts. They hold a banner identifying themselves as "Mormons Building Bridges," a group founded by mothers of LGBTQ children that calls on fellow LDS members to show tenderness to all children. They have adopted the motto "all families matter" and run "hugging booths" at Pride festivals like this one, but they don't typically criticize church leaders or challenge them on the church's policies about same sex marriage.

Huh, that group's a little small today, Sarah remarks to her sister with a sly smile.

Yeah, wonder why that is, Julie responds.

They can joke because they both know the answer: The church's hard line on LGBTQ+ issues has made it almost impossible to be both a Mormon and an ally.

After the last float marches past, they move to a grassy area with long picnic tables for lunch. Soon Nick arrives in a shirt with a progress pride flag—a rainbow with additional stripes for the trans community and people of color—and a green necklace with beads the shape of marijuana leaves. He greets them all warmly and gives Brian a tight hug. They stand and talk while Sarah sits at the wooden folding table, making faces at Vivian. She offers the baby a small spoonful of her own lunch, a rice bowl from an Asian chain. Then she looks up to see Brian and Nick kissing. Her smile never waivers. Nick doesn't stay long, says goodbye to the group and fades back into the colorful crowd. He seems to understand he needs to leave space for Brian's relationship with Sarah.

They are all just trying to navigate this new terrain. As Sarah holds her baby, surrounded by a community so different from the one that raised her, she considers what she gave up to be here. "You know, you lose some of your own identity when you leave the religion," she explains. She also lost, at least in part, a reference model for parenting, as have the many Americans in her generation who have left the religious communities in which they were born.

The freedom to reinvent herself as an individual and now as parent is invigorating but also overwhelming. In a big, heterogenous country like the US, the options seem endless. But the question she ultimately needs to answer is: What parts of her childhood does she want to replicate in Vivian's, and how will she replace the parts she leaves behind?

She and Brian both feel the weight of it. On the way home from the train station they pick up an ongoing conversation about their journey away from Mormonism. Pride was wonderful, they agree, and it reaffirmed their commitment to lead more authentic lives.

I just feel like now, without the church, I'm fighting so hard in the opposite direction that I'm going have to refigure out who I am, she tells him, *redefine myself without that construct.*

He nods.

But you know, she adds, *it is kind of liberating once you finally start to kind of break free of that.*

PART THREE

TSUKASA
JAPAN

———

THE PARK NEAR TSUKASA'S apartment is much too big for her "park debut," a kind of maternal sorority rush where women audition to be included in a local mothers' group. Tsukasa has read articles about debuts that advise women to go to a local playground, perhaps with baby toys to offer to the other mothers, to help ingratiate themselves. But don't come on too strong, they warn— let the other mothers ask for contact information first. Tsukasa doesn't take it all that seriously; she just wants to find some other women with children in the neighborhood to befriend. But as she walks the park's wide boulevards, past a dog run where Shiba Inu prance beneath a lotus root sculpture and a stadium that vibrates with students running soccer drills, she doesn't come across any. Back in Tokyo, she frequently saw women navigating the crowded streets with baby carriers. Now, as she returns home along the narrow road through her new Osaka neighborhood, she passes almost no one. It's so quiet she can hear frogs croaking in the rice paddy between two nearby apartment blocks. With Kaz still working around the clock, she's desperate for female companionship.

Mama-tomo, or mother-friend groups, are meant to provide

that, but they're on the decline both because more women work and also because they developed a dark reputation after a series of tragic incidents in the early 2000s, when Tsukasa was young. The first event to gain media attention involved a group's wealthy "headmother" whose two-year-old daughter passed an entrance exam to get a spot at a prestigious nursery school. Another mother in the group, the wife of a Buddhist priest, was upset her own two-year-old daughter had not gotten in and that the headmother then excluded her daughter from playground activities, wouldn't allow her to play in the sandbox or take a turn on the swing. And so the mother retaliated by strangling the headmother's daughter to death with a scarf. Afterward, she put the girl's body in a bag and took it with her on a bullet train to her parents' home in the countryside, where she buried it in their garden. Several years later, a Chinese immigrant believed her daughter was being ostracized because she herself was having trouble integrating into the group of moms at school. She then murdered two five-year-old children in her carpool with a sashimi knife and tossed their bodies into nearby rice paddies.

The Japanese media portrayed both women as ruthless killers, but newspapers received thousands of letters from mothers who said they could relate to the anger the women felt at the casual cruelty of mama-tomo groups. There was a sense that women who had been shut out of the professional arena were applying exacting standards and aggression instead to things like their children's school entrance exam scores. As more women joined the workforce in the following decades, professional hierarchies replaced playground pecking orders and the dominance of mama-tomo friendships declined.

Still, new mothers like Tsukasa need companionship, and so the government has encouraged parent networks through local kominkan community centers. There are roughly fourteen thousand of these centers across the country, originally constructed as hubs for local rebuilding after World War II. Each has about three staff members and dozens of volunteers, usually retirees, who lead activities like puppet shows, art projects, and gardening. Children's rooms are padded and have shelves full of toys while teenagers get spaces with books and musical instruments, even small recording studios. The government spends about 144 billion yen or a little over ten million dollars a year to operate the centers—an exceedingly tiny fraction of government spending—so they're essentially free to use and extremely popular; many new mothers visit daily.

When Rota is about seven months old, Tsukasa learns that her local kominkan is hosting a mother's salon. "I'll do a kind of park debut there," she says. "It's easier to engage in conversation at a community center anyway." When Tsukasa arrives, she strikes up a conversation with a woman named Ayaka whose son is scooting across the floor next to Rota. It turns out the babies are almost exactly the same age and each are their mother's first. The conversation crackles with possibility, and they're soon making plans for lunch with some of the other mothers. Tsukasa's debut, informal as it was, could not have gone better.

A week later, the group meets again in a private room at a soba restaurant. The babies, in neat frocks and button-down shirts, wriggle across the tatami floor. Their mothers are dressed in dark cotton outfits that seem designed to make them disappear into the background like stagehands.

Tsukasa sits at one of the low tables close to the wall and tries to nurse Rota because she seems fussy. But her milk is slow to come and as Rota cries, Tsukasa complains aloud. To her surprise, the other mothers nod in commiseration. They've had the same problem satisfying their babies, insatiable at this age, it seems. And like Tsukasa, most supplement with formula and have never used a pump. What had felt so intimate, verging on shameful to Tsukasa, turned out to be universal.

She'd craved this kind of support, the company of women ready to dive into conversations about childrearing with the same enthusiasm with which most other people run from them. Such "debriefing" with other new mothers is crucial to psychological well-being, says Aurélie Athan, a clinical psychologist and faculty member at Columbia University's Teachers College. It's similar to what trauma victims require, she says. "They need to process what's happened to them."

When the food arrives, Ayaka tells the group that her husband recently had a day off work so she left the baby with him and went to city hall to look into public daycare options. Tsukasa feels a pang of regret that Kaz can't do the same.

Right, daycare, Tsukasa says, *I should probably get my application together soon.*

She's worried about getting a spot at one of them, when Rota is a year old. Mothers like Tsukasa with full-time jobs have priority, but it's still no guarantee, and they might be assigned to a center across town.

Yeah, you should, Ayaka agrees, *there's fierce competition.*

There's no question that all the women in this group will use government-funded centers; daycare has been a public good for more than a century here. In the 1890s, the country created kindergartens for elite families and day nurseries for low-income families' children. In the following decades, the system expanded to include children of female factory workers, day laborers, and soldiers fighting in the Russo-Japanese war. By 1940, there were twenty-three thousand state daycare centers across the country, and then Allied occupation forces created even more for children orphaned by the war. Today, children can enroll from a month old—and many do start in that first year, because it's easier to get a spot than after the child is a year old—and the centers stay open late to accommodate parents' work schedules. Tuition is based on income. Tsukasa will pay less than thirty thousand yen, or two hundred dollars, a month, and the most any family pays is about seven hundred dollars.

The biggest problem is there aren't enough facilities to satisfy the need. In the last five years, the government increased funding so much that waitlists decreased by ninety percent but there's still a shortage in dense urban areas. Many families move to cities in part for the child benefits, like good schools and plentiful community centers, which only exacerbates the shortage of daycare spots. At some centers in Tsukasa's neighborhood there are thirty or forty families in line.

The daycare conversation makes Tsukasa uneasy, but when she gets home from lunch, Kaz is in his music studio, and she doesn't want to take a lot of his time explaining the situation and all of her anxiety surrounding it, so she tries to distill it for him. "I don't give him detailed reports, just clear bullet points," she laughs. Instead, she agonizes over the insoluble questions alone as she transfers Rota onto the futon to nap: Will she get a spot? Will it be at a center nearby? How can she possibly manage Rota's care on top of a full-time job? Should she just quit? Can they afford that?

Kaz, for his part, is also worried about daycare and how they will manage when Tsukasa returns to work. But he doesn't have much time to come up with a practical solution. He's now teaching four classes a week at the nearby university—the reason they moved to Osaka—and also still writes songs for bands, which means he often returns to Tokyo for part of the weekend. Despite his hectic schedule, he says being a father has grounded him in a way that's also changed him as an artist. "There's a sense of relaxation I've never felt before; to have a family, a wife and a child, I find that it makes me more relaxed in my creative work."

Tsukasa can see some of Kaz's creativity beginning to emerge in their daughter. Rota perks up anytime music plays and, like her father, taps along to the beat. One of her favorite toys is a little piano. "It's interesting to watch," Tsukasa says, "I'm excited to see what kind of child she becomes."

One bright Sunday they take a walk as a family in the nearby park, Kaz in a shirt with a drawing of Lucy from *Peanuts* riding a skateboard and Tsukasa in a long black skirt and sneakers. Tsukasa laughs in surprise as a crane swoops past them and settles on a railing. Tsukasa's joyfulness is one of the things Kaz loves about her, and it's something he now sees in Rota. "I don't think Rota is much like me; if anything she's more like my wife—she laughs a lot. It's not that I don't laugh a lot but I think she's an optimistic girl, that's my impression." They each seem to think the baby is like the other one, perhaps an indication of how much they admire each other. Rota herself is more interested in the bird and stares out from Tsukasa's front pack at its downy gray feathers and sinuous neck. Kaz enjoys watching her begin to appreciate the world's natural beauty. "Even if I'm having a bad day, when I look at her it dissipates; she's my priority now and everything else is secondary, and that's an entirely new feeling. I have fundamentally changed since she was born."

Tsukasa loves this time with him, she just wishes there was more. But the next day, he is back to work and she is on her own again. So when her mother comes to visit a few weeks later, Tsukasa is grateful for her companionship and help. It's hard to remember now why she was so reluctant to accept it when they'd lived together after Rota was born. And why her mother's suggestion that she give Rota formula back then had made her so furious. "I was quite stubborn but I think I'm more relaxed about parenting in general now; I let Rota do what she wants to do and eat what she wants to eat."

Her mom seems to be settling into her new role as well. As Tsukasa goes through the daily routine of feeding and bathing and comforting Rota, her mother offers effusive praise. *You're doing a great job*, she repeats.

Tsukasa is grateful but says that in the rush of daily life, there's no time to dwell on the past. She has to keep up with the constant forward motion of life with a baby. And life is also progressing for her friend Kyoko, who calls from Matsumoto to let her know that she is pregnant, after so many months of trying. Tsukasa is incredibly relieved and happy. Now perhaps they'll be able to reset their strained relationship, and of course, it will be wonderful for Rota to have a close family friend so close in age. It would only be better if they lived closer.

For now, though, she needs to get settled in Osaka. There are still a few things she needs for the apartment, but she has been putting off a trip to the department store downtown because it involves going to Osaka-Umeda train station, the frenetic transit hub that two and a half-million people pass through each day. With her mom here to help, she decides to try, and plans their outing as if it was a military operation. "It's unpredictable so you have to do advance research to know what to expect and how to handle it, like simulate what we'd do if a problem came up." She maps her route, determines the location of elevators, and packs cooling spray and a motorized fan. "I do get a little nervous about all the risks," she laughs.

The next morning, they get a taxi to the station, but on the way, their driver asks with alarm: "Have you heard? About Prime Minister Abe? Is it true?" They don't know what he's talking about. Tsukasa looks at her phone.

Mom, she says softly, *Abe-Sōri's been shot.*

What? her mother exclaims.

But there is no time to figure it out now. They are at the station and their train is scheduled to leave in a few minutes. They hustle to the platform, both still in shock, then board a car the color of plum wine and find seats on the green velveteen bench.

Tsukasa takes out her phone again and this time finds a video of the incident.

Look, she says to her mother, eyes glued to the screen.

There he is, Prime Minister Abe, who's been in office almost a third of Tsukasa's life, giving a speech at a nondescript intersection. Then a bang, a cloud of smoke and a scrum of security personnel.

It doesn't make any sense.

There were just four gun deaths in Japan in 2022 and one of them was Abe's. That's the lowest number in the developed world. That same year in the US there were nearly fifty thousand. Finland, by contrast, has roughly the same rates of gun ownership as the US—about thirty-six percent of households have a firearm—yet gun deaths are more than fifty times lower than in the US. That's partly because Finns own more hunting rifles than handguns, which are involved in eighty percent of violent incidents in the US, and also because after a 2007 school shooting, the Finnish Parliament made a number of reforms: It raised the minimum age to purchase a gun; required a detailed application to get a license; and implemented new safety regulations about firearms storage. It was a far cry from the American political response.

In Japan, firearms are also heavily regulated. Hunters and target shooters are allowed to own shotguns, but must abide by hefty safety and licensing requirements. Japanese police officers are allowed to carry handguns but they rarely use them. Even the yakuza, Japan's mafia-like criminal organizations, relinquished their firearms in the face of harsh penalties. The Prime Minister's assassin made his own gun by duct taping metal pipes to a piece of wood.

"It's horrifying," says Tsukasa, but it seems like an aberration rather than a sign Japan is getting more violent. "If this becomes a place where anyone can shoot a gun, like the US, then that's frightening, but I don't connect it to that at all."

She does have a sense that violence is increasing outside Japan, and that makes her less inclined to leave. Before Rota was born, she and Kaz talked about moving overseas for a while; they thought it might be beneficial for their daughter to learn English and escape the homogeneity of Japanese schools. Now though, Tsukasa isn't so sure. Because along with the cultural rigidity—or perhaps more accurately, because of it—Japan is a society anomalously free of violent crime. A place where lost wallets, even lost umbrellas, are almost always returned to their owners and children walk to school by themselves at the age of six. "I just think it's safer in Japan," she says. So rather than expose her family to potential dangers outside the country, she surrenders to what she sees as an often-oppressive system, for the sake of her daughter's safety.

THE LAST TIME TSUKASA had a haircut was almost exactly a year ago, but she can still viscerally remember the long scalp massage that preceded it, and the freedom she felt to lounge in the chair for as long as it took. It fills her with the kind of nostalgia normally reserved for decades-old memories. It's difficult to believe that until recently, there was room in her life for such indulgences. Like regular visits to the onsen, the curative heat of the public bath tempered by the cool washcloth across her forehead. Now, she only bathes with Rota. The baby will usually allow Tsukasa a moment to shampoo her own hair but never enough time for a longer soak. And she certainly wouldn't have the patience for a hair salon.

So instead Tsukasa shuffles to her small bathroom and finds scissors in the cabinet. She pulls her long bangs between two fingers and chops them straight. She considers her reflection. The cut is passable but her skin has gotten flaky, she notices, another casualty of motherhood. No time for makeup or creams; just sunscreen if she's lucky. She finds her toothbrush and thinks she should also try to get to a dentist.

But what would she do with Rota? They spend every moment together, so Tsukasa can intuit her every need. And Rota cries if Tsukasa leaves her sight; she loves her mother wildly. It is beautiful and bone-tiring.

Kaz would like to help but simply can't find time. "Right now, Tsukasa-san is doing almost all the childcare. I'm trying to strike a balance and cut down on work as much as possible, but my job is so unpredictable. It's really difficult to know what the right answer is."

Tsukasa understands, but now that her mother has returned to Matsumoto, there is no one she can rely on for help. "I don't know where I can leave Rota, there's no place or person I could leave her with," Tsukasa explains. Babysitters are rarely used here; only about four percent of Japanese families have ever hired one. If parents need temporary childcare, they typically enlist their own mothers. None of Tsukasa's friends has used a babysitter, and most of them don't really understand the concept: *A babysitter? What's that?*

Paying someone to look after your children can be seen as a shameful dereliction of maternal duty, a holdover from a time when child raising was more communal. The soul of a three-year-old stays with him until he is one hundred, the saying goes, so how could a parent outsource care in those formative years? "We have this mindset that the mother is the best nanny for the baby," Tsukasa explains with a laugh. The idea puts significant pressure on mothers, but also, in the most optimistic reading, acknowledges the importance of what they do, that they are in some way irreplaceable. It does not, however, give them a break, and Tsukasa desperately craves one. Late one night when Rota is asleep, she takes the remainder of the baby food from the refrigerator and also some shirasu—small dried sardines—to eat as a midnight snack while she scrolls the city hall website, looking for support programs for new moms.

Here's something, she thinks: A service that matches mothers with qualified volunteer caregivers. *That looks promising.* Mothers are required to provide a reason for needing the help, she reads. Pure exhaustion probably isn't sufficient. But she has been considering taking a driving class so she can get her license; the public transportation isn't as good here as it was in Tokyo. She makes an appointment to enroll.

On that morning, she arrives at Toyonaka City Hall, an austere gray building with three neat rows of bike parking and stone dragons standing sentinel, and goes inside to meet with a program administrator. He asks her a series of questions, including why she can't care for her own child herself.

I recently moved to Osaka and my new neighborhood is so hilly that it's hard to get around by foot, so I need to take a class to get my driver's license. It's really out of pure necessity, she says, trying to appear regretful.

He looks at her for a moment, then nods and moves on to the explanatory portion of his presentation. Tsukasa is relieved that he seems to have accepted her rationale and earnestly takes notes: there's a suggested gratuity of five hundred yen an hour, less than five dollars, and all appointments must be scheduled a full month in advance. Finally, he enters her information into the system and it's official. Someone else is going to look after her baby. It is both liberating and terrifying.

The night before the babysitter is scheduled to come, Tsukasa can't sleep. The next morning she can't eat. Can babysitters be trusted? How will Rota respond to a new face? Is she a completely negligent mother, and does she really need a driver's license anyway? She'd waited a month for this visit but perhaps there's still time to cancel.

The woman who arrives at their door, right on time, does not seem homicidal, malevolent, or pestiferous. She is a gentle former daycare worker who tells Tsukasa she does volunteer caregiving because she likes small children. She actually seems quite wonderful. Perhaps it will be good for the baby to spend time with someone outside her immediate family, Tsukasa rationalizes.

She shows the babysitter the little containers of oatmeal porridge she's made for Rota. Carrot and potato; broccoli; and sweetcorn and yams. Orange, green, and yellow. There are also two fish dishes if she prefers: shirasu and sweet potato, and porridge with dried bonito flakes. *And then afterward she can have this*, Tsukasa says, pointing to the formula tin. Rota only breastfeeds at night now so Tsukasa's leash is somewhat longer than it was. And at the moment, Rota seems pretty happy playing on the floor without her. So a few minutes later, Tsukasa feels only the slightest pang of separation as she steps into the world on her own, for the first time as a mother.

It would be a little more exciting if she were on her way to an onsen or a café, but she diligently takes a train to the driving school for a class that turns out to be surprisingly difficult. Her mind feels flabby and unfamiliar. Tsukasa is relieved when it's over and then again when she returns to her apartment to find Rota still happy. The babysitter gives Tsukasa a detailed report of their two and a half hours, complete with pictures. They played, Rota peed, they played some more.

Tsukasa fantasizes about what it would be like to have a babysitter who would watch Rota while she did something more fun than driving school, like go to a movie or even drink a sweet cocktail. She reflects that perhaps Japanese women are too quick to dismiss babysitters. "Most moms don't leave their children unless it's really necessary and certainly not to have a rest or to do something fun," she says. "Now that I've used a babysitter, I don't really understand that, I think it was good for me because I feel refreshed, but the concept of paying money for someone to take care of your child may still be hard for some people to accept."

She does not bring it up the next time she sees her friends, about a month later. They have bigger issues to discuss anyway. *Did you see what the new prime minister said?* Ayaka asks when they are assembled on the floor of her small living room.

Oh, the thing about maternity leave? I mean, what was he thinking? Tsukasa says.

Yeah, here let me find it, Ayaka says and pulls out her phone to read the news report to the group: *He suggested women on maternity leave should learn new skills so they would be better workers when they return to the office.*

He said it like parental leave is a vacation! Tsukasa laughs broadly.

Yeah, like in what extra time am I gonna pick up a new skill? He clearly never spent any time with his own kids, Ayaka says.

Exactly, agrees Tsukasa. *And I loved that storm of moms online, just unleashing on him; mothers definitely aren't afraid to speak their minds anymore.*

They laugh and release shared frustration that their work is consistently undervalued, even as this same prime minister seems so intent on prodding them into increasing the birthrate. The reality is that most of them can't even get a moment alone with their husbands. Kaz is busy all day, and at night they sleep on their futon with Rota "like a river," a reference to the Japanese character: two long lines and a shorter one in between. "It just seems easier that way," Tsukasa explains. "Like when she cries I just pat her back, it's so much more trouble if she's in her own crib."

The country has gone back and forth on bed-sharing: Historically, Japanese families slept together on a shared futon, and in the 1950s, only about two percent of children slept in a separate room. Then in the sixties, as the country abandoned some of its more traditional practices, experts recommended against bed-sharing, but most families still slept in the same room. The number of reported sudden infant deaths began to climb though, and in 1996, over five hundred infants died from SIDS. The government launched an investigation and then a campaign against bed-sharing, and it issued recommendations similar to those in the US and Europe about putting children on their backs to sleep on a firm surface. By 2022, SIDS cases had dropped below fifty per year. Still, the bed-sharing restrictions mostly apply to newborns. Many mothers share a bed with their children starting when they are a few months old and typically share a bedroom until they reach primary school. There is a philosophy that sharing space like that encourages empathy and consideration for others.

Tsukasa is relieved to hear that her friends also bed-share, and that they seem as concerned as she is about the toll it's taking on their marriages. "It's a challenge we all face as Japanese couples: that we don't have very intimate relationships because the baby's there," says Tsukasa. A pair of 2024 studies found that between half and seventy percent of Japanese married couples are sexless or nearly sexless, though most still say their marriages are happy. By comparison, an estimated fifteen percent of American marriages are sexless. A recent advice column in Japan's 39 *Magazine* suggested couples drop children with their grandparents and go to a love hotel to rent a room by the hour. "My in-laws probably just think we're a couple that really likes going to the movies," one woman commented. Still, bed-sharing doesn't seem to be the real problem. The majority of respondents said their marriages were sexless because they spent most of their waking hours working or doing chores, and they were exhausted.

Japan's total fertility rate started to drop in the seventies, and in 2005, the prime minister appointed Kuniko Inoguchi as its first Minister of Gender Equality and Social Affairs, an expansive remit. Inoguchi is an experienced politician with advanced degrees from Yale and she has pushed to keep Japan a pacifist nation, a central tenet of the postwar women's movement. As minister, she diagnosed the birthrate problem as financial: it was simply too expensive to have children. She proposed making maternity care free and successfully expanded the childcare allowance. Those programs showed modest results at first, but fertility fell again after 2015.

Inoguchi is now a member of parliament and has reassessed the issue: She says it's not a lack of money as much as time. Women like Tsukasa have the twin burdens of providing most or all of the childcare at home and also working. That creates impossible demands on their schedules. Inoguchi is advocating for a four-day workweek, and Prime Minister Kishida has been receptive. He sees the threat as existential, declaring in 2023: "Japan is standing on the verge of whether we can continue to function as a society."

The reason leaders like Kishida are so concerned about a decreasing birthrate—when starting in the late 1960s, over-population was declared an existential global threat—is that the new downward trend could be disastrous for a country's future, explains Melissa Kearney, Professor of Economics at the University of Maryland. She explains that a smaller population means diminished power on the world stage and a less dynamic economy—with fewer people to come up with new innovations—and that will make it harder to support an aging population like Japan's. "I actually worry about what's going to happen with an aging population that doesn't have children to take care of them in their old age; the idea that robots are going to step in and do it, I don't find that all that comforting." She says countries can stem the crisis by increasing immigration, but as more countries see

fertility rates decline, that won't work forever. Japan has been particularly resistant to increased immigration, though it has allowed
slightly more in recent years. Mostly though, the country has put
the burden of reversing the trend on women.

When Tsukasa gets home from the restaurant, she lays Rota
down on her stomach in their living room and stacks some colorful blocks in front of her. Rota squeals and extends her arms as
if to fly, little fingers grasping the air. When that doesn't get her
anywhere, she tries a different strategy and pushes herself to her
knees then wobbles there for a moment.

That's right, Tsukasa coos and moves the blocks closer. It seems
as if every day, Rota has something new to show her.

The season is changing as well. The bare trees outside leave
no doubt that fall has turned to early winter. Tsukasa knows she
needs to think about next year. She has not admitted it to her
mama-tomo friends, but part of her hopes she doesn't get a daycare spot when Rota turns one in January so she can stay home
until April—when the school year starts and more spots open
up—or even later. She just can't imagine that in only a few months
she would add a full-time job to their fragile day-to-day. "Who's
going to pick up Rota from daycare? My husband can't do it, so I
guess only me? That means I'll have to be so efficient, like really
manage my time in every aspect of life, so yeah, I really just want
to postpone another year."

Her company has other ideas though: A few weeks later, one of
her colleagues videocalls her to talk about it.

It's so great to see you, we all miss you, the woman tells her.

Tsukasa smiles. It is both strange and comforting to see her
face. They'd been close, shared most of their weekday waking
hours before their lives diverged, as Tsukasa became a mother and
moved twice, first to Matsumoto and then Osaka. Through it all,
it seems, life in their Tokyo office continued.

We were talking about what you might work on when you get back, maybe some more design projects.

Tsukasa smiles and nods. She's heartened to hear her colleagues want her back; she always liked them and also her boss, who let her take on creative work in addition to her administrative duties. When she gets off the call, Tsukasa thinks perhaps she could be ready to return, to reclaim that part of herself.

Suddenly the year is rushing to a close and the city is awash in yuletide spirit. Strings of lights turn Osaka Castle from fortress to gingerbread confection. In a country with so few Christians, Christmas has become a kind of early Valentine's Day, and restaurants on the nearby commercial strip decorate tables with roses to attract young couples. Love hotels are sold out.

Kaz is traveling in the days leading up to the holiday, so Tsukasa celebrates with her mom friends. They rent a small space and fill it with Christmas tree-shaped balloons and small wreaths. Rota smiles at one of the other little girls who is dressed just like her, in a red velvet dress and Santa hat. Tsukasa, in her own plush hat, reads to them from a book. She can feel the time slipping away. "A year ago she was still in my stomach and I look back at photos and feel nostalgic. I just want to spend as much time with her as I can, make all the memories I can now."

After the holiday, her boss calls from Tokyo and makes it clear he expects her back soon. He has some design projects for her to manage, similar to the brochures she helped produce before she went on leave. As he talks, she is reminded again of how much she likes her job, the creative and intellectual stimulation it provides. And while she had thought he would be open to her working remotely from Osaka, he tells her the company would prefer that she be in Tokyo. Tsukasa begins to think maybe Tokyo, and the professional world, is where she belongs. "I can feel my consciousness gearing up to return to work," Tsukasa says. That night, she dreams of being on a train and sees tracks being laid to bring her back to Tokyo. It is inevitable, inescapable. In the morning, she wakes with the clear realization: "Everyone would be happier if we moved back."

She talks it over with Kaz. He'll have to commute to Osaka to teach classes but, he concedes, it's worth it for her to keep her job because they do need the income. And he has been traveling back to Tokyo more often to meet with musicians, so he can probably do the same in the other direction. Still, he's nervous for what's coming. "I'm worried about what will happen with us both working," he says, "how we'll be able to do that and take care of everything at home."

Soon they are on a long-snouted bullet train, thundering past wooden farmhouses and wrinkled green hills toward Tokyo, where they leave Rota with a friend and go look at apartments. They take off their shoes and pad through each one, making note of small, distinguishing features. After several hours, they're exhausted and seek refuge in a local izakaya. It is only the second restaurant meal they've had alone in over a year, but it's short and there's no romance in it. They talk about the expense of Tokyo apartments compared to Osaka, their preferred neighborhoods, move-in dates, floor plans. They try to map out a life they don't yet live in an apartment they don't yet inhabit.

And as the stress builds, they direct their frustration at each other.

I don't know if you'll be able to work this much when I go back to the office, Tsukasa says sharply. *I mean, how am I going to do that and take care of Rota on my own?*

Kaz is upset he doesn't have more to offer Tsukasa, but he is also being pulled in multiple directions, with the extreme demands of work and profound draw of family.

Soon after they get back to Osaka, Tsukasa gets a letter from the Osaka city government: They have gotten a daycare spot. Of course, she thinks, because now it's too late; they are going to Tokyo. She declines the offer, knowing some other mother will be ecstatic to have gotten off the waitlist.

A FEW WEEKS LATER in her Osaka kitchen, Tsukasa looks up from the cake batter she's stirring to see Rota surrounded by a sea of gossamer paper.

Rota, what did you do? Tsukasa yelps, bounding across the room.

She already knows the answer: pulled every tissue from a box Tsukasa hadn't thought to move because the tabletop had been out of Rota's reach until today. Rota looks at her with an impish grin so similar to Kaz's that Tsukasa has to smile back. She picks up the tissues and hurries back to the birthday dinner preparations. Kaz's mom is coming soon and Tsukasa is making tai, a sea bream cooked on special occasions in part because its name is similar to omedetai, a celebratory greeting.

At dinner with Kaz and his mom, Rota nibbles at the fish. She eats almost everything now, from curry rice to fermented soybeans. Tsukasa will just wait until she's three to feed her sashimi. At the end of the meal, when Tsukasa brings out the cake, Rota claps enthusiastically and proceeds to get gloriously messy. Kaz and his mom laugh, and Tsukasa basks in the joy her daughter brings the family. It will be hard to move her again, but she is sure that returning to Tokyo is the right decision—until she gets another call from her company.

Her request to return to her previous position was denied. Her boss lobbied hard to keep her, but it's out of his hands now. She will be transferred by the human resources department to work on something to do with corporate housing, it's not entirely clear what. The whole conversation is surreal.

Transferring female employees when they come back from maternity leave is not illegal but the law does recommend employers try to return them to their previous position or something equivalent. Like Chelsea though, Tsukasa feels little agency—or energy—to push back against such a big corporation.

"Everything I expected about going back is just completely different now," she says. "After all those discussions with my boss and my colleagues, where they all seemed to agree it made sense for me to come back, the top boss denied my request." She had carefully planned her return to Tokyo and after weeks of calling around, finally found Rota a spot in a so-called "unofficial" daycare—not regulated by the government but still heavily subsidized—only to discover that control was an illusion. "I don't want to go back now, I don't really want to see what this job is, I just feel betrayed, you know?"

She knew this was a possibility but didn't think it was likely. Large Japanese corporations have "lifetime employment," a system that dates back to the postwar economy and is still in place, in which university graduates enter as a cohort each year and are pretty much guaranteed a job until retirement. Some companies offer them discounted units in "corporate housing," sex-segregated dorms where they eat breakfast in communal dining rooms and take trains to the office with colleagues. They advance as a group, and one reason men are so reluctant to take paternity leave is that they don't want to fall behind their cohort. Women meanwhile get shunted into lower-paying "mommy-track positions" that don't require the same extremely long work hours as the typical salaryman positions. That helps explain why Japan has one of the biggest gender pay gaps. As Nobel Prize winning economist Claudia Goldin argues, because of such inflexible labor markets, parenthood itself can almost entirely explain gender pay disparities in high-income countries. Men and women earn roughly the same until they have children, at which point women's earnings drop and never catch up again to men's.

In Japanese companies, individuals within each class of hires are mostly viewed as interchangeable and management can assign them to a different division or even a different city at any time. That's what has happened to Tsukasa.

It turns out her new job is assessing young recruits' applications for housing in those company dorms. But she feels entirely unqualified: "I don't have any knowledge of real estate and that business, it's all just totally unfamiliar to me." It also holds very little appeal; her strengths are more creative. "It really has nothing to do with my skills or experience and I can feel myself losing motivation."

The job is also in a new location, which she hadn't anticipated when she signed the lease on their new apartment. So her commute, including drop-off at Rota's new daycare, is ninety minutes each way via three train lines and her new manager, she soon learns, is strict about punctuality. Then a few weeks in, she starts getting frequent calls from Rota's teachers. Rota is new to the school and a prime target for every virus that rips through the young population, so Tsukasa frequently has to leave early or take days off to care for her. She puts in a formal request to work remotely a few days a week, a new option since the Covid pandemic, but like her request to stay in her previous role, it is denied.

Kaz wishes he could be more helpful, but he is still working long hours on compositions and now also commuting to Osaka to teach. It's painful for him to watch Tsukasa try to manage so much.

You know you can leave that job anytime, he tells her. *Maybe you should take a break to figure out what you really want to do. I can try to work more to make up the difference.*

Tsukasa is grateful. And after only two months back at work, she submits her resignation. "It just didn't work with my schedule as a mother, so I surrendered."

Kaz thinks the system failed her. "The government does not give mothers enough support and respect. Financial support is one thing but there's not enough support for mothers to return to work. It's really difficult and in lots of different contexts, I can feel that it's not equal for men and women here. I think Japan is still incredibly behind on gender issues."

In the immediate aftermath, Tsukasa is just relieved to be done trying to juggle everything. She returns to spending every day with Rota because without a full-time job, she no longer qualifies for public daycare. As the weeks go by though, a feeling of destabilization sets in and she doesn't know how to move forward. She never expected be a shufu but that seems to be her fate, at least until Rota turns three and can go to public kindergarten. At that point, Tsukasa will be in her late thirties and she's not sure what will happen.

"If your career gets interrupted, it's very hard to rebuild," she explains. "You aren't judged by your performance like in a meritocracy, you're judged by your age, and the older you are, particularly women, the less a company wants to hire you," she explains. Once she hits forty, she can't imagine any big company will recruit her. "They want young, so I'm struggling to figure out the future of my career and how I can contribute financially."

The future she'd once envisioned—a creative career, more than one child—seems almost unthinkable now. "I do want another baby but with this system and in this environment, we can't afford it," she explains, sitting at her kitchen table with a tray of uneaten senbei rice crackers in front of her. "I don't have family nearby to help and I feel like I've aged a lot with the first one so I'm not sure I have the physical strength for it."

Rota wakes from her nap and Tsukasa lifts the drowsy girl off the futon, her hair still tousled from sleep. Rota's limbs are long enough now to wrap around Tsukasa's waist, and she grips her mother tightly. "You know, sometimes I'd like to have just a little bit of freedom, to read a book or maybe study again," Tsukasa says from within her daughter's embrace. She has sacrificed so much this year to a system that she feels has asked more of her than it should have—preyed even, on her willingness to give. Because there is nothing she would not sacrifice for Rota. "She expanded my sense of love, she is beyond my imagination. This is a creature to whom I would give anything, I would give everything."

CHELSEA
KENYA

TWO WEEKS AFTER SHE was fired, Chelsea is in a narrow retail stall on the busy commercial strip near her home, cleaning red mud from the floor. There's a leak in the roof that needs a patch and she wonders how much it will cost. She put most of her savings into the deposit for this shop, which she and her cousin James decided to rent as partners, and turn into a used-clothing store. They'd been toying with the idea for a while, and when Chelsea lost her job around the same time the space became available, they jumped on it.

The previous occupant had papered two of the walls with gold Gucci logos and a third with Louis Vuitton. Chelsea wants the shop to evoke a different kind of opulence: subtler, more pastel. It should call to mind smooth fairways and trimmed teeing grounds. It's a world with which Chelsea is familiar because just a few hundred meters away is a gated golf club. James works there as a caddie and has to look the part—not hint at the messier reality outside—so their plan is to sell caddies like him quality second-hand athletic wear.

She sources it at the soko, an open-air market next to an

informal settlement, where vendors sell a vast array of goods out of baskets and plastic bags, including so-called fashion waste from Western markets. Some are new garments that didn't sell; others are secondhand clothes. They are called mitumba in Swahili, meaning bundle, because they're typically sold that way, or sometimes kafa ulaya, dead white man's clothes.

It takes Chelsea time to find the solid gray and black T-shirts and athletic pants she needs. A few of the shirts have text that offers clues to their provenance: *Shut up liver, you're fine. Puerta Vallarta*; and *Gecko Bar at Ban Krut Beach, Thailand* encircled by a green lizard. It's hard to predict what customers will want, and she hopes she gets it right. "It's all so scary because I'm putting all the money I have into this," she says.

The bank where she worked has not yet sent her severance pay. They assured her it would post by the end of the week but when it doesn't, a representative tells her flatly that there was a "system glitch" and it will go out by Monday. That's not good. She took out a loan to help cover the rent on her apartment, and every day that she fails to repay it, the lender charges steep interest. Her Wi-Fi has already been shut off and she can barely afford food. Ada now loves banana, pumpkin, avocado, and anything flavored with garlic but that's more expensive than nursing her was. Then there is Zahra, the nanny she hired to replace Florence. Chelsea has been relying on her to look after Ada so she can get the shop running, but Zahra's own daughter has just been diagnosed with a heart condition that requires surgery, so she has to go upcountry to the hospital there and needs to be paid first.

"Everything came all at once," Chelsea says quietly.

She looks down at Ada, comfortable in her arms in a fuzzy gray suit that turns her hands and feet into paws. Having her here makes it more difficult to talk to customers, but Chelsea is still grateful for the time together, and for the companionship. At the end of the day, she locks up the shop and goes to her cousin's house rather than her own. With Zahra gone, her flat feels too quiet. "I don't like staying alone, it makes me overthink my situation and then I get depressed, so yeah, I like a full house."

A MONTH LATER, CHELSEA notices Ada's hair has grown long and uneven. Probably time to shave it, she thinks. But she's reluctant because in her Luo community, shaving a child's head for the first time is significant: The mother-in-law traditionally does it in a ceremony where the father can raise any doubts he has about his paternity. If he doesn't, the baby and mother are welcomed into his family.

Joseph finally returns Chelsea's calls, and she asks him if he has a preference about who should give their daughter her first haircut.

My Kalenjin community's not so traditional about hair, he tells her, *so go ahead and shave it if you want.*

His response reinforces what she already knows: That they have no real, shared community of their own. It makes her worry about how Ada will navigate the world with a Kalenjin name but no meaningful connection to that group and only tenuous ties to the Luo. "I don't want her to be discriminated against or to be treated differently because she's from a certain tribe; I don't know why it happens like that but yeah, it does."

It has been that way since the British declared Kenya a crown colony in 1920 and essentially drew a border around a broad expanse inhabited by dozens of ethnic communities. They relocated those on the most arable land and took it for themselves, and so began a long struggle for farmland and survival among the different communities. During World War II, some Kenyan men were conscripted into the British army and sent as far away as India and Burma. They returned with a new understanding of nationalist movements and with pride that they had fought on the side of self-determination against fascism. That helped fuel a Kenyan independence movement, and the British became increasingly nervous about violent revolution. So they established a network of "rehabilitation" camps to root out revolutionaries, which over time came to resemble the concentration camps the British themselves had helped liberate in Nazi Germany.

They were horrific, violent places. Girls as young as eleven were incarcerated for supposed revolutionary crimes. Women suspected of sympathizing with the independence movement were subjected to torturous interrogations and hard labor, just days after giving birth. Sometimes sick children were strapped to their mothers' backs as they worked in the hot sun, and when their crying stopped, the women would turn to find their children dead.

Reports of those horrors alarmed some British Members of Parliament, most notably Barbara Castle, who led a crusade against the camps, and after she helped reveal a coverup of killings there, the British finally closed them. It was no longer sustainable for the colonists to stay in Kenya, and in 1963, the country achieved its independence. Still, Kenyans who had worked with the British as "colonial chiefs" maintained their wealth and authority. The new independent government was filled mostly with members of a single ethnic community who looked out for their own, and that system persists to this day. Three of the country's five presidents since independence have been from that same community, the Kikuyu. (The other two were from Joseph's community, the Kalenjin.) In general, political parties break along ethnic lines, with each new government directing resources to its own group, rationalizing that it's "their turn to eat," as the common saying goes.

Awkwardly, the current presidential election pits a candidate from Chelsea's community against one from Joseph's. Both sides need to turn out their constituencies to win so the candidates stoke atavistic tensions between the groups.

Most people Chelsea knows are voting for their own community's candidate. "They just say, 'I want Raila because I'm a Luo.' It's so tribal, they're not really looking at the platforms, they just want their guy on top, you see. It's sad." She reads all the campaign manifestos and is most persuaded by the ideas of a third-party candidate, who seems to have a real plan for getting the country out of debt. Still, he has no shot at winning, which only adds to Chelsea's conviction that the entire system is hollow. "You see these old guys who have been in politics for so many years, none of them really care about us; they don't understand how mothers have to struggle to balance a career and motherhood, it's not easy."

As she shaves Ada's head alone, she thinks of her own mom and reflects that she is following the same path she did into single motherhood. She looks at Ada's newly smooth head and tries to fend off her creeping disappointment that Joseph is not here to celebrate with her. "I don't want to be a bitter mom because you know, sometimes when you're bitter, you let the anger out on your child." In her darkest moments, Chelsea's mother would snap at her: *Why don't you just go back to your dad then?* She always apologized afterward, but Chelsea hopes to be different for Ada. "I just want to protect her from everything."

Chelsea remembers how her mother did protect her in 2008, when Chelsea was in primary school and the country descended into violence after a contentious election that involved the very same Luo candidate running again now, Raila Odinga. A US-funded exit poll showed Odinga comfortably ahead and it looked like he was going to coast to victory, but then the election chief called the contest for his opponent. Odinga accused the rival party of manipulating the results and a week days later, the election chief told *The Standard* newspaper he really did not know who had won. Odinga was outraged and encouraged his supporters to protest. Police shot into the crowds and more than a thousand people were killed and half a million displaced as violence spread outward from Nairobi and throughout the country. It got bad enough that Chelsea's mom put her in private boarding school for class five, fifty miles away from the capital. That created a protective buffer so strong that Chelsea didn't learn about the extent of the violence until years later when she watched news coverage from the time on YouTube.

Ada is even younger than Chelsea was then, and remains unaware of her fragile place in this country or the wider problems gripping it: That the economy is suffering the combined blows of the pandemic, a historic drought, and Russia's invasion of Ukraine, all of which have sent food and energy prices skyrocketing and added fuel to the already incendiary presidential race.

"I'm just praying for a peaceful election so that things can go back to normal as soon as possible, so people can just go back to their lives," Chelsea says. It's not a promising time to start a business, and the shop isn't bringing in enough revenue to cover her costs yet. Even after she gets her severance pay from the bank, she's still behind on rent, and Joseph stops responding to Chelsea's entreaties. "He's not in a position to help me, so I think he feels bad and he goes quiet." She doesn't know the particulars of his financial situation but he does tell her that a few land deals have fallen through for him recently.

She turns to friends instead. One has a maize farm and brings her plastic sacks of grain. Chelsea carries them to a nearby store-front where a friendly, round-faced woman pours the kernels into the blue metallic mouth of a mill. With a loud whirr, the kernels move through a tube almost as tall as the woman operating it, and then come out through a funnel as a fine, yellow flour. That evening, Chelsea boils it into ugali, a relatively inexpensive way to fill their stomachs.

She appreciates her friend's generosity. "I've realized I don't need, like, a thousand friends, I can just have two reliable ones and that will be good." Another friend has recently got a job at a call center and agrees to refer Chelsea for a position. It doesn't pay all that well—barely enough to cover her rent—but it's something, and hopefully the store will start generating income as well. She has a phone interview with a manager and he asks her to come in for a training session, after which she will be able to work some shifts during a probationary period. She works out an arrangement with James's wife, Clara, to split coverage at the shop so she can take on another job. But then there is an unexpected snag: Zahra, who'd returned after her daughter's surgery, tells Chelsea she's quitting for good so she can be closer to her own family. Chelsea begs her to at least stay one more day so she can work her trial shift at the call center, but Zahra is adamant she needs to leave.

"I've just been left stranded," Chelsea frets. "You can't miss the first day of a new job." She remembers how things unraveled at the bank after she pushed back her start date a few days following her maternity leave. It begins to seem foolish to even contemplate taking another full-time job with her childcare arrangement so fragile. And it's not clear how to improve it: There is exceptionally high turnover for "house girls" like Zahra, as domestic workers are called in Kenya—sixty percent leave their employers after less than a year.

There are few other options though. Chelsea knows of a daycare on the north side of her neighborhood, but she's reluctant to use it. "Daycare is dangerous, I worry about putting Ada there."

Sabrina Habib, the co-founder of Kidogo, a social enterprise that improves access to quality childcare in East Africa, says, from her office in Toronto, that informal daycares in Nairobi are often unsafe. "It's generally a ten-foot by ten-foot corrugated metal shack with limited ventilation, no running water, and it tends to be quite dark." Most daycares keep their doors closed and the rooms get stiflingly hot. They do that to prevent children from running into the street and also to elude county officials, who check that caregivers have a business license, which typically costs more than they can afford.

Despite the dismal conditions, there's still overwhelming demand: Each daycare serves an average of twenty-two infants and toddlers who can be there from five in the morning to eight at night. Some children even stay overnight if their parents have to work. In such crowded conditions, children can get seriously hurt and some are even trafficked. Their working parents understand the risks but have no other option; and some of them are so poor, they can't afford to send their children with food. "We've heard some parents will bring a tea bag of what's called 'strong tea' to sustain the child for the entire day," Habib says. In these Nairobi daycares, or so-called "childcare parking lots," nearly seventy percent of children aged eighteen to twenty-four months have been found to be undernourished.

As Habib describes it, a lack of adequate nutrition and stimulation in the critical first thousand days can lead to lifelong health problems and cognitive impairment. That means these children are more likely to do poorly in school and then drop out early to engage in menial labor jobs in the informal settlements and have their own children there, continuing the cycle of intergenerational poverty. Habib's goal with these daycares is long-term: to break that toxic cycle.

Still, the issue wasn't even on the government's radar when she first established Kidogo in 2014. Habib recalls that officials would ask her, why aren't these children just with their mothers? Then the pandemic changed everything. "One of the silver linings is that we realized, I think globally, that when you don't have some type of childcare solution, it's impossible to work." Women in Western countries who worked at international aid organizations experienced firsthand the challenge of inadequate childcare, as schools and daycares in their own communities closed during the pandemic, Habib explains. And so those donor organizations began to view it as a priority. Melinda French Gates told *Forbes* in 2023: "We have got to solve the caregiving-problems crisis around the world." USAID pledged more support for early childhood development, and the World Bank published new research that found forty percent of all young children, or 350 million children worldwide, need childcare but don't have access. Instead, their mothers take them to work or leave them with a relative, often an older sister who might have to drop out of school to do it.

Habib decided to reframe her message around economic, rather than child, development. She now tells officials: "By having quality, affordable childcare, we can enable women—half your population—to work and to contribute to the economy." And she points to new research that shows investment in childcare and other care services can yield a three-to-one return for a country's gross domestic product by increasing female labor participation. She says this economic argument has been a much easier sell.

The government needs to recognize something even bigger, says Linda Oloo, a research officer at the African Population and Health Research Center: That the ability to engage in paid work is a basic human right, and the only way women can exercise that right is if there is quality childcare available. The hard part about getting that message across, Oloo says at her office in Nairobi, is that "needs of women are not highly prioritized because the challenges women go through have been normalized." For Chelsea and other women here, a lack of consistent childcare is just part of daily life.

Still, it presents a problem Chelsea isn't sure how she is going to solve. She needs to go to the call center in order to earn more money to provide for Ada, but she doesn't have anyone who can take care of the baby when she does. She vents about it on the phone to a friend as she sits with Ada at her shop.

I might have someone for you, her friend says, *a house girl named Hope.*

Hope is a young woman, barely twenty years old, and Ugandan, like many of the domestic workers here who are drawn to Kenya for its stronger currency and higher wages. When Hope arrives at Chelsea's flat she seems nice enough, but she's only been in Nairobi a short time and Chelsea knows so little about her. And Chelsea is still haunted by a video of a Ugandan nanny assaulting a child that went viral a few years ago.

She summons the courage to leave Ada with Hope to go to the training, though, and arrives cautiously optimistic.

Then the trainer tells her more about the position: *Your job will be to resolve customer complaints,* he says. *Many of the callers are overseas, so you'll be required to work overnight shifts to accommodate the time zones.*

Chelsea feels as if the wind has been knocked out of her. She'll have to leave her baby overnight with someone she only just met? Her baby who still nurses throughout the night and is accustomed to sleeping next to her? And for a job that pays so little it barely covers her rent?

She can't do it.

"You get paid peanuts and then you have the baby to think about," she explains afterward. "It wasn't really making sense for me, so I had to let it go," she says, clearly pained.

She begins searching again for entry-level positions at big financial institutions like NCBA Bank Kenya and KCB Bank. She applies to as many as she can find, just wanting to get back to where she was before she lost her job at the bank. "I'm very, very worried. Obviously the business is not picking up as I had expected and all the bills are on me, and that used to be okay since I had a monthly salary to cover it, but now that's not there, and I don't know if the shop will bring in the same amount, I highly doubt it. So yeah, it's very scary." In a country with vast inequality and limited maternal supports, motherhood has pushed Chelsea over the edge, and there is a long way to fall.

ON THE MORNING OF the election, Chelsea is woken by a phone call from Joseph.

Go vote, he tells her playfully, *I already have.*

Chelsea assures him she will, just needs to get herself and Ada ready. His lighthearted tone doesn't match the strain she feels between them, but she is willing to accept whatever contact he will have with Ada, to try to preserve that relationship.

Who are you going to vote for? he teases.

Chelsea smiles and admits she plans to vote for Odinga, the Luo candidate. She's decided he deserves a chance to finally govern and maybe he'll make good on his promises to improve the economy.

And what about you? she asks.

Ruto of course. But that's okay, he says smiling, *just go vote.*

Let the best candidate win, she responds. *All I really care about is peace.*

In the election and in life.

My building manager says he's going to padlock the door if I don't pay rent, she tells Joseph with some trepidation, unsure how he'll respond. *And he'll do it,* she adds. *There was another woman who was five months behind and she came home to a lock on her door.*

Chelsea shudders when she thinks about that happening to her with the baby. Joseph says he's working on something now and hopes to have money to send soon. Chelsea nods but doesn't count on it; she's already interviewed for a server position at Bao Box, a restaurant in the upscale Westlands neighborhood, and is waiting to hear back.

Two days later, the election has still not been called. The two sides trade accusations of improprieties and it looks like the courts will have to weigh in. "Things are just shaky, there is this silent tension," Chelsea says. She can feel it even as she cleans up after breakfast and tries to stick to a somewhat normal daily schedule for Ada's sake.

Ada herself lies happily on a mattress on the floor, watching "Akili and Me," a Kenyan children's show and her favorite entertainment after Ms. Rachel, an American YouTuber. Ada's little head bobs as an uppercase and a lowercase G dance across the screen. Gauni! they sing as a pink cartoon dress appears. Ada happily babbles along.

Kaki, she declares. *Kaki*.

Chelsea smiles at her. Kaki is her favorite thing to say these days, though it doesn't mean anything in English, Swahili, or Luo, the three languages she's learning. Still, it seems meaningful to her, and she repeats it with a satisfied grin. Chelsea laughs, a welcome release. She and Ada have not gone outside since election day because she's worried about violence. And anyway, there's nowhere to go: most shops like Chelsea's are closed because of the threat of election violence and customers, wary of instability and rising prices, have cut their spending, particularly on nonessentials like athletic clothes.

Life continues that way for a week: The election undecided, the country on edge, her shop closed, along with the restaurant where she interviewed to be a server. Even the big banks seem to be waiting to see how things play out before they make any new hires.

Joseph, meanwhile, has gone silent again, and the slim hope

she'd had for him begins to curdle into resentment. "It makes me very angry. When you're on the verge of being locked out of the house, the least he could do is just communicate that I'll be able to pay by this time, so at least you hold them off for a bit. But when there's no communication and you also don't know where the money is coming from, it's hard, it's hard."

Then Ada gets sick. She vomits all night and can't keep anything down. Chelsea has never seen her like this, but without insurance, she can't take her to the main hospital. She calls her aunt in tears. They haven't been on the best terms since Chelsea gave birth to Ada out of wedlock, but now that the baby's unwell, her aunt sets her judgment aside and recommends a relatively inexpensive clinic where she's taken her own son before.

Chelsea can't afford a taxi to get there so she hails a boda-boda motorbike on her phone. She knows it's risky; her own stepfather died in a motorbike accident, "but we also can't walk all that way because Ada is heavy nowadays." So when the dust cloud settles, Chelsea climbs on behind the driver with Ada strapped to her in a baby carrier and asks the driver to go slowly. He nods, then they merge into the frenzied city traffic.

The clinic is a small Muslim-owned operation, and the doctor seems competent. He diagnoses Ada with a bacterial infection—probably from something she ate, he tells Chelsea. A nurse administers an injection to stop the vomiting. Chelsea isn't feeling great either; her stomach has been sensitive and she seems to catch every passing virus. The staff examine her and determine she has high blood pressure, likely from stress. It doesn't help that she can't afford this visit, though it is cheaper than a hospital would have been. She messages Joseph, and he says he'll try to come up with some money, but then, once again, she doesn't hear any more from him. A few friends help her instead.

Even as Ada convalesces, Chelsea can't calm her own body, and she doesn't sleep for forty-eight hours. She's lost so many people, any hint of illness is distressing. A friend of hers contracted Covid last year and died within a week. "So much can change in a split second, people just collapse, you see, and they die. And that's it. And these are people's fathers, brothers, sisters."

She has no one to reassure her that isn't going to happen to her. No partner. And worse, no mother. Her mom's death, of course, was the most traumatic. And that, she knows, is where this anxiety comes from: the fear that she could leave Ada the way her own mother left her. And that if she was gone, no one would ever love Ada the way that she does. "I just want to always be there for her, don't want her to feel how mean the world is and the only way I can protect her if is if I'm healthy."

The Luo historically relied on people called Jocho, or soothers, to help members of the community in emotional distress. "If somebody experienced a bad moment—the trauma of losing a child or a mother—Jocho would be deployed so there would always be someone there who knew how to help, and they might even stay for months," says William Janak, a mental health counselor in Nairobi. He says Jocho's work could be described in Western terms as psychotherapy. There are only a few of them left today and while clinical psychology and psychiatric medication are now available, they are expensive and there aren't enough practitioners to deal with the staggering need. An estimated one in four Kenyan girls struggles with mental health challenges and there are only an estimated one hundred licensed psychiatrists in all of Kenya.

Chelsea does what she can to keep moving forward, and stay healthy for Ada. Eats a low-acid diet to protect her stomach with more yogurt, cabbage, and other vegetables like okra; also puts garlic in her socks to fend off ringworm and bacteria. And for her mental health, she goes to church on Sunday. It lets her socialize without spending money, and try to fill the hole where her community should be.

A MONTH AFTER THE election, Joseph calls and reports with a wide smile, how pleased he is that his candidate has been sworn in as Kenya's president. He's as voluble and charismatic as ever. "Today he's in a good mood, he got his president, he's fine," Chelsea says.

At times like this, when he's feeling good, they'll text and if she has enough data, even videocall, so he can see Ada. The only reason she lets him remain such a sporadic presence in their lives is that she doesn't want to close the door on him meeting Ada in person. She would just show up at his house with the baby, she says, but he's in Eldoret, the city where they met when she was in university there, and she doesn't have the bus fare. She's grown tired of asking him to come to her. "If he feels like he needs to come, he'll just come. But I'm done with that because he's an adult, he knows what he's supposed to do."

Chelsea simply tells him she's happy the election ended peacefully. Democracy more or less prevailed and hopefully business will pick up now. Still, she needs a bridge to get her through; the last month drained her financially. So she organizes what she calls a "mini fundraiser" and reaches out to family and friends to ask them to contribute. It's uncomfortable to have to ask and makes her feel like a failure, "like I'm disappointing my mom; she said, your children should live a better life than you. I'm trying."

Her uncle agrees to send money but then tells her sternly: *I hope next month it won't be like this.*

In that moment, she realizes she's become a burden to the people closest to her.

"They have their own problems and they get tired and wonder

why my situation isn't changing." What they probably most want to know, she acknowledges, is why Ada's father is not supporting his baby. It's his job, after all, not theirs.

Then Hope, her latest nanny, quits after just one month. "The first time I was shocked that someone would just leave work like that but nowadays, I'm used to it. When they go, you just go look for another one and life continues." She muddles through, carries Ada to the hectic soko market and to her own store, now reopened after the election concluded; carries her as she shops for food and as she prepares meals. And even that much time together isn't enough for Ada. If Chelsea so much as opens the door to the bathroom, Ada gets so fussy that Chelsea relents and brings her inside with her. At night, Ada is uncomfortable from teething and constantly wants to nurse.

It is tiring, but she finally finds a new Ugandan nanny named Lydia, a young woman with a kind face and short braids. As soon as she starts, Chelsea puts all her energy into improving the shop. It's September and the university students are back in session at the nearby agriculture school. When they spill out of its campus, they seem more interested in food than clothes, so Chelsea decides to start selling snacks like hard-boiled eggs and little sausages called smokies.

On a hazy morning a few weeks later, she arrives at her shop early. She shoos a stray dog from out front and it rejoins its pack, a scruffy bunch with missing legs and ragged scars. In the stall next to hers, a man scoops boiled potatoes from an orange bowl into hot oil to fry them into viazi karai. She gives him a fist bump.

Then she goes into the shop and wheels out a small metal trolley that her friend Vee lent her, removes a portable charcoal stove from the bottom shelf and places it in the street to light. She fans the little flame until a plume of white-gray smoke snakes down the street. She sets the bowl of smokies and eggs on the trolley to boil and arrays the condiments on top. Finally, she unfurls an orange and white umbrella to blunt the equatorial sun. She's open for business.

A few hours later, Lydia brings Ada to the shop. Chelsea is delighted.

Hi, Mama, she coos to Ada softly. Mama is her nickname for Ada because she's named after Chelsea's own mother.

She sets Ada on her lap, proud to show her daughter the business she's built: Since she started selling food, profits have increased, and she now takes enough home at the end of the day to buy dinner and some diapers. Perhaps it would have also made her mother proud. She imagines sometimes what a good grandmother her mom would have been to Ada and how her stepfather would have spoiled her. "But God had other plans," she says.

Chelsea still has her own grandmother, Magdalena, or Shosho, as Chelsea calls her. She keeps asking when she'll get to meet Ada. Chelsea would love to bring Ada upcountry to introduce them— and finally get the chief's signature so she can access her mother's bank account—but the bus fare is expensive. Now at last, with the profits from the shop, she can afford it. She doesn't tell her grand-mother she's coming until she has the paper ticket in her hand. Shosho doesn't believe her at first; it seems too good to be true that she'll finally get to meet her great-granddaughter.

Chelsea and Ada leave early the next morning and when they arrive in the afternoon, one of Chelsea's uncles is at the station to greet them. He drives them to her grandparents' property and there is Shosho, finally, in a flowered top and purple skirt, hold-ing a wooden walking stick and offering unconditional love. Her embrace satisfies a craving that has ached in Chelsea's stomach since she'd become a mother: A hunger to be cared for herself. It has been such a lonely fight for so long.

That evening, she eases into rural life. Her grandparents' compound is lovely and green and their home is relatively modern for an upcountry residence, with running water and electricity. Chelsea is glad to see that since she last visited they have installed mosquito nets, so she can stop worrying about Ada contracting malaria. Ada herself is in heaven. She loves watching the cows and dogs and chickens, and crawls happily in the soft grass, so different from the pocked roads of Uthiru.

Chelsea's grandfather Odero, or Kwara as she calls him, follows behind Ada in a short-sleeved button-down and khakis. Then, as Ada wobbles to standing, Kwara gently lays his hands on his great-granddaughter's shoulders to steady her. Ada looks out at this new world and he looks down at her, both enamored.

He and Shosho, who is now seventy-three, raised their own five children here in Nyakach, near the shores of Lake Victoria. He was a plane attendant for Kenya Airways and she worked in the home. Back then, Shosho recalls, "a child didn't belong only to the mother but to the whole community." Other women helped look after her children and there was a group of men called the Nyumba Kumi, a kind of community police group that, she laughs, "would flog any child that was misbehaving." Nowadays though, she says, there aren't those same traditional laws in the Luo community and more mothers are on their own.

Shosho perches on a tree stump and Chelsea sits down next to her. A donkey grazes behind them and wind blows in off the lake. It's so peaceful, the break Chelsea needed from city life. "While I'm here, I don't worry about bills, everything is just nice," she observes.

It seems like the right time to tell Shosho about what's going on in her life. About Joseph.

Has he ever come to see the child? her grandmother asks.

No. And that's actually the part that hurts the most 'cause

I'm like, this is your child too, why is she not important to you? Because I love Ada so much, Chelsea says, her voice deep as if directly from her soul. *And I wouldn't like her to get hurt. I always wanted to see my father and I always asked myself, why doesn't my father love me?*

Her grandmother nods sympathetically. She pauses a moment then asks if Joseph at least supports them financially.

He used to but things have gotten hard for him financially so currently, not really, Chelsea says. She can see the disapproval on her grandmother's face.

What tribe is he from?

He's Kalenjin.

Mmm. You know, Kalenjin only marry from their tribe, Chelsea. The best thing you can do now is find yourself a job. And you're still young, you have time to find another man if you want.

That's not really my priority right now, Shosho. I'm mostly focused on being grounded financially.

I think that's for the best, her grandmother tells her.

It's the kind of clear, loving guidance Chelsea had been seeking. She only wishes she could stay longer, maybe forever. But she has to return to Nairobi to untangle her life there and make the most of the city's economic opportunities. To start, she decides to move from her sunny one-bedroom to a ground-floor studio. It cuts her expenses almost in half and the new landlord doesn't make her put down a deposit; a real kindness, she thinks, since they're not even from the same ethnic community. "I feel like the pressure has been lifted off," she says.

The new flat is mauve, with a small sink, a refrigerator, and a bathroom. Her bed and couch fit but not much else. Lydia comes with her and it's a squeeze for the three of them, particularly at night when the nanny puts down a mattress that takes up most of the small floorspace. Still, it has its benefits: Her door opens onto a small garden where young children play while their mothers tend vegetables. Clothes hang on a line above a bush that blooms yellow and pink. And over the corrugated metal fence is a clear view of layered green hills under tropical skies. It feels like a fresh start. Ada mercifully begins to sleep better as her teething eases and she wakes just twice rather than ten times. In the morning, she calls "baba," looking for Chelsea.

It's sweet, Chelsea tells Joseph when they videochat one rainy evening that week.

He smiles and says he wants to pay the rent on this new place, is just waiting for a deal to come through.

Chelsea nods but doesn't expect anything to materialize; she's learned better than to hope. So she is surprised a few days later when Joseph does send enough to cover her rent. It's hard not to indulge the illusion that it's a first step to him returning to her life. But she stops herself. She remembers Shosho's admonition that she should make her job search the priority and so she continues to apply to full-time positions, though she never gets a response. She knows it can be hard to get a job without a personal connection, but she still keeps trying. As they head into another rainy season, with Kenya Power trucks rumbling through the neighborhood to fix outages from flooding, she tries to stay positive.

Her visit with Shosho was invigorating, so she decides to lean on the family she still has. She calls her cousin William and asks if she can visit. Her cousins have been more compassionate toward her than her aunts and uncles, who expressed so much disappointment and anger when she got pregnant out of wedlock. The younger members of her family like William and her other cousin, James, seem more accustomed to modern, complicated relationships.

When Chelsea arrives at William's place, he asks her warmly how she's been and it all comes pouring out: that the year she lost her parents was the most traumatic of her life but this past year was not much better. And when Joseph paid her rent this month, it made her hopeful their relationship might improve. Still, she's pretty much shut her heart to him, she tells William, and she's not sure when she'll ever open it again.

I'm not saying I've completely blocked that part of my life, but I'm just saying I feel like if I get another heartbreak I'd be so depressed and that makes me lose a lot of focus, she says. *When I'm depressed, I usually just stay in bed, I don't even spend time with my daughter and then I end up feeling so guilty.*

William is sympathetic, he can see the effort she's put into being a good mother and wants her to be happier.

He hugs her.

This year was really hard, dealing with so much loss and also a new baby, he tells her. *But the year is almost over and I am sure better things are coming.*

She believes him.

The only way I can be happy is just focus on myself, you know, at least try and heal, she says. She dreams of a comfortable life, she tells him, of being able to support her daughter. Maybe someday she'll even get a car. She's always wanted a Jeep, she laughs, but really just a house with nice grass where Ada can play.

William wants to help. He works in microfinance and is connected to Kenya's successful fintech scene that's earned the nickname Silicon Savannah. He tells her he's heard that a mobile credit company is looking for new salespeople and encourages her to apply. That same evening, she does, and a few days later, she gets an email: "Dear Chelsea, Good Morning. We have received and reviewed your application for the Sales Associate-Credit Card role, and we would like to invite you for an interview." Chelsea smiles then immediately calls her uncle, hoping he'll be pleased.

Good luck, he says warmly, *I hope you get it.*

His approval, as measured as it is, feels good; he'd been so tough on her when her mom died and then when she got pregnant, but now he can see the effort she's making. "We're beginning to be on the same page," she says happily. "He's still very hard on me but I'm trying to take a different approach and be less defensive."

The next day, she nervously approaches International House, an imposing beige building with blue rails running the length of its frontage. She doesn't know what to expect and is hesitant even to be back in an office after her last corporate experience, but when she gets out of the elevator on the ninth floor, she can tell this place is different. There's a palpable buzz. *It has a good vibe*, she thinks.

Three people meet her in the conference room, including Patricia, the manager of the credit division, who greets Chelsea with a warm smile. She asks her what she did previously and seems impressed that Chelsea worked at a bank.

Why did you leave? she asks.

Chelsea decides to shade the truth and just say that her contract ended. She doesn't want to get into how she'd had to pump in a filing room or the time her manager tracked her to the hospital. As they say goodbye, Patricia is encouraging: "We like you, we'll follow up."

Chelsea glows as she bumps along on the matatu back to her neighborhood. "I don't mind starting from bottom, so long as there's an opportunity for growth. I really need that financial freedom so I'm very willing to work my ass off." She opens her shop at three, doesn't want to miss a full day of sales.

A week later, Chelsea is back at her shop. She had started the day by putting on a bright white shirt with the words *I Run, I Rule* in pink blocky letters. Now, she can feel a wide smile spread across her face as she reads an email from the credit company, inviting her to come back for a second interview. She will need to give a PowerPoint presentation detailing how she'd do the job of saleswoman, it says.

She doesn't own a laptop so she borrows one from a friend, and is so excited that she finishes the assignment that same day. The next week, she waits with other candidates until she is finally called to give her presentation. She's nervous but she steadies herself, and when she's done, Patricia smiles at her. Chelsea feels like she's finally on the right path.

The next day at the shop she allows herself to imagine what life might be like if she actually got this job, and then the buzzing of her phone pulls her back into the present. It's Joseph.

I'm in Nairobi, he tells her, *and I'd like to see Ada.*

Chelsea almost doesn't believe him. For nearly a year, she'd dreamed of this day and now, just as she's begun to move toward independence and let go of any expectations she had for him, he's inserted himself back in her life.

As soon as they hang up, she rushes home to get ready. She still isn't sure what to make of his call but she certainly isn't going to give him time to have second thoughts. She pulls a red and white polka-dot dress over Ada's head and pushes her feet into little pink socks. She could not be more adorable. More lovable. Chelsea hails a motorbike and they speed off in the direction of the mall where Joseph suggested they meet. She wonders whether he'll actually show up.

Then there he is. Tall and handsome as ever, maybe a touch more gray in his full beard. He wears a light blue long-sleeve shirt and a matching blue baseball hat with crisp jeans and boots. And in the next surreal moment, he takes Ada in his arms. They look so alike, with the same radiant smile. Ada is typically reluctant to let people hold her, but it seems like she's almost preternaturally comfortable with her father. Chelsea can't quite believe it.

She feels emotion well in her throat, knows she couldn't speak if she tried.

She follows him to sit down on a bench in the bright atrium of the mall. Joseph tells her he's here on business and has some people to meet, but had also wanted to see Ada. Chelsea doesn't try to dissect it, is just happy this moment has finally arrived.

When they stand to go to lunch, Ada coughs and Joseph gently pats her back. Then the baby calms and burrows deeper into him, her small head tight against his broad shoulder. At the restaurant, Joseph tells Chelsea he wants to spend more time with Ada and put her on his health insurance. After lunch, they walk to a market and he buys them groceries: yogurt, cereal, diapers. Chelsea still feels a connection and watching him with Ada only reinforces it. She knows it isn't rational or healthy, but there's no denying she's drawn to him. He has to return to Eldoret tomorrow, he says, but the next time he's here, hopefully they can see each other again. Then, after half a day together, he's gone. Chelsea decides to think of the encounter as a step in the right direction.

In the next few days though, she doesn't hear from him. All that talk about seeing Ada again. Promises of health insurance. The warmth she felt between them. Was any of it real? She doesn't hear back from the sales job either. Patricia had said they would get back to her immediately and made it seem as if the email would come that same day. But two days pass. And then three. The next day she stops checking, it's too depressing. She tries to focus instead on how to improve her shop so she can support Ada long term without Joseph, without her uncle, without any of the men she knows she can't truly depend on.

Around eight that night, after she's sold the last of her smokies, she sits heavily on a plastic stool and absentmindedly looks at her phone. And there it is: An email from the credit company. She got the job. She is overcome with joy and relief. This moment marks a new beginning, she can feel it.

She messages William, Shosho, her uncle, and, with mixed emotions, Joseph.

He wishes her good luck.

That's it? She thinks. And it seems that it is. They don't speak at all in the month leading up to Ada's birthday. When she does think of him, it's with disbelief that he changed so much this past year. "I never thought it would be like this. He used to be really nice and responsible, I really never saw this coming."

She never thought she would be someone who had to pressure her baby daddy to provide, she says. Never thought she'd need to ask people for rent money or to help pay for a simple dinner. And never thought her child's first birthday would look like this: She still can't afford a party with friends and food and candles, so instead, she buys Ada a cookie and watches her girl excitedly devour it. Ada isn't old enough yet to miss the party. Or her father. Or her grandparents. Or the innumerable other things Chelsea knows very clearly her daughter should have in her life. Ada just delights in the sweet cookie in front of her. It's a lesson, like all the others this year has brought. "I'm not the same person I was before I gave birth to Ada," Chelsea says. "I feel like being a mom has opened up my mind. I'm more responsible, I have clearly defined future goals."

That clarity has led her to a philosophy of interdependence: She now viscerally understands the importance of community, the kind Shosho had when she raised her children. But she can also see how much it conflicts with the individualism of modern city life and the rules she has learned to play by. She hopes that by the time her own daughter becomes a parent, things in Kenya will be different again: That the companies that help set its cultural standards will actually appreciate mothers, and that they'll show it by offering them longer leave and more flexibility.

For now, she'll continue to do the work of raising Ada, whether or not anyone recognizes her efforts. And since she doesn't have the community Shosho did, she'll look to Ada herself for emotional support. At the end of this difficult year, in which she lost so much even as she gained a child, she basks in Ada's love. Chelsea tells herself what any struggling parent would: that it's enough. "It's an achievement that we've come this far and we're still going far because she brings me so much joy. When I've had a rough day, she makes me not think about all my problems. She keeps me going."

ANNA
FINLAND

—————

WHEN LUKA IS SIX months old, to Anna's immeasurable relief, he sleeps through the night for the first time. They wake up next to each on their big shared mattress with the summer sun shining through the sheer curtains as strongly as it will all year. He smiles widely at her, as he does every morning. Anna wonders whether she should move him to his own bed now that he can sleep through, but then again, maybe she'll just keep him with her a tiny bit longer. There's something magical and fleeting about sleeping this way. She knows the risk—kätkytkuolema, cot death or SIDS—but the nurse at their clinic encourages her to co-sleep if it's easier. As with breastfeeding, she should do what works for her.

Later that morning, perhaps fueled by his first full night of rest, Luka begins to crawl. It's as if they've awoken in an entirely new phase of childhood. "He's no longer a small baby; he's a big boy now," Anna coos as she watches him. "It seems like such a short time that I got to hold him in my arms and now he's already doing things on his own." All the more reason to stay close at night.

She is, however, ready for a change to their living situation.

Anna has already submitted an application for a rental flat closer to the city center but in the same school district so Liv won't have to transfer. Anna doesn't think she'll get it though. Landlords typically favor two-parent families. "Even though there's all this equality here, there are still these old, old traditions," she says. So she is delighted when, a few days later, she hears that her application has been accepted. It's such a relief to be moving on from the rocky relationship that defined her time here that she doesn't stop to think about what she's leaving behind until Liv points it out: *This was Luka's first home*, she reminds her mother, *you have to say bye-bye*. Anna smiles appreciatively, struck by Liv's sensitivity.

She herself remains a picture of steely sisu, the Finnish ethos of perseverance developed in response to a century of Russian occupation. She packs for three days straight while her mother watches Luka. The only breaks she takes are to take Liv to school or to soccer practice, short windows of time she gets alone with her daughter these days.

On the morning of the move, dressed in an orange smock dress and work gloves, she tapes a few last boxes closed. Inside one, a Brio wagon, a soft baby blanket, and one of Liv's old dolls, now missing a shoe. Anna doesn't dwell on the significance of these relics until she gets to a box in the kitchen filled with bottles. The sight of them reminds her of the beginning of the year when life had been a blur of boiling bottles and breastfeeding. *Huh, we're getting to the end of that phase*, she thinks; *he'll soon be moving on from bottles*. For a moment, she wants to go back. As hard as it was, with some distance she's nostalgic for those cozy, early days.

Then her father arrives with a black moving van and it's time to go. They load the boxes and drive to her new building, a brick complex across from a well-appointed public old age home. Two of her friends are waiting outside and one finishes a cigarette as they pull up. She is grateful for their help—a moving company would cost a month's rent—and excited to begin their new life here.

She hasn't said anything about the move to Masa but it's clear he's found out when he messages: *I hope Liv likes the new place.*

Liv's father probably told him, Anna thinks, *they've gotten so close recently.*

Masa confirms that, and says Liv's father also told him Anna should have given him their new address but instead "she just disappeared." As it is, Masa still sees Luka at their regular, supervised meetings.

Anna doesn't respond, prefers to let her lawyer do the talking. She's still waiting to hear back from his side about her request to find an amicable, out-of-court solution to their custody dispute.

In the meantime, their supervised visits continue, twice a month. They have one good meeting, when Luka plays happily with his father on the floor, but at the next one, Luka recognizes the building and begins to cry before they even get inside. *This is not good,* Anna thinks. She tries comfort him by getting down on the floor herself to play and then encourages Masa to take over. As soon as she goes in the other room though, the baby howls.

Masa calls to her: *Luka's crying, come back, Anna!*

She's reluctant to return so soon because she wants Luka to get used to Masa. If she goes back now, Luka will only play with her.

When she doesn't return, Masa takes the wailing baby in his arms and carries him to Anna. She's crying now as well and reaches out to take him.

I'm not giving him to you, Masa says, *you just need to come in there so he'll be all right.*

At that point, the supervisor intervenes.

We still have over an hour left in the session, she tries to say calmly over Luka's sobbing, *but everyone's emotions are running so high, it might be best to end early.*

Masa is upset; this is the only time he gets with his son. Anna is dismayed at how difficult the visit has been for Luka and hurriedly straps him into the stroller so as not to prolong it. As she leaves the building with the baby still shrieking, she wonders where she can go to get some space and put the episode behind her.

A few days later, Masa sends a text suggesting they split custody fifty-fifty. They can't even make it through an hour at a supervised visit, Anna thinks, how could he possibly care for Luka on his own; the dressing and bathing and feeding it entails, the need to keep him safe. *It's just not realistic,* she thinks.

Later, in the quiet of the evening, she's more reflective. "I'm trying my best to not block Masa's way, or Luka's right to time with his father." She knows the experience must be difficult for Masa but stops herself from speculating any more than that; she doesn't have the energy for it. "I have to keep my cool head now to focus on Luka and just hope Masa can, as a parent, fix whatever he has to fix." At the start of the year, she was willing to attend to his emotional needs and guide him through parenthood, but now she's ready to relieve herself of that responsibility.

She does what she can to keep daily life calm, and on a mild afternoon a week or so later, she takes Luka for a walk along the river. He sleeps peacefully in his stroller, as he always does in the open air. There's a tradition of Finnish babies sleeping outside, typically on balconies, even in the cold depths of Nordic winter. "Liv slept outside when she was a baby. They sleep well and become hungry when it's a bit cold and fresh; it's good for all of us, even the older people sleep outside," Anna says. As she walks, passenger boats glide past. A sculpture of a Buddha-like figure wearing headphones sits in cross-legged meditation on the riverbank.

Then suddenly, Masa is alongside her. "He just—pop!—came and started asking questions," wanting to know if she'd told officials she wanted fewer than two meetings a month. She tells him she never said that, but he seems unsatisfied.

Masa later says he was riding his bike by the river and happened to pass them. Their visits were so infrequent, he explains, that when he spotted them, he stopped to get a look at his son and also to ask Anna whether what one of the social workers had told him was true, that she wanted there to be fewer visits.

Were you upset after the last one? he asks her. *Is that why you left so fast? You didn't seem okay.*

No, I was totally fine, Anna reassures him, and says she really needs to go. Her heart is still racing from the jolt of his sudden appearance.

I'm sorry about what happened at the last visit, Masa tells her. *Let's coordinate the next one.*

Okay, that sounds good, but I do have to go, she replies as she moves to continue along the footpath.

Their interaction is so destabilizing that it takes her several hours to fully calm down. Then a few days later, Masa sends her a message that shakes her again. He says he'd recorded their conversation by the river because he wanted evidence in case she changed her story about what kind of arrangement she was seeking.

Masa says later that he never hid from Anna that he was recording—she would have noticed he was holding his phone between them, he says—and that he did it because he needed, "some kind of concrete something." He felt like social services and the broader legal system did not fully appreciate his point of view so he wanted a record of everything. "Anna is Finnish, she understands the language, she knows the system, and I'm a foreigner so I needed to do it to defend myself." He had asked his lawyer whether recording his conversations with Anna was legal. She told him that while it was probably not good social practice, it was not illegal. "In this case," Masa says, "it was the right thing to do."

For Anna though, it's unsettling. "In a way I understand he's frustrated because Luka doesn't know him," she says. "But he's blaming me for making him a stranger, so he's holding this grudge toward me and then we cannot work together." That's evident a few weeks later when she hears from Masa's lawyers that he does not want to resolve things out of court, as she'd proposed. Instead, in a new filing, Masa argues that he felt obliged to accept twice-a-month supervised visits for fear of not seeing his child at all, but he actually thinks this is far too little contact. Since he cleans ships in the mornings and evenings, the filing goes on, he's free during the day to spend time with his son. And so he would like to see him three times a week for two hours at "unsupported" visits, meaning without a caseworker.

Anna can't conceive that. There needs to be a supervisor present until Masa learns to care for Luka alone, she says. "He needs to start from scratch and there needs to be support with that." For now, there are no visits scheduled at all because Masa has challenged the existing agreement. That makes Anna uneasy. Masa was so upset with her even when they did have visits; how will he respond to not seeing Luka at all? To cope, she throws herself into legal research and works with her lawyer to craft a response: She'll agree to twice a week visits, rather than twice a month, but only with a supervisor because Masa hasn't yet formed a "safe attachment," as evidenced by Luka's inconsolable crying. The legal work takes time, and on top of caring for Luka and Liv, Anna isn't sure how she's going to manage professional responsibilities when her parental leave ends in two months.

IN SEPTEMBER, THE ASPENS go from green to gold. Luka's round baby face starts to develop the definition of a child's. Only his hair, which still sticks up in patches, recalls his soft infancy. He's also more engaged in the outside world. As Anna pushes his stroller through their neighborhood, he peers into a music shop that sells vintage audio cassettes and a Marimekko store filled with the iconic floral prints. But nothing interests him as much as K-Market, the local grocery store. Every time he sees its colorful, blocky logo, he exhales a satisfied "Ahhh." Like his parents, he seems particularly attuned to art and design.

There was a time, back when she first had Liv, that Anna worried motherhood might stifle her own creativity and she'd lose that part of herself altogether. The author Alice Walker described her own similar fears that having children would diminish the quality of her writing. It was only when Walker became a mother that she realized her mistake had been to believe that she would derive only personal satisfaction from having children but in fact, she found that motherhood had enriched her as a writer too. Children were not the enemy to creativity and ambition, she discovered, the true foes were racism and sexism. And she'd bought into the sexist directive that, "you have to have balls to write," when really, "having a child is easily the equivalent of having balls. In truth, it is more than equivalent: ballsdom is surpassed."

Anna seems to have arrived at the same conclusion. She draws on the strength she's found in motherhood to endure the bitter custody dispute, and the splendor of it to fuel her creativity. With Luka now sleeping through the night, she can feel her capability returning. It seems like the right time to figure out her professional future. So one crisp fall morning, she leaves the baby with her mother and walks twenty minutes downtown to where the streets are lined with baroque buildings more suggestive of St. Petersburg than Scandinavia. She finally reaches Market Square. On one side is a domed Orthodox church built by Tsar Nicholas I, and on the other, a Parisian-style department store.

She enters a building on the corner across from that store and takes the elevator up. It feels good to be back in the office. She and her colleagues catch up, and then Anna's manager asks what her plan is for coming back. Her company, like all Finnish firms, guarantees she can return to her position or something equivalent for three years, so it's up to her to decide when she's ready. Most mothers do come back, at higher rates than their American counterparts, and Anna has given a lot of thought to how much she can handle with everything going on in her personal life.

She doesn't share any of that with her manager, but tells her that she'd like to start working two days a week when Luka's a year old, and when he is fifteen months, she'll return full-time. Her parental leave ends soon but, as most mothers here do, she'll switch from maternity pay to a caregiver allowance, a stipend she can receive for taking care of Luka rather than sending him to daycare, up until the age of three. She's guaranteed a daycare spot as soon as Luka turns nine months, but less than one percent of children start then. By age three, when parents are no longer eligible for the caregiver allowance, almost all children are in public daycare.

Anna is committed to sending him at fifteen months, at a cost of €154 euros a month including food, though she does have a nagging worry it's too early. "He'll still be so small," she says. Small is, of course, a relative term. Sarah's and Chelsea's children were in care starting from three months, a full year earlier. Professional care for children that young can be significantly more expensive to provide, because it requires more daycare workers per child. So one potential benefit of longer parental leave—for both men and women—is that it could actually save the daycare system money.

Anna's manager approves her plan and explains that while she's part time, she'll share responsibilities with a colleague. *And Anna,* her manager adds, *if something comes up, we'll adjust. We can plan for Mondays and Wednesdays for now but if you decide different days are better that's fine, let's just keep in touch about it.*

Anna smiles. Her company employs a lot of women, many of whom have young children, so they understand her situation, she says. "Plus, it's a big office so it's not going to collapse if one person isn't there precisely at eight a.m. Monday morning." That's different from the unforgiving corporate culture that drove both Tsukasa and Chelsea from the workforce and kept Sarah in a full-time job when she would have preferred to go back more gradually. "The whole atmosphere is supporting you and saying these two things—family and career—don't have to be mutually exclusive," Anna says. "I feel lucky to work in a place like that."

Economists had expected that flexible work culture and the country's emphasis on gender equality would lead to a higher birthrate, but to their surprise, that hasn't happened. There was a drastic decline in fertility rates in 2010 and they never recovered, even when the economy rebounded after the Great Recession. Successive prime ministers have asked for an explanation from advisors including Anna Rotkirch, research director at the Family Federation of Finland's Population Research Institute. Rotkirch, an engaging speaker practiced at holding the attention of busy world leaders, says that something happened around 2010 that changed everything: The rise of social media and globalization generally.

As people have started talking more openly and accessibly on social platforms, young people became more aware of both the difficulties of parenting and the benefits of a child-free life, like more time for travel and professional fulfillment. Couples proudly proclaimed themselves DINKS (dual income no kids) and DINKWADS (dual income no kids with a dog). Likeminded online communities such as Finland's Association of Voluntarily Childless People validated those choices and lessened the stigma around not having children, in a way that was never possible before in human history. Researchers describe it as a kind of feedback loop that led more Finns to not have children, a far cry from the postwar jubilation when compatriots encouraged each other to have "a third for the fatherland."

There were others who might have had children but, because social media personalities with picture perfect lifestyles tend to get the most engagement—like Hannah Neeleman, the Mormon woman with eight children, ten million followers, and an idyllic farm life—it can perpetuate the unrealistic idea that people should wait to have children until their own life approximates something close to that. Even in Finland, where parental supports are relatively strong, social media from abroad can make financial success seem like a prerequisite to parenthood. And in that way, Rotkirch says, children became a capstone rather than a cornerstone of adulthood. But, she adds, now some Finns wait too long and miss their opportunity. Still, studies show that for the most part, older people both with and without children do not regret their choice.

Anna was always sure she wanted to be a mother. And as happy as she was to be back in the office for the morning, there is something equally reassuring about slipping back into that role in the afternoon. When she returns home, she thanks her mother for looking after Luka, then dresses him to go out with her to the Turku City Library.

When they get there, she pushes the stroller past rows of Moomin books, a Swedish language section and, at Luka's eye level, a detailed dinosaur diorama. In a corner next to a clothes rack labeled "clothing swap," is a basket filled with knitting sup-plies. There's a half-finished scarf with a sign encouraging visitors to continue the piece in progress. Even knitwork, it seems, can be communitarian.

She and Luka settle into their favorite corner by a window to look at picture books and puzzles. Anna says her fellow Finns shouldn't be scared to have children. "I think the system still works quite well. We don't have to worry that much about the costs or think, I cannot have a child because it's so expensive and how will I take care of everything. The system will lead you, so I think at least in Finland, just do it."

The government has historically been reluctant to openly push people to have more children. That is particularly true of left-leaning administrations, which typically advocate for strong parental sup-ports but don't see it as the government's place to pressure people to become parents. When Rotkirch worked with Prime Minister Sanna Marin's left-leaning government, she says that, "they were very hesitant to say anything about having children at all, they were so worried about offending anybody." Sometimes it was frus-trating, as when she couldn't get the Ministry of Social Affairs to add material to school textbooks about reproductive health and sexuality because the agency did not want it in the same section as population fertility, which could be viewed as a directive about increasing birthrates. Rokirch says she told them it would be fine to include it in a different section then, but they stalled and didn't add the information anywhere. "They're so uncertain about these things, I mean, at some point they didn't know if they could use the word *woman* and that makes it very hard to talk about female reproduction."

Marin was succeeded by the center-right Orpo government that, Rotkirch clarifies, holds positions in line with American left-wing politician Bernie Sanders. Its leaders promised to cut the debt and did reduce public expenditures but they kept most child benefits intact. Those programs are popular and, according to a report Rotkirch wrote for the Orpo government, more Finns have started to view plummeting fertility as a serious issue in recent years, even without the country explicitly pushing the idea that they should have more children. They understand that the country needs young people to work and feed into the social welfare system, to support retirees and others who can't work—that's how the generous system has been able to function since it was set up after the war. There is always increased immigration but as Japanese leaders argue, that might not be a long-term solution because birthrates are trending down across the world, particularly as countries develop and access to family planning increases. "Having lost one-third of our births in thirteen years, it's now seen as a shared problem in Finland," Rotkirch says.

The hard truth is that no one really knows what will increase the birthrate, she says. So it's best not to focus on the numbers but instead on young children who, if all goes well, will live for more than one hundred years and must be productive citizens during that time. In other words, think about the quality of the population rather than quantity and invest in human capital through prenatal and postpartum care, early education and healthcare access. Beyond the economic benefits of a healthier population, the original intent of many of those programs was to improve the quality of life for parents and children, and that remains true today. They are beneficial because they allow individuals more agency in how they live their lives. "All demographers agree this kind of investment in children is the key," says Rotkirch, "and I think Finland has a good track record there and that will only grow in importance."

IN LATE OCTOBER, THE trees are bare, surrounded again by their own discarded leaves. The days are gray and misty and only last until six. It's Luka's first introduction to the country's annual descent into darkness, but as night gobbles up day, he doesn't seem to mind. He's just happy to be inside with his mom, clambering on top of anything he can. Anna can't leave him alone for a moment. "He's super fast and just like total destruction everywhere he goes," she laughs. One afternoon at her parents' house, she's surprised to discover he can climb stairs when she finds him halfway up a flight. She carries him back down, but when she turns around again, he's managed to get himself all the way to the top and has a gleam in his eye she now recognizes. She can tell he knows he's been naughty.

Still, she's grateful he can entertain himself because she doesn't have money to spend on other activities; she just moved from parental leave pay to the childcare allowance of about four hundred euros a month. "Right now I'm really counting every single euro and the more days when we don't spend at all, the better." Even with her rental subsidy and child support it's not enough to live on, in part because food costs are so high with inflation and the war in Ukraine that has led to increased energy prices. So she applies for an additional thousand euro a month "social assistance allowance" for low-income families. It's meant to be a temporary, last-resort form of financial assistance. It's granted a month at a time, and according to official guidelines, everyone who uses it still has an obligation to look after themselves and seek a livelihood. Anna finds it somewhat embarrassing to rely on. "It used to be called 'support for poor people' and they go through your accounts to make sure you really have no resources," she says. She's glad to have it though. "Without that support, I would be stressed out completely."

As it is, she's enjoying these last months with Luka, despite the damp, bone-chilling weather. The only real antidote is the dry heat of a sauna, and her new flat has a small electric one. She turns it to mild and carries Luka inside. He sits on her toweled lap on the lowest wooden bench—the coolest—and watches her splash water on a stack of black and white stones. His eyes widen as it hisses and clouds of löyly, the curling sauna steam, rise to the ceiling. "It's like magic for a child that small," she says.

As they sit together, she imagines what it would be like to stay home with him for three years, as she did with Liv. But she has to remind herself of the toll the long leave took on her career: She lost her pension for that time and thinks her career might have progressed faster, or differently, if she hadn't been gone so long. "I lost a lot compared to my school friends and the colleagues I had then; they were young and ambitious and really wanted the big offices and they got themselves pretty nice lives. But I have to say I don't regret it at all, because I might have worked my way up and come down with a nervous breakdown."

In the US and Europe, paid parental leave of up to about six months has been shown to have a neutral or positive effect on mothers' employment and wages long term; some studies have found the same for up to a year. But leaving for multiple years is a different story: A study found a three-year caregiving allowance in neighboring Sweden reduced gender equality and maternal employment. Such long leaves, as well as temporary employment contracts, might be the reason that almost half of Finnish women who were recently pregnant reported discrimination, fear that leave would damage their careers, or another negative consequence. It was particularly bad among highly educated women in specialized positions.

Sweden got rid of its caregiver allowance in 2017 after that study came out showing it reduced gender equality. And the country now has low rates of workplace gender discrimination and a high rate of female managers, about forty-two percent—roughly the same as the US—compared to about thirty-six percent in

Finland. (Interestingly, in the US, there are actually more female managers than male among workers under forty but after that, the trend reverses, perhaps because of parenthood.)

Anna knows that for the sake of her own career, she shouldn't stay home longer than fifteen months. She'll be ready to go back then: Her mind already feels clearer than it did just a few months ago and she's nearly finished breastfeeding. There aren't pumping rooms at her office anyway, since most Finnish women are done nursing by the time they go back. For now, she focuses on enjoying the remaining time she has with Luka. It feels different than it did with Liv, because she knows Luka will be her last child. "I feel like I'm more present for him; I see the value in it, I can appreciate it, which I didn't before. Not in the way that I appreciate it now."

When he is about eleven months, Anna leaves Luka with her parents to meet Masa in court, where a judge will rule on Masa's request to see Luka three times a week unsupervised. She greets her lawyer outside the courthouse and they enter together through a sleek glass addition that wraps around the historic building, a converted cork factory. Anna has always tried to take a detached "machine-like approach" to their case, but when she gets to the courtroom, she's nervous. The space is surprisingly small for the grandeur of the building, so her seat is not far from Masa's. He's already there, but she feels too awkward to even look him in the eyes. Instead, she makes eye contact with his lawyer and stiffly takes her seat. The judge reviews the documents and then, after less than half an hour, issues an opinion: They should restart the visits twice a week with supervision, exactly as Anna had requested.

She sighs with relief, pleased to finally have some resolution. "When I know things are correct on paper and Luka is happy and developing fine, then it's all good," she says. It's when there's a lack of clarity that the bitterness between them edges in.

Her optimism lasts about a week, until she gets a string of

messages from Masa expressing his dismay. "I haven't done any-thing wrong," he says, "but I was treated almost like a criminal in this country." He's upset that Anna's side brought up his mis-givings about Western medicine and thinks he's being painted as an incompetent parent. All he's asking for is more time with his child, he says. He wants to be able to teach Luka Japanese; maybe one day his son will even be able to read the journal with daily messages he's been writing him.

Anna registers Masa's disappointment, but tells him it's out of her hands and he should contact social services. Still, his texts to her only get longer, she says. She tries to respond succinctly: *Focus on Luka and how to create a relationship with him.* Finally, she tells him that if he keeps messaging her, she'll have to block him.

She can't excise him from her life completely, though, and she feels a cold dread when she thinks about seeing him at their next supervised visit. She tries to reassure herself that it's only until Luka gets comfortable with his father so he can attend the meet-ings without bawling, and after that, she won't have to attend. Mercifully, over the next month, Luka begins to recognize Masa and they can spend fifteen minutes playing with toys and singing songs while Anna is out of view in another room. It's enough to temper the hostility between them. Masa stops messaging her and they even engage in small talk about Luka's development and their Christmas plans.

Turku is already aglow with holiday trimming. The Path of Light festival draws visitors from across the country, who walk across the icy river on bridges lit green and blue, and under lumi-nous parachutes that catch the falling snow. At the Christmas market in the square outside Anna's office, there's mulled wine and a tent where Santa tells delighted children he's come to see them from his home up in Lapland.

Parents also get a welcome surprise this year: The government doubles the child allowance in December for all families, to off-set rising costs of living. For Anna, who's still barely getting by, the timing is perfect. She's grateful for all the support from the Finnish government over the last year, which was difficult in ways she couldn't have predicted. The goal of those programs is to offer citizens the freedom to live as they want, writes Finnish journalist Anu Partanen in *The Nordic Theory of Everything: In Search of a Better Life*. "The system is intentionally designed to take into account the specific challenges of modern life and give citizens as much logistical and financial independence as possible." To provide people that freedom, the government spends about three times as much on family programs as the US does, and also more than Japan and Kenya as a percentage of GDP. It's financed in part by a progressive tax system with higher rates on wealthier citizens. The highest tax bracket is forty-four percent. Anna pays seventeen and with other withholdings—such as unemployment and pension insurance—twenty-five percent comes out of each paycheck. Like most Finns, she thinks she gets her money's worth.

She can have the kind of stress-free Christmas Eve she wants, with Luka and Liv at her parents' house. The baby marvels at the straw decorations tied with big red bows. Then as the sun sinks in the late afternoon sky, she carries him to the outdoor sauna, past pools of candlelight in the snow. Last year, she was scamper-ing across this same cold ground with Masa. She thinks now that they're on somewhat better terms, she should call him so he can see his son on Christmas. When she does, Luka smiles at the sight of Masa's face on the screen. It feels like progress.

Then it's time for them to eat: Christmas ham, fish eggs with sour cream, herring, gravlax, pickled vegetables, potato casserole and a rosolli salad of diced beetroot, onions, and apples served with cream, pink from beetroot juice. Luka tries everything. He wrinkles his nose at the ham but when Liv offers him a taste of butter, he dissolves in satisfaction. For dessert, there is gingerbread. His first piece is so good he gleefully motions for another and then grabs it from Anna's hand, so impatient to get it to his mouth. The world is warm and spiced and filled with new delights.

For New Year's, Anna takes Liv to an outdoor skating rink where the two of them glide across the ice, Liv in a bright yellow helmet, Anna in a black pompom hat. Anna reflects on the year. "The main thing on my mind is I'm quite happy with how things have turned out," Anna says. "I don't long for the past and I'm not making big goals for the future either. I'm enjoying the moment how it is, just being. I think good things are coming but I don't need to know what they are, not just yet."

THE NEXT TIME SHE sees Masa is in the waiting room of the children's health clinic where they have an appointment with an ophthalmologist to assess whether one of Luka's eyes is ever so slightly crossed. As soon as she arrives, she says, Masa begins firing questions at her about their custody case, which they won't have a final decision about for months, and then takes out his phone. Anna realizes what's happening—that, almost inconceivably, he's recording her again. She'd thought they were in a better place.

Masa says that by now he has developed a good sense of when he needs to record their conversations, "meaning when I have to protect myself, and need something she cannot manipulate."

From then on, Anna stops attending their meetings, just drops Luka with the supervisor and leaves. It's hard to do even that, but she knows it's her responsibility as a parent. "You have to keep your calm, be a grown-up for the small person's sake. There are plenty of things mothers have to do besides warming up milk or washing dirty butts or something," she says with a smile.

She pushes forward and accepts that her relationship with

Masa is different than it was even a month ago, when they were on better terms and she'd considered inviting him to Luka's birthday party. For now, she'll celebrate these milestones on her own. The upside is she can throw exactly the kind of party she wants: elegant, with a cheese board, gravlax, and twinkling coupes of champagne. Anna wears a sculptural black shirt and colorful gypsum earrings. Liv's hair is pulled into an elegant ballerina bun and she plays on the floor with Luka, who has on a little green bow tie. There's not a goofy party hat in sight. Theme parties aren't traditional here, she explains. "You just need to give space for people to talk, eat, and be with each other."

All that noisy revelry is a surprise to Luka, though, and he cries when Anna brings him to the living room to greet their guests. Anna's friend, a woman with her own small baby, quickly offers Luka a gift-wrapped box. He forgets he's upset and Anna settles into the couch with him on her lap next to her great aunt, whose braided gray pigtails fall almost to her waist. As Luka tears open the present, Anna sips champagne, just as she did a year ago when she first brought him home to meet her family. She's grateful that since then, she's had the support of this assembled group and the community more broadly. It has meant that her daily life was stable, even when her relationship with Masa was not. At the end of the party, she helps Luka blow out the candle on a strawberry-topped sheet cake.

The next day, another milestone. Luka says his first intelligible word: *kakka*. It means poo, Anna explains with a smile. "He's got a good sense of humor." She's glad to witness this tiny breakthrough, knowing she'll soon be back at work. "This is the last time," she says, her voice breaking before she steadies herself. "So yeah, I'm happy that I've been able to be present for everything that has happened with him this year. And it's time for the next round, when he's a toddler," she laughs. She knows intellectually, if not yet emotionally, that she's ready to move on herself. She can't wait to get a paycheck and contribute to the social welfare system rather than draw from it.

It isn't how Anna planned motherhood—two children, no long-term partner—but she did it on her terms. "It wasn't purposeful," she says, "I just did it my way."

SARAH

US

———————

THE FIRST VACATION THEY take as a family is to Las Vegas for a professional conference Sarah is attending during the school summer holidays. That way Sarah can keep breastfeeding and the hotel room is covered. She's in sessions most of the day, but Brian comes to slip her the baby at regular intervals, and they spend her lunch break walking the strip. It's broiling in the desert this time of year, so Sarah feeds Vivian as much as she can to keep her hydrated. Sarah has never felt more faint but the baby seems fine, thriving even: She smiles at restaurant servers and stares wide-eyed at the whirling towers of Cirque du Soleil acrobats. Sarah enjoys watching her baby get so much pleasure out of life. It inspires a foolish hope that with enough careful planning, she can make sure Vivian is always this happy.

The experience isn't cheap, though and they quickly blow through Sarah's allotted per diem. "I've spent a pretty penny here, most of my overtime pay," Sarah says. Still, it's worth it to be together for such a long stretch. They'll have to wait until the end of the year to do it again.

I wish I could spend more time with you this summer, Brian tells Sarah.

But they both know that given his limited paid time off, he needs to make up for the days they spent together at her conference. So when they return, he's back to his delivery route, now in the summer swelter. It's not so bad, he says, aside from the persistent heat rash.

Sarah never thought it would be this hard to find time together. "Life was definitely more simple back when we were growing up, I don't feel like you had to work quite as hard," she reflects. Money was sometimes tight, but her parents raised seven kids on a single income and her father didn't get his bachelor's degree until their oldest child finished high school. Now, it would be impossible to survive on Brian's salary alone, even just the three of them.

"I think the driving force is capitalism trying to make the most money at the expense of family values, of making sure employees have time at home with their kids," Sarah says.

They are thoughtful about the time they do have together and try to use it to build an authentic life for themselves. And that still includes Nick, Brian's boyfriend. When Brian and Nick talk about gaming and other "nerdy stuff" though, as she gently teases them, Sarah does sometimes wish she had the companionship of other new mothers. She's mostly made do with online communities. And one day she sees a familiar name pop up in one of them: Her old friend Bonnie, whom she knew in her community theater days. Sarah messages Bonnie and they make plans to meet at a local McDonald's.

The restaurant is clean and modern, with blond wood paneling and tall touchscreen menus. But the main draw is the two-story PlayPlace structure. It sits inside tall picture windows that frame the nearby peaks. The informal cost of admission is a Happy Meal.

Sarah's stepson Mason wings down a green slide and Vivian tries to organize her limbs into a crawl. Bonnie feeds her own daughter as she and Sarah swap war stories from the front lines of motherhood. The commiseration is comforting. It's similar to the relief Tsukasa found in the mama-tomo friends she met at the community center, though there isn't the same public investment in parental community building here.

Over the next few weeks, she and Bonnie meet frequently, at each other's houses or back at McDonald's. Afterward, Sarah always takes a long nap with Vivian. It is a lovely way to pass midsummer. But then August crashes in and brings the new school year. Students pour through the heavy glass doors. "It's harder this time than it was coming back from maternity leave," Sarah says. Back then she craved the mental stimulation, but now Vivian is so interactive, Sarah just wants more time together.

Between the baby and work, she is so busy, she almost misses the email from their student loan provider. Sarah took out loans to pay for her master's degree; and Brian is still paying off the debt from his associate's degree at a for-profit college that was subsequently shut down when a judge determined it misled students about their earning potential and ability to repay loans.

Sarah usually ignores these periodic updates, but this message looks different.

Whoa, she thinks when she opens it, this new program will probably completely forgive Brian's student loan debt and at least part of hers.

She's not sure she fully agrees with the policy—she knew what she was doing when she took out her loan and doesn't expect anyone to bail her out now—but this could be transformative for them, and maybe education just shouldn't cost so much, she says. As she drives to get Vivian from her parents' house, she bubbles with ideas for what they could do with an extra three hundred dollars a month that used to go to their loan payments.

I'd actually been thinking that if we did have another baby, we'd probably need a bigger house and all that jazz, she tells her mom. With less debt, they'd probably qualify.

Still, she says, housing isn't the real problem. "I mean, childcare is just in another ballpark." Licensed daycare is nearly fourteen thousand dollars per year on average in the US and only slight lower in Utah at eleven thousand. Sarah is grateful her parents take care of Vivian on the three weekdays Brian works, and she loves how devoted her mom is to Vivian. Still, it isn't easy for them. Her parents are both in their seventies and they also care for her brother Evan, who is bedbound and tube-fed, with cerebral palsy and a seizure disorder. Like Tsukasa's mother, who cared for her own parents at the same time she was looking after Tsukasa and Rota, they are among the grandparents everywhere taking on substantial caring responsibilities.

That makes it hard for Sarah to envision a future with more kids. She and Brian have talked about having another one but she doesn't think she could expect her parents to take care of two young children. "Because my brother's care is so intensive, I don't know that I could in good conscience be like, 'and here's another baby to take care of.'"

A *New York Times* survey found that the cost of childcare was the most common reason Americans of childbearing age gave for having fewer than their "ideal" number of children. "I do think people take the cost of childcare in particular, into decisions about whether to have another child," says Karen Guzzo, director of the Carolina Population Center at the University of North Carolina. She says she has seen many people enter parenthood thinking, how hard could the childcare thing be? "And then once you have that first kid, you're like, holy crap, it's more than my mortgage, more than my student loan payments, and there's a nine-month waitlist." She says it's hard to study because of the US's patchwork system, but lack of affordable childcare probably does play a role in America's declining birthrate, which has been on a downward track since 2007 (with a brief uptick in 2014). "In the United States, you are really on your own to raise kids," Guzzo says. "Don't have kids if you can't afford them, that's sort of the common mantra."

Parents did get a brief reprieve when the Biden administration committed about forty billion dollars to prop up the childcare industry during the pandemic. There were more daycare spots, tuition costs decreased, and workers went from making nine or ten dollars an hour to fifteen, says Anna Thomas, Policy Director at Voices for Utah Children. "It was transformative."

The national reforms were so popular that some of Utah's neighboring states came up with their own programs when federal funding ran out. In 2022, New Mexico became the first state to offer near universal childcare from six weeks, in a program primarily funded by oil and gas development fees. It's been incredibly popular: Governor Michelle Lujan Grisham campaigned on the issue of early childhood education, then won reelection after implementing the first phase of the generous program. And two years after it went into full effect, a survey found that close to ninety percent of families with young children said the program had a positive impact on their well-being.

Still, the Utah legislature and governor showed zero interest in creating that kind of program after federal funds ran out, Thomas says. "They saw it as funding during a crisis, while advocates saw it as funding that always should have been going into the system to make it work for families." Utah's approach reflects a long-held American belief that government should only involve itself in childcare during times of crisis. The first American daycares were set up in the 1820s to allow poor women to seek employment (so they would no longer require government assistance), but once those women were in the workforce and out of financial crisis, they were on their own. That idea persists today. As Thomas explains it, "since we don't have a very communitarian approach to raising children in our country, it's hard to raise people's taxes for it."

Sarah and Brian are essentially on their own. And so they try to support each other as much as they can. Brian takes care of Vivian on his two days off, which fall during the week—different from Sarah's, so they do what they can to find time as a family. And every weekday morning, he preps Sarah's pumping bag to make sure it has the necessary supplies. "I think he's seen how hard breastfeeding is on me and there's nothing else he can do to take that load off," she says appreciatively as she cooks breakfast. She turns to see him holding Vivian in front of the large mirror, pointing at the wispy-haired baby reflection peering back at them.

Who's that baby? he asks her as both babies giggle.

There was one time when the government did step in to provide childcare to families like theirs. During World War II, the national crisis was so acute and female labor so necessary that, somewhat incredibly in retrospect, the government enacted near universal daycare through the 1940 Lanham Act. It authorized over a billion dollars (adjusted for inflation) for childcare facilities, staff, and meals. Despite the program's success and its positive effects on children's development, the government announced that at the end of war, it would close the centers. Parents revolted. The White House was flooded with letters begging that the program be continued, and in New York, hundreds of mothers took to the street in protest. "Leave our childcare program as is! We don't want relief, we want to work!" one organizer cried. Other mothers told leaders they would pay higher fees, even if it was a significant economic burden, to keep the centers open.

The protests were effective—for a time. The program was extended a year, but the two offices tasked with continuing it had differing views on how to proceed, including whether there should be "deference to local communities"—coded language for not interfering with Southern school segregation. They couldn't come to an agreement and so, with no viable path forward for a desegregated, national daycare program, officials announced, yet again, that they would close the centers. This time they meant it: By 1947, almost all of daycare centers shuttered and over a hundred thousand working families lost childcare. It was not the last time racism would undermine efforts to create childcare supports for all American families.

Sarah might have benefited from such a program, but instead she drives almost an hour to pick up Vivian after work from her parents' house. Ideally, she thinks, she'd find a job where she could work remotely and also afford in-home childcare, like an au pair. "We talk about potentially having another child, and it would be much easier if I could just be at home." She wouldn't have to make that long drive and could also nurse on demand, rather than pump three times a day. Pumping is time consuming: cleaning the pieces—and even once or twice driving home to get parts she forgot—then setting up the system and staying stationary, with the pump plugged into the wall (wearable pumps don't seem to work as well for her).

She plans to keep it up until Vivian is a year old and starts drinking cow's milk, and is proud the baby has only had one bottle of formula in her life, at the doctor's office when she was two days old. Still, it would have been easier to get this far with a more flexible work arrangement. Many American mothers feel the same: A quarter have considered a job or career change because of their need to pump. It's a concern mothers in Finland and Japan don't share because they have longer leave and are more likely to be done breastfeeding when they return to work.

Sarah's strict pumping schedule and long childcare commute don't allow for much flexibility when something unexpected arises. Such as the little pink bumps that appear all over Vivian's skin one morning. First Sarah gives her Benadryl, and then a bath. But these are the only two remedies she can think of, and when the bumps persist, she really begins to worry. What is Vivian allergic to? Has she eaten something different or been around something new?

She messages her sister: How long after an allergy exposure do hives develop? Her sister asks if Vivian was sick recently because it could be a stress response to an illness. She did have a cold the previous week, Sarah responds, so perhaps that was it. But even after the bumps fade, Sarah can't seem to control her own physical reaction to the episode. There's a tightness in her body that only gets worse when she learns Brian's phone is broken.

What are we going to do? Sarah frets. *How are we going to pay for a new phone?*

She tries to put it out of her mind as she dresses Vivian for the day.

At work, she begins to feel better when some colleagues invite her to lunch; she could use the laughter and commiseration. They drive to a nearby Chick-fil-A, where two people in headsets outside keep the long drive-through line moving. When they open the door, the smell of fried chicken greets them, along with a grinning portrait of the chain's Baptist founder and a note that the restaurant is closed on Sundays. On each table is a vase of pink lilies.

They place their orders and settle into a red-cushioned booth, where they sip oversized drinks and swap stories of life in the classroom. But midway through lunch, Sarah feels strangely inhibited and can't engage in the lighthearted conversation. Then it gets worse. Her chest tightens and she is unable to speak. The light jazz keeps playing, cars glide past the drive-through window, but she is frozen. She realizes she is having a panic attack.

It has happened once before, during teacher training for a summer camp program when she was so scared of hiking along a ridgeline that she developed severe chest pain and was sure she was going to die. Afterward, her doctor diagnosed her with an anxiety disorder and prescribed medication. That was the first year she didn't have nightmares ahead of the schoolyear. "You mean this is how other people live? Not in a constant state of panic?" she remembers with a laugh. "I just thought it was normal to feel that way." She later backed off the medication and had been fine, up to now.

She sits mutely until the end of the meal, then texts the school secretary that she doesn't feel well enough to be effective at work and is going home. She rationalizes that if she leaves now, she can deal with the stressors that precipitated the anxiety. First among them is replacing Brian's phone.

That phone itself is a long-running source of strain because he's always on it. Just the other night, she snapped while they were watching a movie together.

What did I do? I'm sorry, he sputters when she tells him to stop playing on it.

His response only makes her angrier though.

What are you even apologizing for? Do you even know why I'm upset?

Not really.

It makes her feel so alone. Her frustration in this moment is connected to a more general feeling that she has only herself to rely on, because there's no real indication the wider community cares much about her well-being. In the past, there were attempts to reach mothers and families that needed help. Two decades after parents protested in the streets against ending the World War II daycare program, President Lyndon Johnson created Head Start, a new program that would provide low-income families childcare from birth. But it ran up against significant, racist opposition. Southern conservatives assailed Johnson's program: Mississippi Senator James Eastland, whose state did not even enact public kindergarten until 1986, claimed Head Start was a "device to funnel funds into the extremist leftist civil rights and beatnik groups in our state," and implied the centers were a front for Communism and black militancy. Mississippi Senator John Stennis, a member of the powerful Senate Appropriations Committee, accused the Black leadership of a local Head Start program of being inept, and launched an investigation into its funding. Segregationists led attacks against federally-funded daycare centers. Klansmen lit crosses on local administrators' lawns and burned entire facilities to the ground.

Even as the program inspired violent animus in the South, it expanded across northeastern cities. But by the late 1960s, there were still not enough centers there to satisfy the need. Many children of poor families continued to care for younger siblings while their mothers worked. Black fathers were sent to fight in Vietnam but this time, the government did not step in to provide childcare. Activists like Dorothy Pitman Hughes—who worked for a time as a babysitter for Malcom X's four daughters and later founded an integrated daycare in New York City that Gloria Steinem, then a cub reporter, called a "neighborhood-changing, life changing" place—argued that child care should be a political priority. She was joined by radical feminists who believed daycare should not be provided by for-profit entities, or by employers that could use it to make women dependent on their workplaces. Instead, they proposed cooperative childcare centers where parents could connect for social support and to advocate for shared goals. Along with Pittman Hughes, they pushed to get child care on the national agenda.

And it worked.

In the 1968 presidential campaign, Richard Nixon promised to expand access to public daycare. After he was elected, feminists across the country called on him to make good on it. In 1970, they held the "Women's Strike for Equality" and one of their three demands—in addition to abortion access and equality in employment—was free, twenty-four hour daycare centers. Congressional representatives Shirley Chisholm and Bella Abzug turned their call to action into a bill that helped shape the 1971 Comprehensive Child Development Act, a truly revolutionary piece of legislation. It budgeted over two billion dollars—sixteen billion adjusted for inflation—to create universal childcare based on the Head Start program. Like their counterparts in Finland and Japan, American families would be charged tuition on a sliding scale. The US was again on the cusp of enacting sweeping changes that would improve the lives of American parents.

The bill's sponsor in the Senate, Walter Mondale, was in almost daily contact with Nixon's White House, writes Gail Collins in *When Everything Changed.* When it finally came to a vote, the bill passed the Senate by a wide margin. The vote was closer in the House, where Republicans said it didn't give local government enough control, employing the same coded segregationist language used against Head Start. But in the end, Congress still passed the bill and sent it to Nixon for his signature.

Advocates were certain he would sign it given his campaign promises, but then the conservative flank of his party revolted. Leaders of the Mormon Church publicly worried the bill would upend traditional family structures and, along with other conservative organizations, organized parent groups to write a hundred thousand letters in opposition. Right wing pundits called the bill "Communist" and a "plan to Sovietize our youth." Eager to shore up conservative support ahead of his trip to communist China and the upcoming election, Nixon used his veto message on the childcare bill to do it. He called it "the most radical piece of legislation" that session of Congress had produced. As Collins writes, "the goal was not just to kill the bill but also to bury the idea of a national childcare entitlement forever."

It pretty much worked. After the bill failed, childcare policy became almost taboo. Even feminists were reluctant to bring it up, recalls Marcy Whitebook, founder of the Center for the Study of Child Care Employment at the University of California at Berkeley. She was at Berkeley in the early seventies and remembers the deflation among feminists after the defeat of the childcare bill. "That set everybody back because nobody knew what to do next."

Mainstream feminists shifted their focus away from parental supports. "They were all about getting women jobs that they hadn't had before and they didn't want to be associated with women's work—they wanted to be free from it," Whitebook says. Women's groups would sometimes ask her to set up childcare for their meetings, she says, but didn't make it part of their political strategy. "That was annoying at first and then, you know, infuriating," she laughs.

In retrospect, Whitebook thinks that was a missed opportunity. Cultural attention shifted to workplace feminism, evidenced by the 1980 hit movie 9 to 5, starring Jane Fonda, Lily Tomlin, and Dolly Parton. "But the urgency of what parents and kids and childcare workers were going through never rose to the top," says Whitebook. "Imagine if we'd had a Jane Fonda movie and a song done for us." As women's rights groups largely sidestepped the issue, conservatives claimed the issue of motherhood and it became and associated with submissiveness rather than authority.

The challenge was, and remains, to give motherhood real civic power without essentializing women as caregivers.

Sarah, like many American women, does what she can to succeed professionally without affordable daycare and the other supports that might make it more feasible. And that's on top of carrying much of the mental load for her family—solving the shared logistical problems and making plans—which at the moment means figuring out how to replace Brian's phone. She is relieved to learn it will be less expensive than she'd feared and resolves to put the whole episode behind her when she goes to a wine night her colleague is hosting. She usually enjoys these gatherings, loves chatting with fellow teachers about school and also the challenges of family life. But after helping herself to the potluck buffet, she starts to feel uneasy and can't seem to engage with the other women. It's as if the color has drained from her life and left everything dark and gray. The bright laughter of her colleagues throws her own gloom into relief.

In the early weeks after Vivian was born, her doctors screened her for postpartum depression, but since then no one has really checked in on her. Perhaps that's because for the most part, she seems fine—she masks the sadness well and still lives up to everyone's expectations of her, just as she always has. And now again, she does the responsible thing: she seeks professional help.

The midwife at the health clinic is understanding.

Sometimes symptoms come on really forcefully and those are the people who tend to notice it and get treated early on postpartum, she tells Sarah. With other people it's like boiling a frog, the temperature is slowly turned up until you're cooked, and it sounds like that's kind of the case for you.

Sarah nods and says she thinks there's something bigger as well; that she sacrificed herself because it seemed like that's what was expected of her. "In the LDS community and in America more broadly, we praise moms for giving everything for their children. And that's a problem because then we feel like we aren't good moms if we don't." Before she had Vivian, she prided herself on flouting the expectations of the LDS community and vowed not to repeat the patterns she saw in childhood. She is beginning to realize that she still feels the weight of those expectations but no longer has the support the LDS community could have provided. Or any real public support. That can have a real impact on well-being: In a study that looked at families in more than twenty countries, researchers found that parents are happier in places with stronger social programs, particularly those that lower childcare costs. In Finland, for example, parents are happier than non-parents, while in the US the opposite is true.

Sarah's midwife recommends she start the antidepressant Prozac. Sarah agrees; she had a feeling that's where this was headed.

The change of seasons doesn't help: Fall has come to the valley and with it, more darkness each day. By the time Sarah gets back on the road to take Vivian home from her parents' one evening, the sky is a hazy black and the hillsides are dotted with the bright glow of temples. Sarah thinks about how different her life would be if she didn't have this long commute. "It's killing me, driving to Orem all the time, I would love to be able to reclaim like three hours of my life just by not having to drive there and back."

She certainly does not have time to get out and advocate for herself politically, though if she did she would have some choice words for her elected officials. Grose, the *New York Times* opinion writer, says that's common. Parents still in the exhausting early stage don't have time to get involved in politics, she says. "And once they leave that super stressful five years, they're just like, thank God we got through that, and there isn't the political will to make change because it's not top of mind for them anymore." Then the next group of parents are stuck in the same mess. "So unless somebody else takes that up and there are allies, it's not looking good."

President Barack Obama tried to push Congress to help American parents when, in 2014, he proposed a budgetary item that would fund universal preschool for four-year-olds through a cigarette tax. But tobacco's largest lobbying organization, the Altria Group, protested and the legislation went nowhere. So instead, Obama directed nearly a billion dollars, through a public-private partnership, to states for early childhood programs, which did help produce local public Pre-K programs across the country.

The program also expanded Head Start programs for young children, but they only serve low income families. So private equity saw an opportunity in childcare chains that charge desperate parents college tuition rates for toddler care, while paying low wages to workers. A Goldman Sachs analyst recently told the *New York Times* that the private daycare Bright Horizons was "profitable and throwing off cash." Expanding public childcare would threaten that model. As Bright Horizons wrote in its 2021 annual report: "Government universal child care benefit programs could reduce the demand for our services ... and adversely affect revenues."

Earlier that same year, President Joe Biden had proposed a policy that might have done that. His Build Back Better plan included a provision to cap childcare costs at seven percent of family income and ensure childcare workers a "living wage." It was criticized for being too expensive by pundits on both sides of the aisle and in the end, stripped from the bill to get the support of Senator Joe Manchin, the West Virginia Democrat. "I cannot accept our economy, or, basically, our society, moving towards an entitlement mentality," Manchin said at the time. (The *New York Times* reported that afterward, Manchin received donations from at least six childcare industry executives.)

Whitebook, the Berkeley childcare expert, says this was a predictable end to decades of disregard for parents. "I don't think you can separate what's happening in childcare from what's happening in so many other aspects of American life. It's a market-based system where private equity and corporations are growing and they're going to continue to grow because we never embraced childcare as a public good."

AS SARAH TRIES TO find her way out of the darkness, Brian begins to open up to her about his own struggles, prompted by a television series they're watching. It follows two LDS women who left their husbands for each other. The pain the women endure when they come out to their families is hard for him to watch. He recalls to Sarah how difficult it was to suppress his bisexuality for fear of being rejected by everyone he knew. He can still remember the looming threat of conversion therapy and worse, eternal damnation.

"I've felt this way since I was fourteen," Brian says, "but I never did anything or acted on it because the expectation was, no, God told you to procreate, so I just did my best to kind of push those feelings down and ignore them—you know, this isn't the way I should be thinking, this isn't right."

It's heartbreaking for Sarah to hear and she has a strong urge to protect him. She tells him she remembers learning in church that gay and lesbian people had fallen prey to Satan and needed to resist the temptation. As she got older, that idea made less sense to her and she began to wonder why everyone around her was so willing to accept the teachings of the Prophet unquestioningly. "I look back on that and think there's a reason why people talk about Mormonism as a cult: It is one."

Brian has a harder time seeing it that way. The community was so important it felt like an extension of his own family, but he's finally coming around to the idea that he needs to make a clean break.

Yeah, I really don't want to be associated with this anymore, he tells her.

Sarah is relieved and commits to being there for him as he grieves his old life and navigates a new one. Even if it's a little uncomfortable, like when his relationship with Nick begins to fray.

Brian texts him to see if he still wants to go to an event they'd talked about attending together, but Nick is noncommittal. His work has gotten more demanding and he is also balancing relationships with two other women. Brian has been busy as well, with family commitments and a new dispatch shift on the weekends. He doesn't like dispatch as much as being in the field, but it's a way to move up in the company and even lay the groundwork to start one of his own. Brian tells Sarah he feels like he's in a holding pattern with Nick and so she follows the advice she's read in their ethical non-monogamy books and helps him think things through.

Have you communicated to Nick what's acceptable for you and what's not? she asks. *Are you okay if this is the end of your relationship because your needs aren't being met?*

Finally, Nick stops responding and Brian feels rejected. Sarah tells him she wishes Nick had been more up front, but that in the end, it seems more situational than personal. And perhaps it will give them time to focus on their own relationship; they have been trying to find their way back to the intimacy they once had.

Sarah talks about it with her sister when they catch up on videochat.

Breastfeeding can impact desire because of changes in

hormones, her sister tells her. So for some people there can be a long postpartum period of not feeling that desire.

Right, says Sarah. *And I'm still breastfeeding, so I'm not totally expecting that to have changed yet.*

Then there is her mood. Even with the medication, Sarah continues to struggle. One evening when she is alone with Vivian, a wave of depression crashes so hard upon her that it's all she can do to resist being washed into the warm embrace of her bed. She struggles to hang on until she can put Vivian down.

We're going to sleep right at seven o'clock whether you're tired or not, she tells the baby, *because I just need to be done.*

She wakes up the next morning filled with dread. Work is more stressful than it used to be and she frequently fantasizes about quitting. As she loads her pumping bag into the car, she feels such revulsion for daily life that she longs to bury herself back beneath the covers. The only antidote she has found comes via the Starbucks drive-through window, and so she gets herself a foamy chai latte as delicious as it is exorbitant—eight dollars for this caloric endorphin rush. It's too bad her five-hundred-dollar-a-month insurance premium doesn't cover caffeine.

At her next appointment with the midwife, she reports that her anxiety has diminished but her depression is worse. The midwife gives her a screener. Sarah checks yes to question after question.

Well, we have you on a really low dose, so it could be that we just need to increase it, the midwife says.

Sarah isn't sure.

My sister was on Prozac once and it made her feel suicidal, she responds.

Right, that can happen in rare cases, the midwife acknowledges, *and people do tend to follow familial patterns.*

She prescribes a different medication and asks Sarah to schedule a return appointment. A few weeks later, Sarah isn't sure whether the drug is helping. "It's hard because there are still some days that are really bad and then other days that I'm like, I actually feel more like my normal self. So it's still kind of hit or miss."

The times she feels good typically involve Vivian. At dinner one night, Vivian, dressed in a watermelon printed tank top, watches Sarah intently as she brings a slice of crusty pizza to her mouth. Then she gently grabs Sarah's chin while she chews. Sarah laughs, little hand still on her face, and so does Vivian.

"She's just so smiley all the time," Sarah says with some admiration. "I think part of why I didn't see the depression at first is she was that bright spot and I just enjoy spending time with her and playing with her."

Still, she realizes, she needs to find joy in other aspects of her life.

When she was younger, there was one thing that consistently made her happy: musical theater. It was an accepting community, made up of people who didn't always fit in other places, and acting provided an escape. She messages Clara, a friend who directs community theater, and is happy to discover that she has a baby almost the same age as Vivian.

Clara encourages Sarah to try out for their upcoming production of Cinderella.

I just take my baby with me, Clara says, and if I need to be onstage, somebody will hold her. She makes it seem possible to establish an identity within and apart from mothering.

Finding that balance is at the heart of "matrescence," a term coined by the anthropologist Dana Raphael in 1967 to describe the months, even years-long transitional period to motherhood. As in adolescence, new mothers lose and gain friends, their relationships with their own parents change, and they wrestle with spiritual and ecological issues, like the plastic in baby bottles and the future of the planet their children now inhabit, says Aurélie Athan, a clinical psychologist and faculty member at Teachers

College, Columbia University who has revived Raphael's study of matrescence. Athan argues that the difference is, society allows teenagers to grow into whatever type of adult they wish to be, whereas there's an expectation mothers will fit into the maternal archetype their culture demands. "But there are as many ways of mothering as there are mothers, because they're people."

COLD WIND BLOWS THROUGH the valley as Sarah and Brian prepare to celebrate their fifth anniversary at a nearby hotel.

When they drop Vivian with her parents, Sarah is surprised by her own lack of anxiety. Must be the new medicine, she thinks, and of course the fact that the hotel is only forty-five minutes away.

Remember our anniversary last year? Sarah says to Brian as they turn off the highway, beneath peaks capped with snow just as they were then. *I was so pregnant and uncomfortable*, she recalls, *all I wanted to do was soak in the bathtub.*

Brian laughs and pulls into the parking lot. The hotel is an expansive brick building with an old Western façade that was once the Salt Lake City Brewing Company. In the 1990s, the current owners turned it into the Anniversary Inn and designed each room with a romantic theme: Mysteries of Egypt, Biker Roadhouse, Hawaiian Hideaway. Sarah and Brian choose Treasure Island and are pleased to find the suite is a passable rendering of a ship's deck with a captain's wheel and white ropes braided around a mast. It is transportive, and they ease into a different reality where they have time to leisurely stroll the nearby shopping strip until they find a Mexican place that looks good. It's the first time they've eaten at a restaurant without Vivian since she was born.

The freedom to do what they want prompts a rush of memories from the last time they felt like this—before they had a baby. Sarah asks Brian what he wants to reclaim from that time.

Brian considers the question and tells her he'd like to get back into the trading card game Yu-Gi-Oh!

Okay, good, Sarah says, *so maybe we need to just set apart time where it's like okay, every Saturday you get four hours that are all your own and you can choose what you want to do with those four hours. You can go do Yu-Gi-Oh! stuff or you can to go spend that time with, you know, your other partners.*

Brian recently started seeing a younger man named Tom, whom he met through a friend at work. Sarah tells him, while they're on the topic, that it's been hard on her because Tom doesn't integrate with the family as well as Nick did. And she worries he sometimes leans too heavily on Brian for support.

She tries to offer the advice without applying pressure, as she would for a best friend, because she knows that in ethical non-monogamy, it's frowned upon for one partner to have veto power over the other's relationships.

Tom doesn't have other partners, so it just seems more like a monogamous relationship, she goes on, *so he seems to have the expectation that he should be able to talk to you and see you all the time, so I think that sometimes makes it a little more difficult. And I'm a little concerned you're internalizing his emotional struggle. I don't know, I just don't always get great vibes.*

It's the kind of conversation they had pledged to have regularly when Brian first started dating outside the marriage, but with the demands of new parenthood, they weren't able to find the time. Brian is receptive and promises to be more attentive to Sarah. She can tell he is infatuated with Tom, a phenomenon described in polyamorous communities as "New Relationship Energy" and known to be a challenge for other partners. As Taormino writes in *Opening Up*, "the key to maintaining your sanity is patience, allow [him] the freedom to ride high but remind him he has other commitments." Sarah isn't optimistic much will change in the short-term, but still thinks it was healthy to talk things over.

As she later reflects: "Sometimes I don't really feel my own feelings because of how it will affect Brian's feelings, so then I end up trying to protect Brian by just shoving my own feelings down and never making room for them."

Taormino writes that, "the monogamous partner should never feel pressured to accept the nonmonogamous partners terms... there must be a dialogue where both partners have input about the limits, boundaries and rules. Both people must see it as a choice."

Brian acknowledges what Sarah is saying, and also assures her that she'll get time to herself to pursue musical theater.

They talk for hours and are attuned to each other's needs in a way they haven't been in a long time. Sarah feels a kind of joy she recognizes as the thrill of being emotionally connected.

It seems like they're on a better path, and when they get home, Sarah hears that her audition for *Cinderella* has earned her a part as a member of the ensemble. She is giddy with excitement.

It's a big time commitment though; she's in so many scenes that she'll have to attend four rehearsals a week. When she brings Vivian to the first one at the theater, a stucco building set incongruously among modern commercial spaces, another mother in the cast looks at her and chuckles: *This is my escape from my kids.*

But Sarah is happy to have her baby with her. And the idea that she can't combine creative pursuits with motherhood seems misguided. Athan, the clinical psychologist, says many women get the message that they have to give up their interests, intellect, and time to be a good mother. "The idea is only one of us can survive—the mother or the baby—but actually we're co-developing, growing together, and a lot of the development of the child is moving the mother into a new developmental stage, too."

Vivian smiles happily at Sarah's castmates, and a few of the younger women offer to watch her while Sarah is on stage block-ing a scene.

Afterward, one tells her earnestly: *I've always thought I wanted kids but I also don't want to have to give this up, so it's nice to see that it doesn't have to be the end.*

Another nods and praises Sarah for "doing it all."

Sarah isn't sure. She's reclaimed this part of her life but still feels unsettled in her marriage. She had felt so much closer to Brian during their trip, but now that they're back, it's as if it was all a decadent illusion. They fall back into old patterns.

There are times she allows herself to consider what would hap-pen if she and Brian did split up. But she always comes back to the idea that he is a good spouse and it's unreasonable to expect that their priorities will always perfectly align. "That's just not the real world." Plus, financially, it would be difficult to survive apart.

Most compellingly though, Sarah can't imagine splitting cus-tody of Vivian. "Even though I know having time with her dad would be really beneficial to her overall well-being, I would just really miss that time with her." It's already so limited. Colleen, Brian's ex-wife, always talked about how hard it was for her to be apart from Mason, but Sarah never fully understood that before she had Vivian. Now, the idea of giving up time with her daughter is almost too painful to consider. "I'd rather work through those issues than lose all that time with her and go through a custody battle with her in the middle of it."

VIVIAN'S BIRTHDAY FALLS ON a weekday, and they celebrate that eve-ning at her parents' house with Sarah's nephews, who also live there. Vivian sits expectantly at the kitchen table. At the sound of singing, she throws up her arms in wild excitement as if to grab the entire cupcake. Sarah laughs and gently holds the baby's hands so she doesn't burn herself on the candle. Vivian judders with anticipation and then—as Sarah's mom removes the candle and Sarah releases her hands—she grabs the cupcake and shoves it into her mouth as fast and as hard as she can. Her family roars in delight.

There is something sacred in this moment, in the love that Vivian has inspired here. Athan says parenthood is one route to enlightenment—something that might otherwise be found in a church pew, an ashram, or through travel. But parenthood was never seen to carry the same spiritual weight, she says. Perhaps that's because it was viewed mainly as women's work and a mundane part of everyday life. "Parenthood was always diminished but it's the suffering and the joy of it that stretches and deepens us."

Church certainly never provided Sarah that kind of spirituality, but what it could have offered was community support. As she discovered, not much else did; there was only vast cultural silence on the issue of who would care for new mothers as they navigated the complicated transition.

Vivian smiles widely, delighted to be covered in chocolate and the center of attention. "She's just such a happy kid and wants to make everybody else happy," Sarah says, "so I see a lot of Mason and Brian in her that way, but then I also catch things and I'm like, she's got her mom's spunk like, 'uh-uh you're not going tell me I can't do that.'" At the moment, she has her big cousins wrapped around her little finger, Sarah thinks admiringly. "I genuinely just enjoy watching her. When I think about what brings me joy now, it's spending time with my baby."

In the coming year, she hopes they get more time together. She's considering other careers that offer more flexibility and ideally better pay. She thinks corporate training might be a good path but it would require her to travel and she's not sure the benefits are worth the time away from her family. Most of the trainers are men, she observes, who seem to have an easier time being apart from their children. "I wonder if that stems from a biological thing where men aren't as attached, or is it cultural?" It's hard to untangle these big questions from such close range.

Even admitting that she feels a longing to be with her child—and is willing to make professional sacrifices to satisfy it—is a brave and radical act in a culture that has used that kind of deep personal desire to justify gender inequality and push women into serving as the social safety net. But it is her way of staying true to who she is, just as she encourages Brian and her children to do. She can only hope to find supportive allies so that she can live more fully and maybe even—along with her daughter—thrive.

EPILOGUE

WHEN WE MOVED BACK to the US, it was my children who took the longest to adjust. They had lived their entire lives in Japan and were perplexed that they were now supposed to wear their outdoor shoes inside, and dismayed by the grimy city streets. Their response to a new country made clear just how early cultural norms take hold and why they can be so difficult to shake. I didn't mind that the sidewalks weren't perfectly clean—it implied a certain casualness and freedom I'd missed.

I started to work on this book shortly after I got back and the four women became a kind of parent group for me; one that spanned the world and allowed me to see, to the extent that it's possible, the full breadth of motherhood. There were things that were nearly universal: The physicality of the work and the psychic weight of suddenly occupying the position of parent. And then there were the aspects of one's personal experience that come from a particular national history and culture.

Reporting their stories confirmed for me that I didn't need to conform to any particular expectation about how to parent because there are so many right answers. The role and responsibility of a mother might even be described as a belief system, upon which other aspects of a culture and policy are based. And the agency each mother feels in how to be a parent is derived from those beliefs.

I kept up with the women after 2022, the year in which this book takes place, and saw how that first year of motherhood shaped their experience afterward. For Tsukasa, as soon as she quit her job, she plunged even further into caregiving because around the same time, her grandfather, who was ninety-five and living with her mother in Matsumoto, began to decline. So every weekend, Tsukasa would go with Rota to help her mother care for him. Three months later her mother hurt her knee, and Tsukasa offered to stay in Matsumoto a little longer. But that same week, her grandfather took a turn for the worse. He now needed round-the-clock care and was so weak he couldn't even drink water without assistance. He had been clear he did not want to go into a nursing facility, so instead, home health aides visited three times a week and Tsukasa did almost everything else. For the next month, she took care of him as well as her mother and Rota. He passed quietly at home, just as he had wanted.

Tsukasa was glad to have helped him get that peaceful ending and also that Rota had been there, because her grandfather's death, she reflects, "was an opportunity for Rota to learn about life." Still, her time in Matsumoto left her so drained that when she returned to Tokyo, the idea of immediately finding another full-time job was inconceivable. She needed time to recover from the work of caregiving. And the experience confirmed her decision to wait to go back to work until Rota turned three and could go to youchien, public kindergarten. "Then I will have my own time to plan my own future," Tsukasa says, ever hopeful.

Perhaps she has reason to be; things are changing in Japan. The year after I followed Tsukasa, the rate at which Japanese men took paternity leave nearly doubled, from seventeen to thirty percent. That's largely because a new law went into effect requiring companies to disclose paternity leave usage. It was designed to encourage them to be more parent-friendly in order to attract prospective employees, and is an example of how policy can move culture forward, just as happened in Finland.

As for Chelsea, during her first year of motherhood she also felt limited agency in her own life, in part because she lacked strong community support and dependable childcare. The issue of childcare directly relates to the ongoing international conversation about declining birthrates, because the suggestion that the only way to produce more economic innovation is by increasing the sheer number of people on the planet ignores the fact that so much existing capability is being squandered. Nairobi's lack of adequate childcare is creating a generation of children with stunted growth and development. The loss of human potential in that city alone is staggering, and there are hundreds of millions of children worldwide who similarly lack access to quality care.

Modern city life had weakened the traditional care networks that Shosho and Mama Asande Bonyo relied on as young mothers. Still, Chelsea did have friends like Vee and Jen who were there for her, and cousins willing to lend their support even when their own parents—Chelsea's aunts and uncles—mostly turned their backs. And it was through one of those cousins that she got the job at the credit company. Even with it though, she continued to struggle financially. The salary from the commissions-based system was low and she had a hard time making ends meet. She survived thanks to the additional income from the store, which she continued to run with her cousin and his wife. It was a stressful existence and she was frequently at the local clinic for medicine to treat her ulcers and migraines. When she was feeling well though, she allowed herself to indulge her dream of one day enrolling in a computer coding course to learn data science or software development. She had enjoyed coding when she was at university and an additional credential could be a pathway to a more stable career. Like Tsukasa, Chelsea remains hopeful she can gain more control over her life as a mother. As for Joseph, he blocked her calls and so she finally resolved to let their relationship go.

There were some parallels between Chelsea's story and Sarah's. They each lived in countries with significant income inequality and so the stakes of parenting felt particularly high: the wealthiest families in both places have access to better healthcare, parental leave, and childcare than everyone else. Falling out of the middle class would mean losing even the minimal social protections they did have. Sarah's workplace had a lactation room, unlike Chelsea's, but perhaps even the pressure she felt to breastfeed exclusively is tied to the American fear that one's children will fall behind, into poverty even, if they're not given every advantage from birth. The US—the wealthiest nation on the planet—still operates from a mindset of economic scarcity.

After Vivian turned one, Sarah started to look for part-time daycare for her so they wouldn't have to commute to Sarah's parents. But all the nearby centers were full or astronomically expensive or both. Finally, Sarah asked a colleague where she sent *her* son, who was six months older than Vivian, and the woman told her he went to a home daycare that only charged five hundred dollars a month for fulltime daycare. Sarah couldn't believe it. That's still significantly more than Tsukasa or Anna pay, but a fraction of what most centers in Sarah's area charge. The home center is run by a husband and wife, along with their adult daughter, and when Vivian started there at eighteen months, it changed Sarah's life. She has even begun to think she could have another child because with Vivian in daycare, her parents would only need to look after the new baby.

Then another promising development: Sarah heard from the union rep at her school that the state legislature was working on a bill that would require that teachers get three weeks paid maternity leave, a bid to increase teacher retention. It would mean that if Sarah had another baby, she wouldn't have to burn all her sick days as she did when she had Vivian. She is planning to wait until she is sure the policy is in place to start trying for another child, showing again just how impactful family-friendly policies can be. Rather than try to push women who don't want children to have them, it makes more sense to focus on the many American families that stop short of their ideal number of children because of the high cost of having children in the US.

Brian would still have to use his sick days of course, because he's still not entitled to any paid leave. As Rep. Jimmy Gomez and his Dads Caucus argue, there needs to be support and permission for fathers and non-birthing parents to be more involved. Gomez wants to bring to the US a version of the Finnish philosophy that men and non-birthing parents have a right to time with their children, and that children have a right to time with their fathers. The appetite for such a culture exists: In California, as soon as men and partners were given the option to be more engaged parents through parental leave, they took it. And California remains the center of global innovation, so the policy did not have the damaging economic impact corporate interests warned about.

As proven by Latte Pappas—and Gomez himself, with his viral moment on social media—involved fathers can be aspirational figures and even romantic archetypes, desirable for their warmth and caring. Importantly, they can also be fully human; allowed to experience the splendor and difficulty of parenthood that, as the clinical psychologist Aurélie Athan argued, can provide a path to enlightenment. (And they avoid becoming, as the Japanese characterization goes: nure-ochiba, wet leaves stuck to their wives' shoes.)

A more parent-friendly system would also produce healthier children, according to the philosophy espoused by the Finnish maternity system, which has had some of the best child health outcomes in the world for over a century. And those children will hopefully live for the next century, exactly the kind of long-term investment societies should be making.

Anna and Masa now have a custody arrangement in which Luka is with Masa about two full days a week. They both say they are happy with that outcome. "There is mutual trust between Luka and his father and me and so communication is good and Luka feels really safe and healthy," Anna says. She recently took a new job producing the Turku music festival, an annual classical music event, and has also started a degree program in urban design. To her delight, Luka now teaches her and Liv Japanese words—colors and also more complex phrases. "I love this little boy, who is like two and a half and already teaching us," she smiles.

Masa has settled into Finnish life and is busy with several performance art projects, including one based on his transition to fatherhood that examines how men are affected by being raised in patriarchal societies. "I had my own difficulty fitting into those typical gender roles when I was younger so I find it very interesting," he says. And he also has a new partner, who does not want her own children but is open to helping him raise Luka. The experience of introducing his partner to parenting has helped him understand Anna's experience in their early days of parenthood. He describes one day, as he and his partner were giving Luka lunch, when he realized she had gone off to make herself lunch and he was alone taking care of Luka and also preparing the baby's food. "My partner has allergies, so it's understandable she was making her own lunch, but the timing of it, I was like, 'oh wow, now you're doing your own thing while I'm dealing with all this,' so I totally understood it from both sides in that moment."

That is the kind of broad perspective some members of this generation are bringing to parenthood. And so a new social movement seems to be forming: a kind of inclusive feminism that advocates for more freedom and fulfillment for both women and men, and for both parents and non-parents. That's important because the idea that women with children are more or less worthy of a place in civic life has historically been used as a way to divide and marginalize all women. It is what Grace Onyango, the first female Kenyan parliamentarian, pushed back against in the sixties, when that cynical Labor Minister said married women should be home with children, and yet single women were unsuitable for leadership. In a truly inclusive movement, women would have a voice regardless of their reproductive status and use it to act as allies for one another. That would mean advancing the shared goals of protecting reproductive rights and creating supports for people who do choose parenthood.

Onyango and other leaders paved the way for the activism we see today. From the 1919 International Congress of Working Women that demanded protections for female workers, to the American mothers who protested in the streets for daycare, to the first Finnish female parliamentarians, whose legacy is evident in that country's robust family supports, to the Japanese postwar women's movement that pushed for protections there, they set the stage for modern activists. Generations before ours worked to create better systems for themselves and also for us, their children. It is part of what Tsukasa described as the divinity she found in the chain linking generations, so natural and mundane that it could be overlooked but also thoroughly mystical.

The goal now should be to create societies in which having

children is not driven by war, colonialism, or capitalism but by people's genuine desire to be parents, with all the difficulty and joy that can bring. And then to honor parents' work with support so they can make the choices that allow them to live full, rich, modern lives.

TSUKASA
Japan

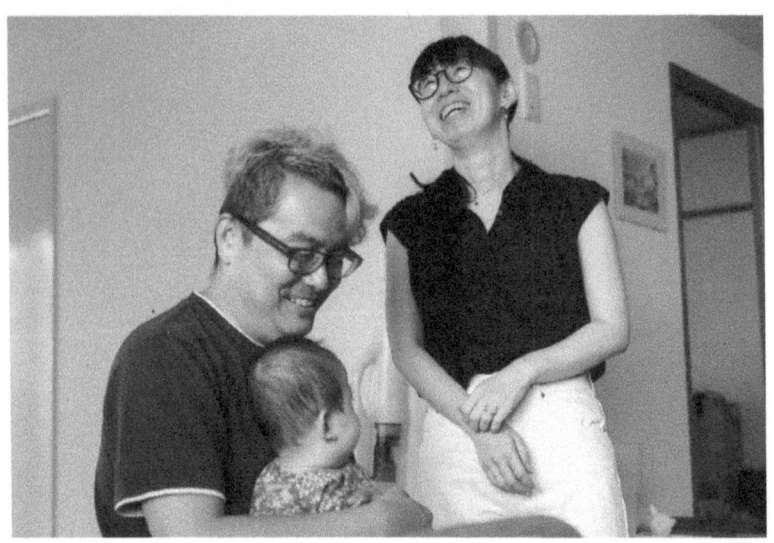

CREDIT: TOSHIKI SENOUE

CHELSEA
Kenya

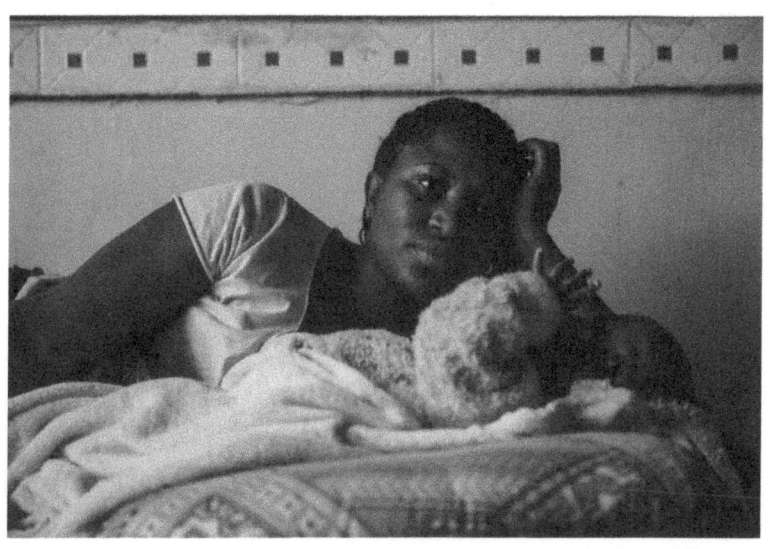

CREDIT: SARAH WAISWA

ANNA
Finland

CREDIT: SONJA SIIKANEN

SARAH
US

CREDIT: KIM RAFF

ACKNOWLEDGMENTS

THIS BOOK TOOK INNUMERABLE hours to write and I would not have been able to do it if my husband, Pete, had not been there to take over our shared parenting responsibilities. For so many reasons, he is why this book exists at all, and has been a singularly enthusiastic champion of it. I am extremely grateful.

My children remain my inspiration. As C. S. Lewis observed, "girls [and boys] grow quicker than books," and now that I have finished writing this one, I no longer have any small babies of my own but rather big, wonderful kids. Phin, Hannah, and Nat, you have brought so much joy and magic to my life, and kept me laughing even when writing was a challenge, I love you to the end of the universe.

This book was a true collaboration and I am grateful to the brilliant international journalists who worked on it with me: Rael Ombuor, who went above and beyond to record the daily life of Kenyan mothers and made sure I had a full picture of that country's history to help inform the portraiture. Edwin Okoth, a talented investigative reporter, was with me from Nairobi's informal settlements to Kenyan Parliament. Makiko Segawa, my friend and collaborator, and a tireless advocate for independent journalism in Japan helped me not only report the book but also translate interviews from Japanese. Hiroko Moriwaki and the FCCJ team provided detailed research about the Japanese maternity system. And Mari-Leena Kuosa, a talented Finnish storyteller helped me find a wonderful mother to profile. Also the photojournalists Sonja Siikanen, Kim Raff, Sarah Waiswa, and Toshiki Senoue, who created beautiful images of the families profiled here. Heidi Schultz provided meticulous fact checking on a tight schedule. And I am very fortunate to have had the most unbelievably talented research assistant, Anja Nilsson, who put her considerable skills toward sifting through historical documents and government records as well as translating documents from Swedish and German, among other explorations.

Thank you to my agent Heather Carr, who saw something special in this project when it was still in its infancy and has been a tireless collaborator and advocate ever since. And to my outstanding editors, Madeline Jones and Charlotte Humphery—and their teams at Algonquin and Sceptre—who consistently offered smart feedback and patient handholding. Your guidance made this book so much better.

Thank you to Val Gryphin for doing such a careful read of some chapters, and also Kanoko Matsuyama for reading other portions of the manuscript and providing insight into a country I still struggle to understand, even after nearly seven years living there. Similarly, thank you to Lauren Cochran for consistently supporting this project and offering insight into East African culture and history. And to Irene Muchunu for helping me understand the Kenyan employment system as well as Bright Shitemi, Treza Uduny Owino, and Mukami Munyoki for explaining Kenyan mental health care and the staggering need for more support in that area. And to Kate Woodrow, for offering thoughtful and generous guidance about how to get these stories into the world.

Michael Okwu was there when I needed him on this project and is one of the journalists who raised me, along with the incomparable Brenda Breslauer, Judith Wolff, Karla Murthy, Maria Hinojosa, Stephanie Smith, and John Siceloff. Thank you for teaching me how to build a narrative and do the rigorous reporting stories like these deserve.

I probably would not have survived my own first year as a parent without the love and support of my partners in motherhood: Yuni Hong Montgomery, Ashleigh Owens, Renee Hulsmann, Liz Patridge, Cy Duss, Jillian Hoffman, Vivian Song, and Bex Kelly. And on the other side of the globe, the group that supported me through the effort of writing: Katie Morris, Sarabeth Broder-Fingert, Louisa Revitte, and Hannah and Sarah Baker-Siroty. Thank you to the Hennessy family, whose men are shining examples of involved, loving parents—and in particular to Michael and Hugo Hennessy, who sent much needed encouragement (and nourishment) in my final months of the writing process. Zoey Alexander offered thoughtful design advice. Also to Mimi Mejia, my children's other mother. And of course to Sam and Jesse Leonard, who understood immediately what I was trying to accomplish here.

Prapti Mehta the kindest and most intuitive soul I have known, encouraged me to embark on this project from the beginning, and Jim and Ally Whitney helped me envision what it could be.

Most importantly, I am forever grateful for the women who let me follow them for their first year of motherhood. Tsukasa, Chelsea, Anna, and Sarah: What brave, thoughtful, and loving mothers you are. Thank you for allowing me to share your stories.